Not Monsters

Not Monsters

Analyzing the Stories
of Child Molesters

Pamela D. Schultz

ROWMAN & LITTLEFIELD PUBLISHERS, INC.
Lanham • Boulder • New York • Toronto • Oxford

ROWMAN & LITTLEFIELD PUBLISHERS, INC.

Published in the United States of America
by Rowman & Littlefield Publishers, Inc.
A wholly owned subsidiary of The Rowman & Littlefield Publishing Group, Inc.
4501 Forbes Boulevard, Suite 200, Lanham, MD 20706
www.rowmanlittlefield.com

P.O. Box 317, Oxford OX2 9RU, UK

Copyright © 2005 by Rowman & Littlefield Publishers, Inc.

British Library Cataloguing in Publication Information Available

Library of Congress Cataloging-in-Publication Data

Schultz, Pamela D.
 Not monsters : analyzing the stories of child molesters / Pamela D. Schultz.
    p. cm.
 Includes bibliographical references and index.
 ISBN-13: 978-0-7425-3057-7 (cloth : alk. paper)
 ISBN-10: 0-7425-3057-4 (cloth : alk. paper)
 ISBN-13: 978-0-7425-3058-4 (pbk. : alk. paper)
 ISBN-10: 0-7425-3058-2 (pbk. : alk. paper)
 1. Child molesters—Psychology. 2. Child molesters—Case studies. 3. Child sexual
abuse—Psychological aspects. I. Title.
 HV6570.S43 2005
 362.76—dc22

                                                                    2004015962

Printed in the United States of America

♾™ The paper used in this publication meets the minimum requirements of
American National Standard for Information Sciences—Permanence of Paper for
Printed Library Materials, ANSI/NISO Z39.48-1992.

For Eileah Miriam,
who reminds me how wonderful childhood can be.
I have been privileged to see the world through her eyes,
and I am forever changed because of it.

This book is dedicated to the victims of the offenders
I met during the course of this study.
I wish you peace.

Contents

~

Acknowledgments

Since it seems that I have been working on this book my entire life, it is impossible to thank everyone who has helped me on my journey. There are a few people, however, who contributed extraordinary energy to this project. The first people I must acknowledge are my parents. This book won't be easy for them to read, so I want to take the opportunity to tell them here how much I love them and that, without their influence, I could never have become the strong, committed woman I hope I am. They have always supported me unconditionally. My gratitude has no words.

The next people I need to thank are two wise, compassionate corrections counselors who taught me more about empathy and dedication than books ever could. I only hope this book reflects the profound influence Jim and Doug have had upon my research and my life.

I am indebted as well to the following people for their invaluable assistance in this project: Dr. Bernard Brock, my mentor from Wayne State University, whose insight has been truly inspirational; Susan Meacham, who spent countless difficult hours transcribing these depressing and frequently horrifying stories; Rowman & Littlefield editor Brenda Hadenfeldt for recognizing the potential value of this study; and my friends at Alfred University, in particular Sandra Singer, who was always willing to listen, and Michael McDonough, who helped arrange my teaching schedule to give me time in which to finish this book. I also want to thank the succession of AU students who were patient when their professor took every chance to weave observations about sex offenders into class discussions.

Finally, I want to acknowledge the support and sacrifices of my husband, Brien. I didn't realize until it was almost too late the toll this project took on our life together. I'm deeply grateful that he stood by me, even when his feelings about the subject matter sharply diverged from my own. His faith means the world to me.

~

Preface

Let me establish one pertinent issue at the outset: I am a survivor of child sexual abuse.

I was molested by a neighbor for years. Freed from the necessity of employment due to a mysterious chain of work-site accidents that left him on perpetual disability, The Man Who Molested Me was a fixture in our neighborhood. Since this was the 1960s and '70s, he enjoyed his status as the only man on the block during the day. After the other men left their tidy suburban tract homes early and went to work, this affable, boisterous man held court at various women's homes, drinking coffee and flirting shamelessly, always ready to lend a hand in assorted chores such as baby-sitting. He had unfettered access to any number of potential victims. I doubt I was the only child he molested. In fact, I know that I wasn't, since years later, when I began to deal with my memories of molestation, I discovered that he had victimized my sister as well.

He's dead now, so it doesn't cost me anything to share this information. I'm not betraying a confidence or destroying a family. No one can accuse me of being a liar. The Man Who Molested Me has been dead for twenty years. The memories of what he did, of whom he hurt, ought to be buried with him. The other children in the neighborhood, the countless kids who lived on my block in the other cookie-cutter brick homes, have long since become adults and moved away. I imagine many of us now have children of our own, and that we spend a lot of time worrying about how to protect our sons and daughters from terrorists, serial killers, and child molesters. I imagine some of us remember how it felt when we were sexually abused.

I managed to disentangle myself from my abuser once I became a teenager. No doubt I became less attractive to him once I entered puberty and, as my involvement in after-school activities increased, I was able to avoid him on a regular basis. However, I ended up acting out the trauma, over and over, until my late twenties. I was a textbook example of an abuse victim. I used food and sex to sublimate my inner pain; I put a wall of fat around me to keep me safe; I approached each day as though I was on stage, carefully constructing a role to play. I did not directly confront the proverbial demon that dictated my ultimately self-destructive behavior. Somehow, I managed to function well enough to double major in college and go on to graduate school.

While I was in my first year of my master's program, The Man Who Molested Me died suddenly. My mother called to tell me the news. She seemed surprised, even saddened, when I made up a lame excuse not to drive the two hours home for the funeral. Then I proceeded to have a rather loud, swift, emotional breakdown. For a couple of months, I did a fairly good job of keeping my temporary insanity to myself, before I slipped back into the dizzying routine of studying, partying, and sleeping that defined graduate life. If I drank a bit more heavily, or began to smoke bowl after bowl of marijuana on my own, often mixing it with hashish to achieve utter numbness, no one really noticed. Most people go through some sort of emotional plunge while in graduate school. For some of us, it is a rite of passage.

For a few more years, I was able to stave off dealing with the rotting mass of memories that clung to the back of my consciousness. If someone had outright asked if I had ever been molested, I would have quickly and sincerely answered no. I truly did not fathom that I had been sexually victimized, although of course I knew it had happened. I felt as connected to the memories of abuse as I would feel to images recalled from a disturbing film. Although I could recall the plot, and even some of the actual events, it had no emotional resonance. So it was an utter shock when, one night during the first year of my doctoral program, a wave of crystal clear memories came washing over me as I slept. I went to bed the night before never suspecting I had been molested. When I awoke the next morning, I was a victim.

My graduate stipend included insurance, so I sought out a psychiatrist. Although he didn't automatically inspire trust—he was a dark, swarthy, and energetic man who was uncomfortably reminiscent of my abuser—he was able to prescribe some excellent drugs to quiet the shrieking in my head. Then the potent mixture of tranquilizers and Halcion pushed me over the edge. One day I began to weep uncontrollably. When I was finally able to stop crying a week later, I realized that I wasn't going to be able to once again willfully forget what had happened. I had to figure out some way to cope with it. So I weaned myself off the medications, albeit regretfully, and focused on working out my problems through therapy.

I don't think I was a very good patient. Despite the psychiatrist's earnest efforts to lead me along the acceptable regimen of denial/anger/grief/acceptance, I irascibly followed my own path. I tried to feel anger toward The Man Who Molested Me, but it didn't last long. Instead, I had to admit that I still loved him, not in a sexual way, but as a father figure or perhaps a valued friend, who must have been terribly wounded himself to have hurt me so badly. This attitude perplexed and eventually frustrated the psychiatrist, who seemed to feel that I had to hate The Man Who Molested Me before I could heal. I didn't know how to explain to the psychiatrist how I had become an accomplice to the crime, that The Man Who Molested Me had wheedled me into participating in my own abuse through little gifts and extravagant compliments that made the underlying threat seem bearable. By the time I had realized what was happening to me, it was too late to break free. I felt trapped, enmeshed in guilt. So I kept silent. I didn't tell anyone what was happening to me because I thought it was my fault. I wanted to protect my parents from knowing what a terrible child I was.

The psychiatrist also couldn't accept the lack of animosity toward my parents, who for years hadn't recognized their daughter's suffering. Yet why would they ever suspect the helpful, friendly, funny next-door neighbor of such heinous behavior? In the '60s and '70s, an aura of innocence still surrounded suburban life. Sexual abuse was hardly the trendy household phrase it has since become. Parents dutifully warned their children not to talk to strangers, but they never specified what those dangerous strangers might actually do. How could my parents suspect their friend of a crime that, at the time, was nearly inconceivable?

Despite the psychiatrist's ultimately unsuccessful struggle to squeeze me into an acceptable semblance of a sexual abuse victim, he did help me make some tough realizations about my life to that point. I knew I had tried to kill myself in the past, although I never consciously defined it as such. I was frequently compelled to test fate by driving my car recklessly, drinking and smoking too much, sleeping with men I barely knew, experimenting with marijuana, cocaine, amphetamines, whatever drug was available at the time. Experiencing a slight headache, I'd swallow two aspirin, then four, then nine or ten, and wait with detached interest for whatever would result. I had always suffered bouts of low self-esteem, feeling uncomfortable in my flesh, hating the way I looked. Sometimes, I would dig at my arms or my thighs with a safety pin, a thumbtack, or even a pen cap. Watching the blood well up felt good, somehow, because the wound was something I made myself and could control. I had to admit that I had spent the greater part of my life running and hiding—from my family, from people who could hurt me, from myself. I thought I knew who I was, but suddenly I had to accept the wrenching realization that everything inside me existed because of—or in spite of—my childhood victimization.

Unwilling to dig too far into the emotional ramifications of my abuse, I did the next best thing: I intellectualized it. I devoured books on child sexual abuse, even turned class projects into a chance to further explore the issue. I desperately wanted to understand why this man had used me. I felt that if I could comprehend the motivations behind molesting a child, I could come to terms with the ambiguous feelings that haunted me concerning my own abuse. While I researched the subject, I kept regular sessions with the psychiatrist. This went on for almost two years, then the psychiatrist said something disturbing that made me leave and never return. Almost casually, one day he told me, "The issue is not how an adult male can be turned on by a little girl. Little girls can be sexually provocative, and any healthy man can become aroused. The issue is whether the man follows through on those feelings. There's a fine line between feelings and actions."

I couldn't accept this. How could children be sexually provocative? As a woman, I had certainly never been sexually aroused by a young boy, so why would I believe all men were sexually aroused by little girls? The image was more than disgusting—it was absurd. And yet, from all the reading I had done up to this point, I knew that child sexual abuse was hardly an isolated phenomenon, nor something new to modern society. All that has changed is our willingness to acknowledge it. The psychiatrist's comment fed my need to understand why an adult could be sexually attracted to a child. I had to know why, how, what it all meant to me and to the countless other victims struggling to overcome their childhood degradation.

At the time, I had been working on putting together the prospectus for my doctoral dissertation. Since I had entered the program with the intention of pursuing a focus on organizational communication, my initial dissertation topic was to be an analysis of individual accountability in corporate settings. This was a safe, unemotional issue that suddenly seemed pretty dull in light of what was happening in my life. Midway through amassing mounds of research on the topic, I abruptly stopped and decided to wrestle with the issue of sexual abuse instead. When I presented a short synopsis of my new topic to my adviser, he gamely agreed to read through it. He took it home with him that weekend, and I waited in both anticipation and fear. Although I felt compelled to pursue the topic, I was also desperately worried that my adviser, who was also my friend, would be appalled, dismayed, or in some way recoil from me, now that I was openly admitting to having been molested. When I met with him the following Monday, he was polite but distant, and suggested I change to another adviser. This wasn't his area of expertise, he said, not meeting my eyes. Haltingly, he admitted that, while he was reading my manuscript, his young daughter had been playing in the same room. The thought of some man's thick fingers touching her, fondling her, reducing her to nothing but an object, made him physically ill. He knew that if he agreed to go on working with me, he'd be forced into such comparisons all too often, and he simply couldn't do it. I really did understand. He was a minister's son from the Midwest, where people didn't do such things. At least, they didn't talk about it when they did.

So he recommended I ask another professor to be my adviser, a venerable fixture in the communication program who was known for his high standards and crusty, demanding manner. I had taken only one class from him at that time, and I found him intimidating. But I also felt instinctively that under all that lofty talk, he was open-minded and empathetic. I was right. Drawing him into my struggle to put my childhood trauma into perspective proved to be immensely valuable. We had long discussions about not only my research, but also my feelings surrounding the project and my own quest for understanding. Once or twice, as we talked, he even appeared to be on the verge of tears. At those times, I couldn't always relate to his compassion, because the further I got in my research about sexual abuse, the more I was able to once again distance myself from my own pain. Packaging my experience as an intellectual exercise made it easier to box up all those intrusive feelings of hurt, betrayal, and grief. I had found another potential means of escape.

A couple of years after embarking upon my dissertation, I finished my doctoral course work and began the nerve-wracking task of job hunting. I was offered positions at a couple of different colleges, but one in particular intrigued me. The position was as an instructor of communication studies at a small, isolated college in New York. When I arrived that March to interview, my plane circled the airport as the pilots debated whether to land in the midst of a snowstorm—which, I later learned, was a fairly typical occurrence. During the long drive down to campus, which took a good two hours through blinding snow and sleet, I had a lot of time in which to form an impression. I settled into bed that night certain I'd spend the next day being squired around a campus I had every intention of hating. Yet when I awoke the next morning and peered out of the window, I saw blue skies, crisp piles of snow, and quaint little buildings that already felt like home. Although the people I spoke with that day were more eager to impress me than expecting me to try to impress them, they didn't need to work so hard. I instinctively felt that

I needed to be there, that this was the place where I could renew my energies after the exhausting, tumultuous years I'd just spent in therapy.

I finally completed my dissertation in the fall of 1994. At that time, New York was considering adopting its own version of Megan's Law. Although the idea of having policies informing people of convicted perpetrators living in their neighborhoods ought to have comforted me as a survivor of sexual abuse, it didn't. In fact, the more I thought about the implications, the more uncomfortable I became. I decided to add my voice to the din. On November 13, 1994, the *Rochester Democrat & Chronicle* published my opinion piece, titled "New Law Won't Stop Sex Offenders." I wrote:

> As a survivor of sexual abuse, I am intimately acquainted with its horrors, yet I cannot believe that convicted molesters are beyond redemption. Society's attitude that child molesters cannot be reformed simply strengthens an abuser's conviction that he will never be able to control his impulse to molest. If society holds no hope for a molester's redemption, how can he learn to trust himself?

My column inspired some dissent. The newspaper printed a few of the more interesting letters people wrote in response. Some were politely indignant (albeit sympathetic to my admission of victimization), and a few were downright strident, even accusing me of being an advocate for pedophiles. Mostly, my views were received with bemused disbelief. How could a victim speak out for the offenders? Was she brainwashed, or just plain deluded? At the time, I wasn't completely certain myself. I was still struggling with a deep-seated need to understand the motivations of The Man Who Molested Me. I knew he had loved me, in his own way. I wanted to believe he would have felt guilty about his actions and would have tried to make amends, if only someone had intervened. I wanted to believe that I was more than just a convenient vessel.

As a result of the article, I received a telephone call from one of the counselors at a nearby correctional facility. He told me about the sex offender program they had begun in the prison, and he invited me out for a visit. On a gray December morning, I headed out to the facility. When I pulled my car into the visitor's parking lot, I noticed uneasily that the tall fences surrounding the prison were topped with barbed wire. When I rang at the gates, the guard buzzed me in, and then the door banged shut behind me. For a split second, I felt an impulse to flee. I focused on the fact that I had become a very public survivor of sexual abuse, and that none of the men I'd be meeting had any control over me. They couldn't—I was no longer that helpless little victim who kept blindly reacting to her abuse, over and over again. At the end of the day,

I'd be able to leave the fences and barbed wire and guards behind. I was free—in every sense of the word. I wasn't letting my abuser dictate my life anymore.

An hour later, I was shut in a small, stuffy room with a couple of counselors and an astonishing variety of sex offenders. Ranging from exhibitionists to aggressive rapists, they all had one thing in common: they looked so normal. Some peeked at me nervously as they haltingly described their crimes. A few tried to stare me down. "Why are you here?" one man asked bluntly. I had to think about that one before finally admitting that I was simply curious. I told them that I wanted to get to know them, to try to understand why they hurt people. I wanted to know what pain in their lives had made them capable of inflicting such degradation on other people.

They all knew I had been molested. The counselor who called me had made copies of the newspaper article and passed them around. If I expected that this knowledge might give the offenders power over me, I was wrong. It actually had the opposite effect. They were curious, too, and they were grateful that I was willing to speak candidly to them about my experience. In their self-help group, they were being taught how to show empathy. They wanted to know what it was like to be a victim; they wanted to know what their own victims must have felt. So after the initial awkward silence, their questions spilled out like a flood. At the end of the two-hour session, I felt drained, but in a sort of buoyant, giddy way. It was a catharsis to sit in that close, dank room and share the impact of my abuse with men who might have done the same things to similar little girls and women. I even felt like I might have left a lingering impression on a few of them.

Although I had publicly pontificated on the need to help offenders find treatment rather than indiscriminately punishing them, I hadn't really thought through the implications to that point. Seeing this group in action, talking to the counselors who were spending long, emotionally exhausting hours to make their treatment program work, made me realize that perhaps there was some hope for their redemption. When the counselors I met with told me I should consider putting together a research plan and working with their inmates, it seemed only logical. Ever since I had begun my recovery, ever since my own victimization, I had moved toward this opportunity. Yet before I embarked upon this research, which entailed spending hours alone with individual offenders with nothing but a tape recorder between us, I had to wrestle with my motives. Why was I compelled to do this? Did I view studying child molesters as a form of self-therapy? Was I too subjective, did I have too many expectations, would my bias twist whatever I might discover? Was I simply masochistic?

The answers to these questions became irrelevant as the interviews unfolded. The men who have spoken to me are not monsters, however monstrous the crimes they committed. They all have their own stories, with unique sets of circumstances that led to their crimes, yet there are many similarities as well. Identifying these patterns can give us glimmers of why people molest children and how we should treat offenders to keep them from repeating their crimes. Most importantly, listening to these stories can show what steps we need to take to prevent children from falling victim to these predators.

Spending time with these men has taught me a lot, not only about them, but about The Man who Molested Me. Oddly enough, the more I've come to understand his weakness, lack of character, and warped value system that gave him permission to molest me, the easier it's been to forgive him. I know now that he was trapped in his own web of deceit and inner angst, woven from a pattern that was probably passed down from generation to generation. There's no excuse for what he did to me, but there were reasons for it. Understanding the reasons has given me a measure of peace.

The stories in this book are presented pretty much the way they were expressed to me. I've edited them for the sake of clarity and cohesion and changed specific names and places to protect the anonymity of both the offenders and their victims, but I think they speak clearly about the circumstances and motives that led the offenders to commit their crimes. Read these stories with an open mind. When you're finished, despise their actions. Hold these men in contempt for their willingness to give into their darkest impulses. Condemn them for being weak, violent, impulsive, or cruel. But remember the children that they once were and the lessons they learned that shaped their adulthood. Try to imagine what can be done to keep other children from growing up to become just like them.

CHAPTER ONE

∿

The Impact of Child Sexual Abuse

"While I was doing it, it made me feel good, I was able to get satisfaction. To me, it was just like having intercourse with a lady, with a woman. I enjoyed it. I wasn't too worried about what they felt, I wasn't worried about whether I was hurting them—you know, I just didn't care. It was just for myself."

The man across from me is in his early fifties, with graying, greasy hair, thick glasses, and an oddly innocent expression. His weathered face is pleasant, the eyes crinkled at the corners, almost twinkling. He has a pronounced lisp that softens his words, making his story sound more soothing than shocking. He is a convicted sex offender, a child molester, a man who admits to fondling—and raping—at least a dozen boys and girls. And I am alone with him in a small, windowless room, my tape recorder placed on the desk between us. The whir of the tape recorder sounds strangely loud as the man stops speaking, offering me a gentle smile. You want to trust that smile. I'm sure his victims did.

Between 1995 and 2000, I conducted countless one-on-one interviews with incarcerated child molesters. I also co-facilitated in-prison self-help groups consisting of child molesters and rapists. After years of study, what once seemed incomprehensible has begun to gain clarity. I have been given glimpses into why an adult would sexually molest a child. The reasons on the whole do not fit the public's image of all child molesters as perverse or simply evil. As a society, we've been willing to view sex and sexual crimes through a lens distorted by the misperceptions perpetuated by media, religion, and superstition. Our self-righteous, self-conscious sense of morality has

1

been dictated by our squeamishness. We gratefully embrace longer prison sentences and community notification policies as a panacea for our fears, unable—or unwilling—to explore the roots of this crime. But child molesters are not freaks of nature. They are not aberrations or mutations. They are humans, most frequently men, who are driven to their actions by potent stresses and even more potent messages equating sex with power and control.

The impulse that inspires some people to molest children doesn't suddenly appear out of the blue as an inexplicable, uncontrollable desire. Rather, this impulse is programmed into them—and us. This is not to say that everyone is capable of molesting children. For most of us, the prospect is inconceivable. Yet we influence, and are influenced by, pervasive images that present youth and innocence as provocative and even erotic. If we truly want to address the problem of child sexual abuse and protect our children from sexual predators, then we have to admit our own complicity in the crime. If we want to learn the truth, we must be willing to explore the limits of our own value systems, even as we question those of society's latest bogeymen.

This book is my contribution to the controversy surrounding child sexual abuse and sexual abusers. I offer the stories of nine convicted sex offenders, incarcerated at the time of their interviews. These men represent the most common form of child molester, which is not the morally depraved, defiant NAMBLA (North American Man–Boy Love Association) card-carrying member, nor the sort of predatory, exploitative criminal who sets up and supports the child pornography rings that infect the internet worldwide. Nor is the common type of child molester a sadistic kidnapper and killer of children. The most common type of child molester is generally a fairly innocuous, unexceptional individual who doesn't look any different from you or me. He may lead a life that seems very similar to our own, except that for whatever reason, for whatever purpose, out of some mystifying and perverse impulse, he sexually molests children. If we really want to understand this crime, then we need to accept this fact—that most child molesters are not monsters. They are human beings who might have more in common with us than not.

I do not make this observation lightly. As the preface states, I was the victim of a child molester. I spent long years trying to come to grips with the myriad ways in which that experience radically shaped my perception of the world. I empathize with the victims of men such as those presented in this book. I sympathize with the public confessions of victims, in which they express their anger, outrage, and unremitting pain, because I've experienced those emotions myself. I still struggle with keeping the frightened, lonely child inside of me safely stifled beneath the weight of adulthood. But wallowing in fear and disgust is not helping us to solve the problem. We have openly talked about child sexual abuse from the victims' perspective for the past twenty years. Now it is time to listen to what the offenders have to say.

Although I am an academic, and as such have my own ideas about what methodology might help us dissect the crimes of child molesters, my goal is to simplify the intellectual jargon so that we can't hide behind lofty language and obscure, erudite philosophy. Child sexual abuse is not an issue that benefits from the emotional distance provided by forms of quantitative analysis and intellectually sophisticated theories. The social panic that surrounds the crime attests to the way in which it horrifies us on a primal level. Yet to truly understand this issue, we have to attempt to control our visceral reaction so that we may identify how offenders rationalize their behavior. To help accomplish this task, I am presenting the offenders' stories in their own words, so that the reader can see the situation through the offenders' eyes. The men who have shared their life stories here were willing to open themselves to public scrutiny in an effort to overcome the misunderstanding and derision that follows this crime, but the reader is left to determine how much—or how little—truth is in their tales. Their autobiographical accounts, which I refer to as self-narratives, are enlightening more from the form they take, the structural elements they contain, and the premises that construct their actions than from specific names, locations, and other "facts" that may be loosely interpreted as objective. Although each self-narrative contains unique observations, the ways in which the subjects describe their experiences, and subsequently how they understand them, are defined and constrained by socially constructed presumptions of behavior. Their perceptions of themselves, their actions, and their motivations are most fundamentally reflections of social mores and taboos. Indeed, the existence of the crime itself is predicated on the social context. We form our reactions to child sexual abuse from the social conventions that construct our worldview. Although we certainly prefer to consider acts of child molestation as aberrations from the social order, the existence and understanding of child sexual abuse is socially dictated. Therefore, the focus of this book is to show how the troubling statistics surrounding child sexual abuse, and its impact upon victims, perpetrators, and society, take on new meaning when viewed through the framework of narrative, which captures the nature of a discursively created reality.

The Problem of Child Sexual Abuse

Over the past few decades, public attention has been drawn to a flood of statistics and horrific stories about child sexual abuse. The public hysteria surrounding child sexual abuse has been fueled by sensationalized media coverage of the crime that frequently intimates perpetrators are lurking in every playground and park, waiting to feast their evil desires on unsuspecting boys and girls. From the tone of much media coverage, one might think that the presence of sexual predators in the United States is a new phenomenon, yet there were actually two other periods in the twentieth century in which sex crimes and sexual criminals dominated the public consciousness. One peak was between the years 1937 and 1940, when J. Edgar Hoover, in a move aimed at stirring up nationalism, racism, and anticommunism, declared a war on the sex criminals who threatened American childhood and womanhood. The years 1937 to 1940 saw a marked increase in media coverage of child sexual abuse when a series of apparently sexually motivated child murders became a topic of public outcry and legislative action.

The next peak of hysteria over sexual offenses occurred between 1949 and 1955, following the publication of Alfred Kinsey's *Sexual Behavior in the Human Male* in 1948 and *Sexual Behavior in the Human Female* in 1953. Among Kinsey's influential—and shocking—findings was that sex between adults and children in the United States seemed surprisingly frequent. Nearly one-quarter of the four thousand women surveyed said that they either had had sex with adult males when they were children or had been approached by men seeking sex.[1] Once again, citizens groups mobilized and mass media publicized lurid accounts of sex crimes against children. Newspaper and magazine articles offered numerous theories about the psychology of "sex fiends" and psychopaths. Also presented to the public were the views of psychiatrists and psychologists who claimed that the detected offenses were but a fraction of the actual incidence. These assertions helped stoke the panic. State legislatures took action by commissioning sex crime inquiries, setting up special task forces on habitual sex offenders, and passing new "dangerous" or "mentally disordered" sex offender laws.

In the panics of both the 1930s and 1950s, psychiatrists and psychologists played a prominent role in defining the social problem of child molestation. They claimed that the core problem was not the sexual contact per se, but rather the public expression by offenders of socially deviant sexual desires. Little attention was paid to the needs of victims; in fact, until the 1950s, studies of child victims were sparse and tended to report little injury to victims. Researchers also hypothesized that a victim's personality traits displayed before the offense, as well as the victim's environment, could contribute to the aftermath of sexual abuse, since these factors could affect a child's vulnerability at being sexually approached or even contribute to the offense's occurrence. Thus, it was difficult to make a causal relationship between a sexual offense and emotional or behavioral disturbances observed afterward.

Ultimately, contributors to the sexual offense research did not portray all legally defined child victims as actually sharing a victim status. There was no collective narrative of sexual abuse to provide a context for public discussion and comprehension of the effects on victims; therefore, it was difficult for victims to publicly talk about their experiences. Victims began to experience a more welcoming atmosphere for their stories of sexual abuse when the field of family therapy arose in the late 1950s as a challenge to psychoanalysis and the clinical methods derived from it. Family therapists reinterpreted problems that were traditionally treated with individual psychotherapy as part of a greater context. For example, they argued that father–daughter incest was the offshoot of a system in which wives and daughters played pivotal roles. This perception was important, since it played a part in later feminist reaction to the existing literature on child molestation. Family therapists made the child–victim a subject of treatment and created new, highly publicized programs and self-help groups, including ones for adult survivors. In the 1970s, the tenets of family therapy directly influenced legislative changes at both the state and national levels.

Articulating a category of sexual abuse did not stem from the rise of family therapy, however; this originated in the child protection movement. In 1956, Vincent De Francis, a long-time activist with the American Humane Association (AHA), published a report entitled *Child Protective Services in the United States*, which helped to put child protection on the agenda of both private child welfare agencies and the U.S. Children's Bureau.[2] In the late 1950s, the Children's Bureau began to fund a small group of child abuse researchers, including C. Henry Kempe, whose influential article, "The Battered Child Syndrome," thrust child abuse into the public's consciousness in 1962 and mobilized the child protection movement. As the 1960s progressed, the definition of abuse began to expand, and ownership of the issue slowly shifted from medical doctors to other experts such as social workers and therapists. A study launched in two New York counties in 1965 by De Francis and the AHA was instrumental to this change. The new study was radical because it focused on child victims of sex offenders and the response of parents and the criminal justice system to them. Four major breakthroughs occurred with this study. First, De Francis examined more cases with a much higher percentage of offenses not committed by strangers and a higher level of victim harm. Second, De Francis used a broader definition of "incest" and subsumed all cases under the term "sexual abuse." Third, De Francis argued that child victims were also victims of a community that neglected their plight, and that not only the victims but also their families required professional help. Fourth, De Francis suggested that incidences of child sexual abuse might be many times higher than reported incidences of physical abuse.

As the 1970s dawned, child sexual abuse emerged as a pressing social problem when it joined rape as a focus of feminist outrage. In April 1971, the New York Radical Feminists held the first conference on rape. At this conference, Florence Rush, a former staff member of the Society for the Prevention of Cruelty to Children, told her own story of being sexually molested as a child and adolescent. In a set of recommendations for victims published with the conference proceedings, Rush said feminists needed to make the issue of child sexual abuse part of their framing of rape, and to "think of children's liberation as being the same as women's liberation."[3] Theorizing power, not sex, as the crucial dynamic behind child sexual abuse thus established unequivocally victim innocence and offender intention of harm. Rejecting both the traditional psychoanalytic position, which affixed blame on the victim's unconscious desires, and the family therapeutic approach, which looked at incest within the family dynamic, the feminist-driven conceptualization placed sole blame for the crime on the perpetrator. Victims were always coerced as a result of patriarchal structures that permitted, inspired, and sustained sexual domination.

Rush's compelling statements, which she reiterated in her influential book *The Best Kept Secret: Sexual Abuse of Children* (1980), and the feminists' subsequent outcry inspired the "conspiracy of silence" issue that still tends to surround child sexual abuse. This belief has contributed to the present panic over sexual abuse, since it has publicly framed a new definition of the abuse victim, in which themes of innocence, betrayal, silence, isolation, powerlessness, and emotional trauma play heavy roles in media descriptions of the "crisis." Ideologically, the feminist perspective holds that rape and child sexual abuse express the broader pattern of patriarchal domination and are means of disempowering women and children. Rape is a political act of oppression and social control designed to put constraints on women's freedom. By extension, so is child sexual abuse, particularly of girls, as it instills fear, guilt, and shame and socializes girls to accept a subordinate role in society. Thus, a new orthodoxy emerged in the early 1970s in which child sexual abuse was conceptualized as the most potentially destructive experience a child could have.

Legislative efforts focused on researching and combating child sexual abuse ensued. In addition, a flood of media attention occurred, focusing on both rape and child sexual abuse. In 1977 and 1978 alone, almost every national magazine ran a story highlighting the horror of child sexual abuse. A national campaign against the making and sale of child pornography gained national attention in a matter of weeks, and in record-breaking time, protective legislation was passed nationally and in thirty-five states. Following the arrests of alleged members of a "sex ring" in Jordan, Minnesota, and the emergence of the McMartin Preschool case in 1984, media interest in the issue intensified.[4]

The constant stream of stories presented in the media over the past thirty years has been effective in presenting sexual abuse as a distinct risk for every child. The claim is that sexual crimes, and sex crimes against children in particular, have been on the rise. A commonly accepted estimate is that one in five girls and one in ten boys suffer sexual abuse before age eighteen.[5] The statistics change depending on the type of variables, such as the population surveyed, and the definition of sexual abuse employed by the researcher(s). The term "sexual abuse" is used to describe acts ranging from voyeurism and exhibitionism to sodomy and intercourse. Although it is difficult to prove that sexual offenses against children have increased, there has certainly been a radical shift in attitudes and beliefs regarding the prevalence of child sexual abuse, and this may have encouraged more reporting of sexual abuse cases. Until the mid-1970s, some researchers suggested that the incidence of incest was one in a million.[6] In 1976, only six thousand cases of sexual abuse were referred to U.S. protective services agencies; ten years later, this number had risen to 132,000 cases of sexual abuse.[7] By 1992, nearly 500,000 rape and sexual abuse cases were reported annually in the United States.[8] Even though it is hard to prove that this astounding rise in the number of reported cases reflects an increase in actual sexual abuse, it is true that more people, primarily male, have been convicted for sexual offenses against children. In 1980, 20,500 people in the United States were serving prison time for sexual offenses. By 1990, this figure had risen to 63,600 people serving time for sexual offenses.[9] In 1994, state prisons held 88,100 sex offenders.[10]

This startling upswing in the number of imprisoned sex offenders may be due to a variety of factors, whether an increase in the number of crimes being perpetrated or a greater commitment by law enforcement to incarcerate sex offenders. However, many researchers have noted that, in actuality, victim underreporting is a significant barrier to understanding the extent of sexual abuse. To make a report, a child victim must make public an event that involves personal shame, fear, or anticipation of negative consequences. In cases of intrafamilial sexual abuse, victims may experience significant conflict about making disclosures that implicate caretakers or family members. In addition, charges of child molestation are notoriously difficult to prove. Since there is not always definitive physical evidence and there are often delays in reporting the offenses, investigators need witnesses to report a detailed description of the scene to support the allegation. As a result, child sexual abuse cases often rely on circumstantial evidence and word of mouth. Beyond the legal ramifications, child sexual abuse is an undeniably compelling social problem. The self-reports of convicted rape and sexual assault offenders serving time in state prisons indicate two-thirds of such offenders had victims under age eighteen, and 50 percent of those—or nearly four in ten imprisoned violent sex offenders—said their victims were age twelve or younger.[11]

Some researchers propose that new media, particularly the computer, have contributed to the rise in reported sexual offenses against children. In the 1980s and 1990s, video games were a way in which some sexual predators lured potential victims to their homes. By the 1990s, the internet opened virtually limitless opportunities for child molesters to pinpoint and stalk their victims. Public imagination has been stirred by the prospect of countless perverts using e-mail to correspond with unsuspecting youth and setting up elaborate websites with which to share child pornography. The assumption seems to be that a person who would look at sexual images of children must also physically molest children. If this is true, then the number of child molesters worldwide must be staggering. A number of high-profile law enforcement stings in the United States and abroad have publicized the pervasiveness of child pornography on the internet. On September 13, 1995, after a two-year investigation into alleged illegal activity through America Online, then the United States' largest commercial on-line service, the Federal Bureau of Investigation (FBI) arrested twelve people and searched more than a hundred homes in a nationwide crackdown on computer child pornography. The investigation, code-named "Innocent Images," marked the first time federal agents investigated an on-line service on a nationwide basis. According to CNN, by April 1997 the ongoing probe "Innocent Images" had netted ninety-one arrests and eighty-three felony convictions.

Another FBI investigation, code-named "Operation Candyman," was launched in January 2001 after an undercover agent identified three E-groups involved in posting, exchanging, and transmitting child pornography. In February 2001, the FBI shut down the Candyman E-group. By July 2002, the FBI had reported that over one hundred individuals had been arrested since Operation Candyman's inception. A particularly shocking revelation of computer-based child pornography came in August 2002, when U.S. and Western European authorities arrested twenty people for running an international child pornography ring. The acts of sexual abuse and exploitation, which often involved the alleged perpetrators' own children, were captured in images that were then circulated via the internet.

On May 7, 2003, another shock wave reverberated through the media when Pete Townshend, guitarist and songwriter of the legendary band The Who, was "formally cautioned" and entered on the Sex Offenders Register in Great Britain after four months of investigation by Scotland Yard's Child Protection Group. Townshend admitted that he had looked at the front pages and previews of child pornography sites three or four times in 1999 before accidentally stumbling across one. Although Townshend claimed that he accessed the site as part of research for a book he was writing, the police arrested him anyway. In Britain, it is illegal to look at such sites, even under the noble guise of "research."

In the United States, legislative efforts to curb computer-based child pornography have often infringed on First Amendment rights. For example, in 2002, the U.S. Supreme Court rejected a federal law that would make illegal any image that "appears to be" of a nude child or teenager under eighteen years old. The majority of the justices wrote that Congress's first try at banning "morphed" porn was akin to prohibiting dirty thoughts. Undeterred, two weeks later, Attorney General John Ashcroft and several members of Congress revealed the Child Obscenity and Pornography Prevention Act (COPPA). The new COPPA bill referred to any computer-generated image that was virtually indistinguishable from that of a minor engaging in sexually explicit conduct. In June 2002, the House voted overwhelmingly to pass the rewritten bill, which would outlaw photographic digital images of children, unless they were proven to be computer-generated simulations that did not portray actual underage sex.

Efforts to curb child pornography on the internet were just the latest attempts in the United States to adopt legislative means of combating sexual abuse. The demand to curb child molestation reached its zenith in the mid-1990s with passionate, hotly debated, and highly publicized attempts to step up efforts to ferret out and isolate sexual offenders, which culminated in the introduction of registration legislation and "Megan's Law." On May 17, 1996, President Clinton signed a tougher version of the federal Megan's Law, which was named after Megan Kanka, a seven-year-old New Jersey girl who was raped and strangled in 1994. Megan's Law allows for either making information about sex offenders available to the public on request or authorizing probation and parole departments, law enforcement agencies, or prosecutor offices to disseminate information about released offenders to the community at large.[12] By 1997, all states had devised their own versions of Megan's Law.

In general, sex offender registration policies share six principal features.[13] First, the registry is usually maintained by a state agency. Second, local law enforcement is generally responsible for collecting information and forwarding it

to the administrating state agency. Third, information typically includes the offender's name, address, fingerprints, photo, date of birth, social security number, criminal history, place of employment, and vehicle registration. Fourth,
the most common time frame for registration is twenty days or less from the offender's prison release date. Fifth, most states require registration for over ten
years. Sixth, most registries are updated only when the offender notifies law enforcement that he has changed residences. Megan's Law is an addition to this
registration procedure, which allows for certain information about sex offenders to be made available on request to individuals and organizations. Some
state statutes mandate proactive notification, while others merely authorize it.
Some state statutes assign responsibility for conducting notification to state or
local criminal justice agencies, although at least one state requires that the offenders themselves do the notification. This mandate acts as further punishment and demands offenders take personal responsibility for their actions.

Another legislative response to the panic over child molesters is
Stephanie's Law, named after a nineteen-year-old girl from Kansas who was
sexually assaulted and killed in 1994. Stephanie's Law, which some states
have adopted in various forms, allows for detaining in mental institutions sex
offenders released from prison who are deemed likely to recommit their
crimes. For example, between 1998 and 2000, approximately one hundred
men in Illinois were detained in mental institutions indefinitely following
their release from prison.

Although Megan's Law and Stephanie's Law were aimed at assuaging fear of
child molesters by exposing offenders to public scrutiny, a scandal that erupted
in 2002 showed how some perpetrators were able to hide their activities behind
powerful, paternal institutions—in this case, the Catholic Church. The "pedophile priest" crisis had its roots in the 1980s, when incidents of clergy sexual
abuse became socially defined as a pressing problem due to the "celibacy" issue.
This played out against the feminist interpretation of sexual abuse that focused
on patriarchal systems as primary contributors to the exploitation of women
and children. The pedophile priest panic of 2002 seemed to fit into this interpretation of sexual abuse. The crisis was precipitated by public revelations of
the prolific crimes of former Boston priest Father John J. Geoghan and the
ways in which Church officials apparently covered up the incidents. The pedophile priest crisis peaked with the June 14, 2002, announcement that the nation's Catholic bishops had approved an expansive policy for dealing with sex
offenders in the church. In late February 2004, a study prepared for the U.S.
Conference of Catholic Bishops by the John Jay College of Criminal Justice established that 4,392 priests sexually abused nearly eleven thousand children
younger than eighteen from 1950 to 2002.[14]

In the midst of national concern and shock over the scandals in the Catholic Church in 2002, yet another source of fear set the nation's temperature soaring. The summer of 2002 seemed fraught with child kidnapping and sex crimes. Although raw statistics suggested that child abductions and sex crimes had not been on the rise in the United States, some high-profile cases touched a nerve in the nation. On August 6, 2002, after a couple of horrific crimes in which young girls were snatched and later found murdered, President Bush called for a White House summit on child safety. In his comments, President Bush observed, "Unfortunately, as we work to make our children feel safer by fighting terror, America's children and parents are also facing a wave of violence from twisted criminals in our own communities."

The impact of these scandals and shocking revelations has been to focus public awareness on the palpable presence of child sexual abuse in America. Yet, for all the frenzied media coverage and incessant commentary, public understanding of the effects of child sexual abuse on victims and perpetrators remains superficial. The greatest attention has been focused on exploiting the most horrifying—and titillating—aspects of the crime for public consumption. The end result is that, although we are more aware of child sexual abuse, we have limited understanding of the real impact on both victims and offenders, and of the subsequent ramifications for the rest of society. We've permitted the media to choose what elements of the crime to focus on, and consequently, our perspective of child sexual abuse is one-dimensional. The dramatic image of helpless innocents trapped in the clutches of evil sex fiends is compelling, but it draws attention from the more mundane, yet perhaps even more insidious, everyday reality.

Impact on Victims

> The first time I had sex with the man I'm now married to, I was terrified that I'd look up and see his face turn into the face of my abuser. Even now, after five years of marriage, I feel like there's a third person sleeping in our bed. It's become a big problem between my husband and me—that I've brought this creep into our marriage. Even though the guy who molested me is dead, he's still fucking me over.[15]

The woman who related those words to me was a victim of childhood sexual abuse. Her victimization wasn't unusual, nor was the lingering reminder of childhood trauma that threatened to undermine her adult interactions. Adults who were molested as children aren't difficult to find, although they may try to hide their experiences for fear they will be ridiculed, pitied, or worst of all, disbelieved. Child sexual abuse is the sexual exploitation of a child who is not capable of resisting the abuse; therefore, the sense of powerlessness survivors felt as children can construct the reality they enact as adults. In *The Courage to Heal*, a popular self-help guide for sexual abuse victims first published in 1988, one woman is quoted as saying:

> People have said to me, "Why are you dragging this up now?" Why? WHY? Because it has controlled every aspect of my life. It has damaged me in every possible way. It has destroyed everything in my life that has been of value. . . . I don't care if it happened 500 years ago! It's influenced me all the time and it does matter. It matters very much.[16]

The effects of childhood sexual abuse can be devastating for both the child victim and the adult survivor, since the essential element of sexual abuse is the physical, psychological, and moral violation of the child. The original effects of abuse on children can lead to lingering adult problems, including eating disorders, alcohol and drug abuse, prostitution, sleep disturbances, self-mutilation, masochism, and other antisocial, self-destructive behaviors. As a result, even if we are not directly acquainted with a survivor, we are affected by its social implications.

Research studies have described numerous potential effects of sexual abuse on children and adults. These include physical, emotional, and behavioral effects in addition to influences on beliefs, attitudes, and values. These effects can be linked to the post-traumatic stress disorder frequently experienced by victims of violence. As psychiatrist Judith Lewis Herman relates in her book *Trauma and Recovery*, post-traumatic stress disorder consists of three stages: hyperarousal, intrusion, and constriction. Each of these stages has been observed in survivors of child sexual abuse, and each can manifest itself through childhood into adulthood. *Hyperarousal* is the persistent expectation of danger. Because sexual abuse is the misuse of power and control, a child may be left with lingering feelings of insecurity, which can carry over into adulthood. As one sexual abuse survivor described to me: "After that first time when he touched me, I don't remember ever feeling safe again. I can't walk down the street without feeling as if I'm being followed. I can't go to sleep at night before checking all the closets, for fear someone will attack me when I turn out the lights."[17]

Intrusion is reliving the event as flashbacks and nightmares, often triggered by small, seemingly insignificant reminders. A casual brush of the hand, the scent of a man's cologne, or the particular texture of a carpet can bring memories of the event rushing back in an uncontrollable flood. Survivors can rarely predict when these intense reactions might occur:

Once I was walking along in the mall with my daughter. We were eating ice cream cones. Anyhow, all of a sudden as I licked my ice cream cone, this wave of panic just crashed over me, right out of nowhere. I must have blacked out for a moment or two because when I came back to my senses, I was crying and my daughter was clutching my arm and the ice cream was in a puddle on the ground. It took a couple of minutes before I could stop my heart from pounding. It had just hit me—I was seven years old and my grandfather had spread whipped cream on his penis so I would lick it off. The taste and texture of the ice cream must have reminded me of that incident.[18]

Constriction is a state of powerlessness in which the survivor feels helpless to cope with the event and may alter consciousness, either self-defensively or unknowingly, rather than facing the pain. Deliberate attempts to numb or distort perceptions may be exacerbated by alcohol, narcotics, food disorders, or other means of escape. Efforts to block out the memories rather than directly confront them may work temporarily, but eventually many survivors are forced to acknowledge their experiences: "I always feel panicky. I never know what I'm feeling. I never know what I should be feeling. I'm afraid if I do feel something, it will be too frightening and horrible to deal with. So I try to ignore the screaming in my head so I can just get through the day."[19]

Victims of sexual abuse may restrict their lives through social isolation, self-mutilation, and self-destructive behaviors. In this way, they keep punishing themselves for their abusers' actions. Acting out their trauma through destructive behaviors may be an attempt to overcome the helplessness and lack of control they had over their bodies as children. Yet paradoxically, the more they attempt to gain control of their experiences through acting out, the more helpless they become. They are walking a tightrope, precariously poised between intense emotion and numbness, between amnesia and reliving the trauma. As sexually victimized children, they were given contradictory messages. Because they were taught to trust adults, they were sent the message that they must endure the abuse. The abusers might have insisted that they loved the children while threatening, coercing, or forcing them into sexual acts. Thus, as adults, victims may experience difficulties in trust. Sexual abuse survivors may doubt their ability to accurately assess and predict the behavior of another person, so they sabotage relationships because they fear intimacy and being hurt. Survivors may become involved in abusive relationships because they feel they deserve them, or they may completely isolate themselves from other people.

Some victims cope with sexual abuse by "splitting" or dissociating. Victimized children may figuratively split away from their abused bodies, removing themselves out of conscious consideration of the situation, which allows them to suppress both the physical and emotional impact of the abuse. This defense mechanism may help the child endure the experience, but can be carried over into adulthood. An adult survivor describes how she experienced only a fragment of the memory of her abuse:

> For years, I never consciously remembered how my stepbrother molested me. When he was abusing me, I disconnected from my body—it was like I floated around the room and watched him doing the deed from a distance. For the next twenty years, I never thought about it again, except there were lots of times when my hands would go numb. I went to a lot of doctors, but they never found the cause. After I began in therapy, I discovered that the numbness was a memory. My stepbrother would hold my hands over my head, and I was remembering the pain from it, even though I didn't consciously recall it at the time.[20]

The traumatized person who dissociates from the experience may feel intense emotion but without clear memory of the event, or may remember everything in detail but without emotion. Denial and dissociation can lead to a sense of unreality. Survivors may construct an image of "normality" they portray to others but rarely feel inside. In some cases, sexual abuse survivors may become extremely high self-monitors, which is defined as self-observation and self-control guided by situational cues to social appropriateness.[21] Some sexual abuse survivors exhibit high levels of theatrical ability because they learned to cope with their abuse by hiding behind a succession of masks. For these survivors, extremely high levels of social sensitivity stem from the desire to avoid genuine self-disclosure. Careful self-monitoring is a defense mechanism for covering innate feelings of unworthiness and low self-esteem.

The effects mentioned thus far stem directly or indirectly from the impact sexual abuse has on self-concept. Since children develop their self-concepts through interaction with the significant people in their lives, sexual abuse victims may base their perceptions of self on the messages received from their abusers. By showing children that their feelings do not matter, and that they will receive love and affection through sexual performance, abusers encourage victims to identify themselves in such terms. The child's lack of control over the abuser, the environment, and the child's own body engenders passivity. Children possess little power to stop their abuse, since they are put into situations where they are completely at the mercy of a much more powerful person. Sexually abused children are objectified and used; hence, they can grow into adults whose fragile self-esteem is a result of this powerful lesson. The low self-esteem of survivors contributes to their silence and shame;

hence, the social construction of child sexual abuse as taboo is reinvigorated, since it continues to be perceived as a source of secrecy, self-recrimination, and misunderstanding. Thus, the violent cycle—or system—of abuse continues.

Consequently, despite society's newfound outrage emanating from the recent "discovery" of child sexual abuse, a culture built upon a structure of superior/subordinate relationships harbors sexual violence as a form of indoctrination and control. The patriarchal social system that feminists decry has sustained sexual abuse through carefully constructed realities of power differentials and engendered inequalities. This lesson about who possesses power and how power can be wielded has been further supported by the way in which society has subtly held children responsible for their own abuse. Thanks to the deeply rooted influence of psychoanalysis in Western culture, sometimes children have been viewed as accepting of, even instigating, sexual contact. For example, in a 1988 study, researchers found that encouraging and passive children were thought to be more responsible for their abuse than resisting children.[22] When society implicitly blames children for their abuse, the children often come to believe they are responsible as well. As one study reported, unlike physically and verbally abused children, sexually abused children almost always blame themselves, regardless of the severity or frequency of the abuse.[23] This self-blame leads to feelings of guilt and inadequacy in adult survivors of sexual abuse. Looking back as an adult on his childhood trauma, one survivor observes:

> When I finally did say something about what my uncle had done to me, nobody believed me. I was too calm about it. It just sounded so unbelievable. This guy was my uncle, for Christ's sake. He was a big deal in the family. I guess if I had showed more emotion about it, they would have taken me more seriously. As it was, I shut up about it real quick. I figured it was my fault to begin with, so I just had to deal with it myself.[24]

As author Florence Rush observed over twenty years ago in *The Best Kept Secret: Sexual Abuse of Children*, "The dilemma of the sexual abuse of children has provided a system of foolproof emotional blackmail. If the victim incriminates the abuser, she also incriminates herself. The sexual abuse of the child is therefore the best kept secret in the world."[25] Sadly, although more victims have been willing to speak out about their abuse, society still feeds the secrecy surrounding sexual abuse through fear and disdain. In a society that drapes the sexual abuse of children in taboo, it is easier for a victim to remain silent than to risk public exposure. Yet blaming a child for being abused is like blaming a tree for getting struck by lightning. A tree can't hide from the elements; its very nature leaves it open to attack. So it is with children. The very things that make children so precious—their innocence, trust, and dependence—are what make them vulnerable. Yet all too often, adults who were molested as children look back across the expanse of time and feel responsible for their own abuse. Perhaps this is because it is less painful to believe they had some control over the circumstances than to believe they had no control at all, even if it means taking responsibility for their abusers' actions. Or perhaps it is better to think they were at fault than to admit they were completely, utterly powerless. It is difficult for a person to admit to being nothing more than a victim, a ready receptacle for someone else's lust. Feeling guilty may be better than feeling helpless.

In addition, the fact that the majority of victims were molested by someone they know adds to the dilemma. Adults convicted of felony sex crimes rarely have a criminal history and are increasingly less likely to be strangers to their victims. Up to 90 percent of sexual abuse victims know their abusers; they are the children's parents, siblings, relatives, or trusted family friends.[26] So sex offender registration policies and community notification procedures may address only one-tenth of the problem. The frightening reality is that the majority of perpetrators are able to commit their crimes because they already have access to the potential victims. Nine-tenths of these offenders could be acting out right in front of us, but we might never suspect them because they are so skilled at what they do.

Defining the Perpetrators

So how can we recognize these sexual offenders? Frankly, it isn't easy, since the mass-mediated stereotypes we tend to associate with child molesters can draw our attention from the actual perpetrators. We don't even use the terms associated with the behavior correctly. Pick up any article on child sexual abuse, and you may find that the perpetrators are alternately referred to as child molesters and pedophiles. In 1979, A. Nicholas Groth wrote a groundbreaking book entitled *Men Who Rape: The Psychology of the Offender*, in which he defined having a sexual attraction toward prepubertal children as *pedophilia* and sexual attraction toward pubertal children as *hebephilia*, sometimes spelled *ephebophilia*. Although sexual attraction to children by adults has the obvious potential for criminal activity, it does not necessarily constitute a sexual perversion as defined by psychiatry. Technically, pedophilia is a paraphilia, one of the psychosexual disorders including acts of exhibitionism, fetishism, sexual masochism, sexual sadism, transvestitism, and voyeurism, and diagnosis can be made only by qualified psychologists and psychiatrists. A child molester is an individual who sexually molests children. A pedophile is an individual whose sexual fantasies and erotic imagery are focused on children. Many child molesters are pedophiles and many pedophiles are child molesters, but they are not necessarily one and the same.

The stereotypes of child molesters perpetuated by mass media have blurred these distinctions because the most dramatic image is of depravity feasting on innocence. In *Erotic Innocence: The Culture of Child Molesting* (1998), James Kincaid concludes that the stereotypes associated with child sexual abuse victims and perpetrators are hopelessly gothic, since the cultural narratives are populated with evil monsters and helpless victims. Taking this narrative to its extreme, the plot revolves around the potent theme of innocence versus degradation, good versus evil. Unsettlingly, in stories of sexual abuse, good does not inevitably prevail. The monsters stay monstrous, since the assumption is that we cannot prevent child molesters from molesting. The image that haunts us is of an elusive, irredeemably depraved antagonist who cannot be vanquished. We might bravely fight the monster to protect the innocent, yet triumph—if any—may be fleeting as the monster simply fades back into the shadows, only to reappear in the infinitely more depressing sequel.

The sinister character Kincaid conjures is actually a contrast to the more benign, yet paradoxically perhaps more dangerous, stereotype of the child molester that has persisted in American culture until recently. From the vague warnings given to children not to speak to strangers to the graphic exploits of "Chester the Molester" in *Hustler* magazine, child molesters have traditionally been caricatured as "dirty old men"—sometimes harmlessly lascivious, sometimes openly dangerous, yet always readily recognizable. Because it is more comforting to imagine that child molesters look like "Child Molesters," this stereotype has been difficult to dismantle. Despite an outpouring of stories that show abusers as relatives, friends, and even spiritual leaders, it is hard to break the stereotype of the child molester as the creepy individual who moves in down the block or the seedy-looking character lurking in the alley. Even politically expedient legislation such as Megan's Law seems to rest on the premise that child molesters should be easy to identify.

Then, in 1993, this image was shaken when an entertainment icon, Michael Jackson, was publicly accused of molesting teenage boys. Eventually, the case was settled out of court. Ten years later, in late 2003, Jackson was once again thrust into notoriety when he was accused of child molestation. The Peter Pan of the entertainment world, whose persona as soft-spoken, gentle lost boy always seemed a bit perverse, was once again portrayed in the press as a pedophile who preyed on the young boys he invited to Neverland, his palatial estate and fantastic playground. At his arraignment on January 16, 2004, Jackson pled not guilty to seven felony counts of lewd and lascivious acts with a child under the age of fourteen and two counts of administering an intoxicating agent to a child to commit the alleged molestation.

Ironically, or perhaps appropriately, the allegations against Jackson came as Hollywood announced plans to make a new version of the popular 1971 film *Willie Wonka and the Chocolate Factory*, which features another powerful, puckish man who invites children into the bizarre yet alluring world of his imagination. Although the first adaptation of Roald Dahl's 1964 book *Charlie and the Chocolate Factory* might have been a zany interpretation of Dahl's vision, in the wake of the nation's panic over child sexual abuse, the power and control Wonka holds over the children now seem even more sinister. Wonka's world appears calculated to seduce the gluttonous, greedy children who enter. Wonka's ending speech to Charlie, the wide-eyed blonde cherub who wins the contest and Wonka's heart, expresses the desires of a man who distrusts the motives of adults, preferring the pliable naiveté of youth:

> Wonka: How do you like the chocolate factory, Charlie?
>
> Charlie: I think it's the most wonderful place in the whole world.
>
> Wonka: I'm very pleased to hear you say that because I'm giving it to you . . . that's alright, isn't it? . . . Who can I trust to run the factory when I leave and take care of the Oompa Loompas? . . . Not a grown-up. A grown-up would want to do everything his own way, not mine. That's why I decided a long time ago that I had to find a child. A very honest, loving child, to tell all my most precious candy-making secrets.

Fans of Willie Wonka (and I confess that I am one) may shudder at the thought, but Wonka personifies the qualities many pedophiles share: isolation from peers, an intense connection to children, and the ability to manipulate circumstances and potential victims.

So if the commonly accepted stereotype is not based in reality, who are these perpetrators, anyhow? According to conviction records, the average first-time sex offender is a white male between the ages of thirty-three and thirty-five.[27] Note, however, that this is the offender's age at the time of conviction and not necessarily the age at which he perpetrated his first crime. The vast majority of convicted sex offenders are male, although we do know that females also molest children. In a statistical report using data from the U.S. National Incident Based Reporting System, one researcher found that between 1991 and 1996 in twelve states, 4 percent of those charged with forcible rape and 8 percent charged with sexual offenses were female.[28] Overall, studies hypothesize that females commit approximately 20 percent of sex offenses against children.[29] However, on the whole, these crimes are rarely reported, let alone convicted. This may be due to conflicting social expectations, which vilify male offenders while obliquely excusing females for similar crimes. After all, traditional cultural stereotypes view women as those who care for others, not as individuals capable of harming or abusing other people. The idea that women could exploit children for sexual gratification is practically unthinkable. In fact, in its discussion of paraphilias, the 4th edition of the *Diagnostic and Statistical Manual of Mental Disorders* indicates that "except for sexual masochism . . . paraphilias are almost never diagnosed in females."[30] The lack of recognition that females can and do molest children is the result of traditional sexual scripts that depict women as incapable of committing sexual offenses.[31]

For example, consider the case of Mary Kay LeTourneau, the teacher who was thirty-six years old in 1998 when she was convicted of having sex—and a baby—with an adolescent boy. She was initially given a scolding, then served six months in jail. As LeTourneau's lawyer, David Gehrke, observed in *Time* magazine, "She found the man of her dreams, but he was thirteen."[32] Soon after this slap on the wrist, LeTourneau violated her probation when she was found to be yet again pregnant with the boy's child. Even still, LeTourneau seemed to evoke more sympathy than outrage. She was labeled as emotionally disturbed, which she most probably was, but that should not constitute an excuse for manipulating a child into a sexual relationship. If LeTourneau had been a man in his thirties convicted of sexually molesting an adolescent girl, he would have been subject to public outcry and a hefty prison sentence.

Pedophiles are individuals who turn to children for sexual gratification. This happens for a number of reasons. For years, researchers have attempted to classify these individuals into some sort of coherent typology. The goal, of course, is to illuminate the essential question: What motivates a person to molest a child? But the answer to that question has proved to be as maddeningly elusive as it is complex. In general, child molesters are divided into several broad categories. As early as 1892, psychologist Richard von Krafft-Ebing classified child molesters into those with acquired mental illness, senile individuals, chronic alcoholics, and those suffering from paralysis, epilepsy, head injuries, apoplexy, or syphilis. Antisocial offenders were found to have committed sexual offenses with adults and children, and to have committed more nonsexual crimes. In the twentieth century, some researchers described child molesters as men who felt rejected by society and impulsively molested strangers when they felt especially stressed. Some researchers claimed that child molesters were actually just men with weak personalities and not necessarily sexually depraved.

Over the years, researchers have proposed that child molesters offend because they are senile, trying to regain their youth, lonely, emotionally and sexually isolated, or impotent. Some researchers have identified another type of offender as individuals unable to relate to adult sexual roles, claiming that these are immature, underdeveloped people who show marked anxiety over potency and inferiority, and who thus establish sexual relationships with children.[33] Another group of offenders consists of individuals whose crimes are reactions against sexual or emotional frustration, labeled "heterosexual aggressors against children."[34] Typically, perpetrators in this category are incest offenders and have a history of poor marital relations. They sexually abuse their children as substitutes for—or means of revenge against—their wives.

In *Men Who Rape: The Psychology of the Offender*, A. Nicholas Groth presents a typology of child molesters that consists of two parts. One concentrates on the degree to which the behavior is entrenched; the other stresses the basis of psychological needs. The first part of Groth's typology distinguishes between *fixated* child molesters and *regressed* child molesters. Fixated child molesters have been attracted to children throughout their lives and have been unable to attain any degree of psychosexual maturity. Regressed child molesters have related sexually to peers at some point in their lives, but a variety of situational stresses may undermine their confidence in themselves as men. Oftentimes, the source of this stress is unemployment, which not only increases financial pressures but also undermines the aspect of male identity that revolves around a job. Physical illness may also impair regressed offenders' sexual self-image and inspire them to rebuild their sense of security by molesting children, who are less threatening and judgmental than adults.

The other part of Groth's theory addresses the degree of force used in the assault. This is related to the psychological needs fulfilled by the act. A *sex-pressure offense* utilizes enticement or entrapment. This offender, who is pursuing love and affection as well as physical contact, attempts to elicit the victim's cooperation and is usually dissuaded if the child resists. These individuals often state that they are "in love" with their victims. In contrast, a *sex-force offense* uses intimidation or physical aggression. These offenses can be divided into exploitative assaults, which utilize threat or force, and sadistic assaults. These individuals are drawn to children primarily because they are easily overpowered and may present less resistance than an adult. The most frightening type of child molester—as well as the most dangerous—is the sadistic offender. This individual has eroticized violence and must inflict pain, degradation, and even death on the child in order to achieve sexual gratification. Although this type is the most feared of all sex offenders, it is also the most rare.

The FBI has developed a typology of child molesters loosely based on Groth's work, but expanded to include seven subgroups.[35] This classification system is designed for use in criminal investigations. Elaborating on the concept of the regressed child molester, the concept of the *situational* child molester refers to an individual who does not have a defined sexual preference for children and includes the following types:

- *Regressed*—emotionally immature, socially inept individuals who relate to children as peers. These individuals may be experiencing a brief period of low self-esteem and turn to their own children or other available juveniles.
- *Morally Indiscriminate*—antisocial individuals who use and abuse everything they touch. Their victims are chosen on the basis of vulnerability and opportunity, and only coincidentally because they are children.
- *Sexually Indiscriminate*—referred to in the psychoanalytic literature as "polymorphous perverse." These individuals have vaguely defined sexual preferences and will experiment with almost any type of sexual behavior.
- *Inadequate*—individuals who are social misfits and may be developmentally disabled, psychotic, senile, or organically dysfunctional. They see children as vulnerable objects with which to satisfy their sexual curiosity. These individuals have been known to murder their victims.

Preferential child molesters correspond to the fixated offenders in Groth's typology. These individuals show a strong sexual preference for children, and this preference has characterized their sexual attraction patterns throughout their lives. The subgroups include:

- *Seduction*—these individuals have exclusive sexual interest in children, and they court and groom them. They are usually able to identify potential victims who will not divulge their behavior.
- *Introverted*—they have a fixed interest in children, but do not have the social skills to seduce them, so they typically molest strangers or very young children. These individuals may also marry women with children in the age range of their preference.
- *Sadistic*—these perpetrators' sexual preference for children is coupled with a need to inflict pain in order to achieve sexual gratification.

Given these typologies and others, it is clear that child molesters may be motivated by a variety of factors to commit their crimes. But while it may be easy to dismiss the fixated offenders as warped sexual perverts, we are still left to wrestle with the reality that many perpetrators are seemingly "normal" people who inexplicably molest children. What makes them do this? Why does one man, newly unemployed, with a drinking problem, an unhappy marriage, and a host of other stresses in his life, molest a child while a dozen other men in similar straits never even contemplate the prospect?

One theory is that sex offenders on the whole have experienced inconsistent attachments with significant others.[36] This perspective suggests that traumatic disruptions in a child's early formative years may be a contributor to sexual offending in later life and may play a key role in the motivation behind the offense. In this sense, sex offending is not only a behavioral disorder but a relational disorder as well, since it is an extortion of intimacy in an attempt to restore damaged self-esteem and establish an interpersonal connection. Self-esteem, as it is understood in this context, means more than just feeling good about ourselves. Rather, it constitutes the fundamental source of selfhood, the energy that drives initiative and motivation. A person with healthy and resilient self-esteem is able to regulate the flow of energy from high to low and recover from narcissistic injuries. When experiencing an assault on our sense of self, those of us with resilient self-esteem turn to the people and things we love for reassurance and a sense of connection. The consistency and quality of those attachments profoundly affect our sense of self and our ability to form future positive attachments. A sex offender may have unstable self-esteem and lack the cognitive or emotional ability to build self-worth in healthy, mature ways.

This damaged self-esteem can lead to another factor that may motivate child molesters: cognitive distortions and lack of empathy. People with fragile self-esteem are motivated to protect their sense of self-worth from further erosion, therefore they are more likely to engage in self-serving biases when interpreting events and their behavior. Sexual offenders may deliberately distort their perceptions of their victims' distress in order to be able to continue offending without feeling guilt or remorse.

Another theory focuses on the deviant fantasies of child molesters. Sigmund Freud hypothesized that every fantasy is a correction of unsatisfying reality; fantasies are a means of meeting unmet needs. Research has postulated that child molesters are driven by deviant fantasies that show significant relationships with negative emotional states, especially loneliness and depression. In addition, evidence exists to show that some perpetrators were themselves abused as children. Considering the variety of short- and long-term effects of sexual abuse, it seems apparent that adult survivors often repress their memories or punish themselves for their childhood victimization, internalizing the trauma. Yet some victims may cope by externalizing the trauma, becoming "vampires" who repay others for their own victimization. In a cruel role reversal, the vampire may gain the power and control he lost as a victim by victimizing other children.

Hypotheses, elaborate research studies, and educated guesses abound as to what motivates people to become child molesters. But the impulse to molest is often born of such complex factors; it is risky—albeit tempting—to squeeze offenders into any tidy classification system. Maybe the crime is so complicated, it is futile to focus on any possibility of rehabilitation. Perhaps this is why the law enforcement and corrections communities have tended to throw up their hands in helplessness, claiming that treatment programs can't work, therefore punishment through incarceration and public scrutiny are the only means of keeping these perverted, purportedly unrepentant bastards away from our kids. Ultimately, it seems that truly understanding the nature of this emotionally destructive and psychically debilitating betrayal of innocence rests not so much in the statistics surrounding the crime, but in the way we talk about it. Through mass media and moral panic, we have constructed a persuasive image of child sexual abuse and sexual abusers that has become more influential than the facts. We've concocted a widely accepted "truth" about sexual abuse that directs the ways in which we make assumptions about the perpetrators, their motives, and their potential for redemption. Deconstructing the ways in which child sexual abuse is socially constructed can take us a step closer to stopping the crime at its source.

Notes

1. John Crewdson, By Silence Betrayed: Sexual Abuse of Children in America (Boston: Little, Brown, 1988), 24–25.

2. Barbara J. Nelson, Making an Issue of Child Abuse: Political Agenda Setting for Social Problems (Chicago: University of Chicago Press), 40–41.

3. Florence Rush, "The Sexual Abuse of Children: A Feminist Point of View," in Rape: The First Sourcebook for Women, ed. Nancy Connell and Cassandra Wilson (New York: New American Library, 1974), 74.

4. Katherine Beckett, "Culture and the Politics of Signification: The Case of Child Sexual Abuse," Social Problems 43 (1996): 60.

5. David Finkelhor and Jennifer Dziuba-Leatherman, "Children as Victims of Violence: A National Survey," Pediatrics 94 (1994): 413–20.

6. See, for example, S. Kirson Weinberg, Incest Behavior (New York: Citadel, 1955); Alfred M. Freedman, Harold I. Kaplan, and Benjamin J. Sadock, Comprehensive Textbook of Psychiatry (Baltimore: Williams and Wilkins, 1975).

7. American Association for the Protection of Children, *Highlights of Child Neglect and Abuse Reporting* (Denver: American Association for the Protection of Children, 1988).

8. Matthew Parynik Mendel, *The Male Survivor: The Impact of Abuse* (London: Sage, 1994).

9. Jodi Brown et al., *Correctional Populations in the United States, 1994,* 1996, at www.ojp.usdoj.gov/bjs/pub/pdf/cpius94.html (accessed March 10, 2004).

10. Kim English, Suzanne Pullen, and Linda Jones, "Managing Sex Offenders in the Community: A Containment Approach," *National Institute of Justice Research in Brief* (Washington, DC: U.S. Department of Justice, Office of Justice Programs, January 1997), 1.

11. Lawrence A. Greenfeld, *Sex Offenses and Offenders: An Analysis of Data on Rape and Sexual Assault,* 1997, at www.vaw.umn.edu/documents/sexoff/sexoff.xml (accessed December 18, 2003).

12. Peter Finn, "Sex Offender Community Notification," *National Institute of Justice Research in Action* (Washington, DC: U.S. Department of Justice, Office of Justice Programs, February 1997), 1.

13. Scott Matson and Roxanne Lieb, *Sex Offender Registration: A Review of State Laws* (Olympia, WA: Washington State Institute for Public Policy, 1996), at www.sexcriminals.com/library/doc-1029-1/pdf (accessed February 18, 2004).

14. *Rochester Democrat & Chronicle,* February 28, 2004, 1A, 5A.

15. W., personal communication, January 21, 1996.

16. Ellen Bass and Laura Davis, *The Courage to Heal* (New York: Harper and Row, 1988), 33.

17. T., personal communication, October 9, 1992.

18. C., personal communication, August 29, 1997.

19. J., personal communication, January 15, 1996.

20. K., personal communication, February 18, 1996.

21. Mark Snyder, "Self-Monitoring of Expressive Behavior," *Journal of Personality and Social Psychology* 30 (1974): 526.

22. Sylvia D. Broussard and William G. Wagner, "Child Abuse: Who Is to Blame?" *Child Abuse and Neglect* 12 (1988): 568.

23. Philip G. Ney, Christine Moore, John McPhee, and Penelope Trought, "Child Abuse: A Study of the Child's Perspective," *Child Abuse and Neglect* 10 (1986): 512.

24. J., personal communication, December 10, 1995.

25. Florence Rush, *The Best Kept Secret: Sexual Abuse of Children* (Englewood Cliffs, NJ: Prentice-Hall, 1980), 104.

26. Stop It Now! "Child Abuse: A Public Health Epidemic," *About Stop It Now!* at www.stopitnow.com/about.html (accessed April 12, 2004).

27. A. Henderson, "The Sexual Criminal," *Governing* (August 1995): 36.

28. Howard N. Snyder, *Sexual Assault of Young Children as Reported to Law Enforcement: Victim, Incident and Offender Characteristics,* 2000, at www.ojp.usdoj.gov/bjs/pub/pdf/saycrle.odf (accessed January 16, 2004).

29. Association for the Treatment of Sexual Abusers, "Reducing Sexual Abuse Through Treatment and Intervention with Abusers," Policy and Position Statement 1996, at www.atsa.com/pptreatment.html (accessed January 16, 2004).

30. American Psychiatric Association, *Diagnostic and Statistical Manual of Mental Disorders*, 4th ed. (Washington, DC: American Psychiatric Association, 1994), 524.

31. See, for example, Peter B. Anderson and Cindy Struckman-Johnson, *Sexually Aggressive Women: Current Perspectives and Controversies* (London: Guilford, 1998).

32. "Mad about the Boy," *Time*, February 16, 1998, 103.

33. See, for example, J. H. Fitch, "Men Convicted of Sexual Offenses against Children: A Descriptive Follow-up Study," *British Journal of Criminology* 3 (1962): 18–37; W. N. East, "Sexual Offenders," *Journal of Nervous and Medical Disease* 103 (1946): 626–66; E. Revitch and R. Weiss, "The Pedophiliac Offender," *Diseases of the Nervous System* 23 (1962): 73–78.

34. Paul H. Gebhard, John Gagnon, Wardell B. Pomeroy, and Cornelia Christenson, *Sex Offenders: An Analysis of Types* (New York: Harper and Row, 1965).

35. Kenneth V. Lanning, *Child Molesters: A Behavioral Analysis for Law Enforcement Officers Investigating Cases of Child Exploitation*, 1992, at skeptictank.org/nc70.pdf (accessed February 18, 2004), 6–9.

36. See, for example, Tony Ward, Stephen M. Hudson, and Julie McCormack, "Attachment Style, Intimacy Deficits, and Sexual Offending," in *The Sex Offender: New Insights, Treatment Innovations and Legal Developments*, Vol. II, ed. Barbara Schwartz and Henry R. Cellini, 2–9 (Kingston, NJ: Civic Research Institute, 1997).

~

CHAPTER TWO

"Truth" and the Social Construction of Child Sexual Abuse

I am obligated to begin this chapter with a confession: this study has become a vastly different project than I originally conceived. The exhaustive, self-consciously academic proposal I labored to create that the Department of Corrections approved in 1995 turned out to be unworkable as the study progressed. This occurred for a variety of reasons, not the least of which was the dawning realization that, although the Department of Corrections gave me permission to gather the information, they didn't necessarily want me to disseminate it to a wider audience. I came to the conclusion that if I continued to conduct the study as I had proposed, any written reports of my work would never be published. So I radically altered the purpose of my research, abandoning the desire to produce quantifiable results in favor of a more personal approach.

My decision to change my research program was not based solely on the frustration I experienced with the Department of Corrections' policies (and note that my frustration was not directed at any individuals who worked for the Department of Corrections, since they were as constrained by these policies as I was). My decision also stemmed from the growing recognition that my original goal had profoundly changed as I learned more about the subjects and their crimes. The original purpose, which was to apply rhetorical methods to offender self-narratives in order to coax patterns out of their stories, was based on my assumption that the motivations of child molesters could be discerned by forcing a typology of offender characteristics. The more time I spent with the men I interviewed, the more I had to admit that my initial assumptions about them were naïve. I had to take the study into a completely new direction if I wanted to be true to what the offenders were teaching me. When I began my one-on-one interviews, I did so with a blithe expectation that I could enter into the troubled world of sex offenders and maintain a safe emotional distance. As I began to spend countless hours listening to their wrenching stories—hours that stretched into weeks, months, and finally, years—I struggled to be objective, because I assumed that objectivity was a canon of social science research. Yet the more time I spent in prison, surrounded by electrified fences and barbed wire, locked in tiny rooms with men who reeked of defeat, defiance, and despair, I gradually recognized that objectivity was impossible. My personal values inevitably tainted my interaction with those men and subsequently the ways in which I interpreted their stories. So I faced a difficult dilemma: Do I incorporate my own biases into my work? Or do I hypocritically pretend that it hasn't affected every stage of this research, from the initial interviews to the book I now write?

Although I remained fundamentally an outsider to the prison system, an "unescorted official" who could enter and leave at will, I became more involved with my subjects than I ever expected. I could only interview subjects who volunteered to speak to me; consequently, my sample of offenders was completely arbitrary and primarily made up of men who had expressed a desire for rehabilitation. In addition, the way in which I chose subjects for the interviews was hardly unbiased. I firmly refused to talk to anyone with victims under the age of three. Although molesting a three-year-old was bad enough, I felt instinctively that any person who would molest a baby was beyond comprehension. This was a completely emotional reaction, not one I could statistically defend. However, I could not overcome my innate revulsion and, I must admit, I did not try all that hard. I knew I had abandoned all semblance of objectivity when I made the decision to share my own story with the offenders I interviewed. Incarcerated child molesters are necessarily a wary lot. To accomplish their seductions, they learn to be subtle, crafty, suspicious, mistrusting. To survive in prison, they have to sustain this cunning because men identified as "baby rapers" don't last long. In the curious pecking order that structures prison life, child molesters have less status than murderers. Men incarcerated for horrific crimes—men who may torture, rape, or kill; men who may openly lust after teenage girls and degrade women as "bitches" and "cunts"—these men cling to one final taboo, that molesting a child is unpardonable. In their moral universe, killing a baby raper is an honorable act. Consequently, in order to accomplish this study, I had to earn the subjects' trust. I chose to interject my own experience to inspire their cooperation, with the rationale that they would feel more comfortable sharing their stories with me if first I shared my story with them.

This was a difficult decision to make. I knew when I joined the first group meeting and took my seat in the midst of eight hardened, suspicious, predominantly misogynist rapists and child molesters that they saw me as little more than a piece of meat. My breasts and genitalia took precedence over my academic credentials. The biggest hurdle I faced was proving to them that I was neither victim nor enemy. This was a precarious task, since it meant that I had to share my story of sexual victimization with them without showing vulnerability. Because I was a woman, they expected me to be weak. I had to show them that I was in touch with, yet impervious to, my pain while simultaneously expressing acknowledgment of their own. Eventually, I became comfortable with the idea that I could not—and would not—be objective. However, this initially caused me some sleepless nights, because blatant subjectivity can be difficult to defend. Even as I write this book, bringing my own childhood victimization into the foreground makes me nervous. It is essential to the narrative because it originally motivated my research interests and has been inextricably entwined ever since. Yet I can't help but feel a tiny twinge of anxiety, a sneaking fear that my colleagues may revile me and consign my research to the book aisles at Wal-Mart, shoved between lurid true-crime novels and the latest bodice-ripping romance.

Ultimately, however, the risks I took when engaging in this research program actually made me even more aware of the intense stigma that surrounds child sexual abuse and the ways in which that stigma forces offenders into silence. Early on in this research, when the debate over the relative merits of Megan's Law was at its peak, I felt a social responsibility to take a public stand on the issue, and it quickly became apparent that a dissenting voice was viewed with suspicion. My motives were questioned, sometimes in colorful terms. I was accused of being an advocate for child molesters, a deviant, godless woman who obviously did not understand the stakes involved since she didn't have children of her own (of course, the fact that I was once a child myself, and a sexually abused one at that, didn't count). When I became a mother toward the end of conducting this research, those same critics tended to view me with even more suspicion, unwilling to recognize that a woman with a daughter of her own might actually believe a child molester could be anything but an evil aberration of nature. In prison, I was obliquely threatened by some inmates, none of whom were sex offenders but rather were those who stalked child molesters and consequently the civilians they suspected worked with them. At various tense moments over the years, I felt my university job could be jeopardized because my work didn't fit into the safe, theoretically tested niche favored by some of my colleagues.

So I had something in common with the offenders I interviewed. We each took significant risks by challenging the stigma that has discredited those who attempt to break the silence surrounding the crime. On a professional level, I risked losing my credibility. On a personal level, I risked opening myself to painful reminders of the abuse I experienced as a child as the men described to me, in excruciating detail, the ways in which they physically and emotionally assaulted their victims. The offenders had their own risks to shoulder. On a public level, the men I interviewed risked disclosing intimate aspects of their crimes to a public that already labeled them monstrous. On a private level, they risked their own personal safety, because if other inmates recognized them as child molesters, they could face rejection or even physical violence. Since I was willing to accept the risks, I had to acknowledge the possible repercussions my subjects could experience as a result of talking to me. So I overstepped the bounds of academic passivity and involved myself with the subjects of my research. I shared salient aspects of my personal life with them, and I tried to show interest in them, so they would believe that I considered them more than mere lab rats or stereotypes. The prison system, and the world outside the prison walls, might view them as worthless, but I wanted them to feel that I valued their contribution to my research.

I was able to find support within the academic community for the ethical issues I faced. One researcher I have always admired is Jack Kay, who became chair of the Department of Communication at Wayne State University when I was a graduate student. Kay has conducted research on hate groups. To gather information, he actually attended some groups' gatherings, which he had to do under false pretenses since these organizations jealously guard their private rituals. Although Kay, too, wrestled with the ethical ramifications of his fieldwork, as he notes, social scientific research has long dealt with ethical issues. Medical experimentation by Nazi doctors, CIA involvement in academic research, the failure to treat patients in the Tuskegee syphilis study, Milgram's infamous pain studies, and other examples give ample reason to be suspicious of research.[1] Gross violations have led to rigid, sometimes hysterical regulation of academic research. Behavioral investigation committees, human subjects committees, and research conduct codes by universities and professional associations have developed to adjudicate tension between research and the individual's right to safety and privacy, even when those individuals are incarcerated.

Kay identifies four major themes related to ethics in qualitative research: (1) codes and consent; (2) deception; (3) privacy, harm, identification, and confidentiality; and (4) trust and betrayal.[2] I had the subjects sign consent forms. The Department of Corrections required this, but I would have done so anyhow, since I needed to have, in writing, the subjects' clear permission to document their stories and disseminate them to the public. So in this sense, the offenders knew that they had some control over participating in my study. Perhaps the most difficult dilemma I faced in gaining their trust was the interplay between confidentiality, trust, and betrayal. A canon of inquiry assumes that the researcher must carefully protect the privacy and confidentiality of her subjects. Although the Department of Corrections was keenly interested that I maintain the confidentiality of my subjects, ostensibly for the inmates' protection, I also had to agree to break that confidentiality under certain conditions. For example, say one of the men I interviewed insinuated that he had more victims than those involved in his conviction. If he divulged any particular details regarding these other offenses, such as specific names or locations, I was required to report this information to the authorities. The men I interviewed were aware of this, and had to remain on their guard during their interactions with me. If I sensed they were becoming too relaxed, I cautioned them not to reveal too much. This certainly detracted from their self-narratives and left me frustrated. At times, I felt close to uncovering information the courts couldn't address, but had to back away from the knowledge for the subjects' sake, even though it could mean obstructing justice for the unidentified victims. When the offenders signed the consent forms, I promised I would guard their words and therefore protect their lives. Yet I couldn't ignore that these were convicted criminals incarcerated for horrific acts against children. There were a few dark moments when I considered abandoning the study, since I felt that the project threatened to make me an accomplice to their crimes—that, ironically, I was actually feeding, even encouraging, the silence that sustained child sexual abuse with my promise of confidentiality. But I had to continue my work, out of my unwavering belief that society cannot effectively combat child sexual abuse until it understands the perpetrators. I had to find a place to shelve the discomfort, to accept the tension between confidentiality and unwilling complicity.

My goal in documenting these self-narratives is to explore how these particular child molesters perceive themselves and their actions. Self-narratives have an evaluative point to make about the self. Rather than merely describing an event, a self-narrative includes the narrator's understanding of that experience. This understanding is gleaned from the narrator's identity, or sense of who he is. The narrative form used to express a person's identity is a discursive structuring of experiences such that they are connected logically and temporally.[3] However, narrative order does not necessarily reflect the order of actual events but rather the perception of the narrator. So, although self-narratives may be expressed within a logical sequence, they may not be directly relaying the objective facts of a situation. Ultimately, narrated identity is moral identity, which means that it offers an explanation for deeds done.[4]

Since discourse acts as a socially produced system for the production and circulation of knowledge, it expresses both the realm of its object (what the knowledge is of) and its environment (the social order within which it is produced, within which it circulates its knowledge, and upon which the effects of this knowledge may be traced). Hence, self-narratives reflect a *discursive* reality. I believe it is possible to theorize a "reality" with a nondiscursive existence, but discourse is the means of expressing this reality, therefore discourse makes it meaningful. The underlying premise to this study is that *the act of discourse produces an apprehensible reality*. Discursive reality is a process, and the knowledge it produces is socially bound.

Embracing this premise has allowed me to accept the unabashedly biased way in which I've conducted this study and written this book. I consider myself to be a rhetorical critic, and rhetorical studies inevitably contain a moral element. We study sources of rhetoric, such as these offender self-narratives, not only to interpret what is, but also to illuminate what can be. This goal is hardly value-free, and the conclusions to any study are dependent upon the perspective of the researcher. Traditionally, common knowledge has been that researchers in the humanities explore possibilities, while scientific researchers—including social scientists—focus on facts. Yet more recently, many researchers, particularly feminists, have rejected the idea that even scientific inquiry can be value-free.[5] They claim that researchers need to acknowledge their personal, professional, and political interests. For example, rather than as a fact-finding mission, these researchers view the interview approach as an active relationship that occurs in a context permeated by issues of power, emotionality, and interpersonal process. As a result, interviews are viewed as collaborative, communicative events that evolve their own norms and rules. This approach to interview research, called *autoethnography*, is especially useful when exploring sensitive topics that are intimate, may be personally discrediting, and normally are shrouded in secrecy. From this perspective, emotions and personal meanings are legitimate topics of research, since the interpretation of events by both the interviewer and interviewee reflects a discursively produced reality.[6]

Undeniably, the interviews I conducted were heavily influenced by the sensitivity of the subject matter, not to mention the context and setting. The fact that the subjects were incarcerated and the interviews took place inside the prison meant that a clear power relationship was already established. This made it even more important for me to clarify to each man that, although he was confined and physically constrained—by the prison gates as well as by the monitor in the interview room, which allowed guards to keep the inmate under constant scrutiny while he spoke to me—he did have some control over the information he chose to share. I needed to close the hierarchical gap between us so that the inmates felt comfortable enough to be as honest as possible (although the ultimate "truthfulness" of their accounts would be impossible to measure and was not the ultimate goal of the interviews). First, my gender seemed to encourage them to become more open when telling their stories. Perhaps my femininity was less threatening, or possibly they felt that I would be a more sympathetic listener because I was a woman. Second, because they knew my own story of victimization, it seemed to build common ground between us. They knew I could empathize with their victims, but also that I might be able to relate to their own abusive past histories. I suspect a few of them also viewed the interview as a chance to speak indirectly to their victims, to justify their actions in an effort to seek understanding and perhaps absolution.

Once they overcame their initial anxiety, some of the perpetrators I interviewed were pathetically grateful for the attention, shyly offering up the details of their stories. Sometimes these men looked to me for encouragement, as though they wanted to please me, and other times they even broke down in front of me, their tears ripped from someplace deep inside. At such moments, I couldn't help but feel sympathy for their pain. It was an odd emotion that took some time to reconcile: that I would feel kindly toward a child molester, a man who crudely stripped away his victim's innocence in a warped quest to fulfill some unfathomable desire. I never dreamed that I could feel sorry for a child molester. Yet I often did. I felt sorry for the children they once were who were emotionally maimed, stunted in such profound ways that they grew into adult predators. Suffering through a lousy childhood is not an excuse for committing any sort of crime, particularly one so heinous, but it certainly can shape an individual's perspective of the world.

Not all the men I interviewed were willing to be open from the start. These offenders told their stories warily, occasionally embellishing the events with dramatic flourishes and elaborate lies—lies I often suspected they actually believed. It is the dialectical tension between truth and lies that forms the core of this book: lies about sex and sexuality; lies about what it takes to feel strong, powerful, in control; lies that can turn an innocent child into a dangerous adult. As I listened to the litany of abuses some of these men experienced as children, I felt grateful for my own upbringing. I had parents who instilled in me a strong set of values that I was able to use to overcome the aftereffects of sexual abuse. There was not a remote possibility that I would grow up to become a sexual abuser myself, but maybe I took for granted the gift of a loving, supportive family, since within that context I was able to perceive an existence for myself beyond the boundaries of victimhood. Perhaps that is the real lie: that victims don't have power to fight back. That victims are doomed to repeat the cycle of abuse, whether their pain is directed inward or flung outward into the world, where it can create yet another victim.

True Lies

> Truth is not to be found inside the head of an individual person; it is born between people collectively searching for truth, in the process of their dialogic interaction.

> —Mikhail M. Bakhtin

Given the various perspectives that produce knowledge of child sexual abuse and its perpetrators, how do we operationalize the concept of "truth" in offender self-narratives? Certainly, the assumption within the legal system is that the truth of a perpetrator's actions—the objective, dispassionate recounting of sin—may be neatly recorded for posterity within a presentence report. This report, which is put on record within the Department of Correction's massive database, is a narrative that constitutes the offender's identity for the legal community. The presentence report presents the basic facts of the case and invites speculation of the offender's motivations for committing the crime. Essentially, a presentence report includes the following elements:

- Description of offense and the circumstances surrounding it
- Victim statement
- Prior criminal record of the offender
- Educational background of the offender
- Employment history of the offender
- A "social history" of the offender, covering family relationships, marital status, interests and activities, residence history, and any religious affiliations
- Medical and psychological or psychiatric report, if applicable
- Sentencing recommendations.

Since the judge uses this report to make a ruling in the offender's sentence hearing, the goal of presentence investigators is to make the report as exhaustive as possible. They use the account to label the subject as a certain type of offender, hint at any trauma or psychoses that might have triggered the offense, and map out the offender's connection to family, friends, and society at large. Once investigators fashion the account into a coherent structure and it is entered into the Department of Correction's database, there is little alteration. The narrative is assumed to be the truth—or at the very least, the only reality that matters in determining the offender's future within the legal system.

Yet consider the variety of perspectives that go into shaping this account. First, there are the admissions of the perpetrator himself. Then come the observations and assessments of victims, witnesses, family members, neighbors, police and other law enforcement officials, and mental health professionals, among others, who are requested to comment on the offense and the offender. Finally, there are the assumptions of the legal system, which stem from the categories and levels of severity attached to the offense(s). The end result is a report that molds this cacophony of perspectives within a coherent narrative structure. Who did what to whom and to what effect is carefully recorded to be used in successive legal proceedings and to determine sentencing. However, aside from the meticulous recounting of the events that took place, the rest of the report is persuasive as it attempts to present enough evidence to build a basis for educated reasoning. Ultimately, issues of motivation can only be extrapolated from the evidence, since even the offender may not be able to articulate why he committed the crime.

Therein lies the quandary. Unless we are willing to accept the material evidence as sufficient motivation for committing a crime, we end up struggling with the slippery concept of truth. Who possesses it? The legal system? Society, whose social conventions dictate morality and ethicality? Or the offender himself? We attach labels to offenders, based on their crimes, that automatically assume specific characteristics about the individuals in question. This is the way in which we define them as "Other"—that is, not "Us." For example, the label "Child Molester" tends to bring to mind the image of creepy-looking, shifty sexual predators who linger around places where children gather, such as playgrounds and schools, where they can randomly choose unsuspecting victims to kidnap, rape, and murder. This commonly accepted image of the stereotypical child molester is fairly simple to generalize, and it safely places him into the category of "Other." Yet statistics say that although some murderers are also child molesters, the vast majority of child molesters are not murderers, so making this sort of broad-based assumption can be dangerous, since it draws attention from the more common sort of offender. These individuals, who tend to be fairly unremarkable in appearance and already have some sort of relationship with the potential victims, are harder to characterize as "Other" because they might have a good deal in common with "Us." So it might be comforting to ignore them and focus on the offenders who are more dramatically antisocial. This type of violently damning image can also make it difficult for the majority of offenders to articulate their stories, since there is no context for them. Their narratives don't fit into the formulaic structure the public assumes, expects, and demands of "Child Molesters." Thus, with little or no input from the perpetrators as to what motivates their actions, we've concocted a widely accepted "truth" about child sexual abusers that actually draws attention from the more common existence of the crime.

Inevitably, we can only function under a presumption of truth. What determines the efficacy of such an approach, however, is which version of the truth we choose to formulate our assumptions. Overwhelmingly, we are influenced by mass-mediated depictions of child sexual abuse. During the past twenty years or so, there has finally been an audience for the stories told by sexual abuse survivors, so at least we have shown some willingness to understand the crime from the victims' viewpoint. "For narratives to flourish there must be a community to hear; . . . for communities to hear, there must be stories which weave together their history, their identity, their politics."[7] Yet, primarily, the voices of offenders are still silenced. We've compiled a wealth of statistics regarding the crime and even constructed hypothetical typologies of offender characteristics, but the information has been kept at a distant, comfortably quantitative perspective. The general public has little desire to understand what motivates child molesters, because understanding requires empathy. Reconceptualizing the "Other" as "Us" would lessen the power of the stigma surrounding the phenomenon. However, as legal and political efforts of the past decade should attest, such as the populist Megan's Law and its offshoots, means of combating and preventing the crime based upon statistical or superstitious assumptions are ultimately stop-gap measures that do not address the roots of the behavior. We need to listen to what individual offenders have to say about why they commit their crimes, and we need a context in which to interpret and evaluate this anecdotal evidence.

The Social Constructionist Use of Narrative

Although researchers and social critics have attempted to explain the preponderance of child sexual abuse in Western society utilizing a variety of perspectives, ranging from statistical analyses to criminal profiling, perhaps the most enlightening way to look at it is through the lens of social constructionism. Social constructionism has its roots in narrative psychology, which looks at the ways in which humans discursively construct their experiences through narrative forms. Social constructionism focuses on the way in which humans use transactional forms of communication to shape their perceptions. Employing this perspective can help put the self-narratives of individual offenders into context. The goal is not to fashion a pattern in which to squeeze offenders so we end up with a tidy typology. The goal is to show how the disparate elements of individual narratives are entwined with other, similar stories that arise out of social constructs. The self-narratives of sex offenders may express the offenders' personal understanding of identity, but they ultimately show how this sense of self is inextricably connected to the social milieu. Therefore, while it is important to use some method to identify a narrative's structure, the ultimate goal of this study is to show how this structure is rooted in, and reflects, a dominant, socially dictated, discursively produced reality. In approaching narrative from this direction, the perspectives of both narrator and analyst come into play, since objectivity is less important than performance. Verification of facts is less important than the meaning of events for the individuals involved and how these events are located in history and culture. Personal narratives are transactional units of discourse and highlight the ways in which the narrators interpret, rather than reproduce, the past.[8]

Social constructionism is rooted in Peter Berger and Thomas Luckmann's influential book *The Social Construction of Reality* (1967), which defined social construction as a blend of social reality and symbolic interaction. Berger and Luckmann contended that the reality we collectively experience has been constructed by our social interactions. Beginning with the universal need for meaning and order, Berger and Luckmann proposed that as individuals engage in the construction of their personal meaning, collectives engage in the construction of a social reality. Maintaining this sense of social reality requires communicating this structure to each new generation. Berger and Luckmann called the process of integration into the social reality *legitimation*.[9] Legitimation is the process whereby people construct explanations and justifications for the fundamental elements of their collective, institutionalized traditions.

Human beings "think, perceive, imagine and make moral choices according to narrative structures."[10] This book takes the premise that narrative is the representation of real or fictive events in a sequential fashion. Narrative is a way of organizing episodes, actions, and accounts of actions, bringing together facts and fantasies. The narrative structure allows for the inclusion of the storyteller's reasons for actions as well as the causes of the events. The narrative structure also presents the ways in which the storyteller symbolically makes sense of experiences. Ultimately, since we cannot separate the way in which we order our world from our perception of it, all knowledge is self-referential, and therefore all narratives can be broadly considered self-narratives. Our identities are not random residue from some startling, unique, and unanticipated event, but the sensible result of a life story. As rational human beings, we are compelled to make sense of unique events by putting these experiences into what we perceive is a rational structure. We get our ideas of how to order experience within a socially guided account, and this is how we assign meaning to that experience. In developing a self-narrative, "we formulate a story in which life events are systematically related, rendered intelligible by their place in a sequence or unfolding process."[11]

Therefore, an offender's identity takes shape as he verbally accounts for his behavior. Accounts of deviance are "linguistic forms that are offered for untoward action."[12] Identity is structured via "the layering of judgments that emerge from being accountable for events."[13] As Erving Goffman suggests in his work, which stems from a dramaturgical metaphor, social actors stage performances of a desirable self in order to manage potentially "spoiled" identities.[14] Oftentimes, these performances are rooted in gender expectations, which are produced for and by audiences in social situations. To describe these accounts as performative is not to suggest that these identities are inauthentic, however. They are situated and accomplished in social interaction, and the accounts that troubled people tell about their lives reflect their desires to fit their experiences into what they perceive to be social expectations and conventions. As Catherine Kohler Riessman explores in her extensive work on narrative, individuals do not "reveal" an essential self as much as they perform a "preferred" self, "selected from the multiplicity of selves or persona [sic] that individuals switch between as they go about their lives."[15]

Narrators can position themselves in multiple roles within their stories in order to present themselves in a desired light. For example, they can describe themselves as passive victims of circumstance or as active beings who can initiate and control events. Inevitably, the self-narratives of incarcerated child molesters describe difficult lives, rife with trauma and uncertainties, filled with calamitous events that conspire against their efforts to be moral, sexually stable, emotionally healthy individuals. Some offenders' self-narratives are drenched with paranoia, in which various cruel forces conspire to thwart their best efforts to live well-adjusted, crime-free lives. Other offenders' stories express a vicious struggle between illusion, delusion, and disillusionment; they have carefully constructed, socially inspired images of what their lives should be, yet cannot reconcile the reality with the fantasy. In all cases, when incarcerated inmates tell their stories, we are confronted with narratives that are riddled with inconsistencies, vague longings, frustration, anger, and desire. Sometimes, these self-narratives coincide with the offenders' presentence reports; oftentimes, they do not. Assuming that offenders' personal narratives are repositories of facts and documented events is naïve, yet their stories can contain compelling hints about motivation, attribution, accountability, and justification. Whatever the ultimate validity, and how much significance you place on the role "truth" plays in the narratives, these stories offer insight as to what forces shape a child molester. Identifying these themes within the narratives can suggest more efficacious approaches to punitive measures, treatment, and prevention.

The goal of social constructionism is to show how narrative expressions of self-identity arise from social interaction and are then shared via discourse. Until fairly recently, the dominant viewpoint in psychological research was focused in either the study of the inner dynamics of the individual psyche or the discovery of the supposed already determined characteristics of the external world. These two approaches constituted the ways in which human beings supposedly thought about themselves. For example, in psychotherapy, one traditional way of dealing with incest was to view it as a family dynamic and attempt to identify how intrafamilial relationships contributed to the existence of sexual abuse. This approach is less popular today, despite evidence that family dynamics most certainly do play a role in incest, because no one wants to be accused of placing blame on the nonoffending members of a family. In recent years, the emphasis has shifted from focusing on an "incest relationship" to the psyche of the individual offender, although family therapists still emphasize a systemic approach in which individual pathology is a local manifestation of problems inherent in the functioning of family units.

The social constructionist approach to psychotherapy makes the assumption that the contents of our inner lives are not so much "inside" us as individuals as in our experience—and expression—of our lives within a social context. From this perspective, our private lives are not so private, nor are they as logically sequential as narrative constructivists might postulate. Our thoughts only become organized as we express them within a dialogue, because the organizing center of any experience is not within the individual but outside, in the surrounding environment. "It is not experience that organizes expression, but the other way around—expression organizes experience."[16] The social constructionist approach is rhetorical in that it attempts to elucidate not only an understanding of how we constitute and reconstitute a common-sense "background" in our relational encounters, but also how we can—and do—create and re-create ourselves in the process. As Walter Fisher observed in his influential book *Human Communication as Narration* (1987), rhetorical experience may be viewed ontologically as well as epistemologically, as it is most fundamentally a symbolic transaction in and about social reality. "Knowledge is ultimately configured narratively, as a component in a larger story implying the being of a certain kind of person, a person with a particular worldview, with a specific self-concept, and with characteristic ways of relating to others."[17] Discursive rhetorical experience is the way in which shared understandings are developed, negotiated, or socially constructed between participants over a period of time. So, while it is possible to formulate a rigid structure in which to analyze these offenders' self-narratives, this would ignore the dialogic nature of expression that social constructionism celebrates. For this reason, it is important to approach each offender's self-narrative as an individual expression, but one that is contextualized within a social framework.

I am interested in looking not only at the conventions that offenders employ when expressing their narratives, but also at the spontaneous utterances they interject into the stories. An "utterance" is the most expressive type of dialogue, rather than the grammatically well-formed, preponderd sentence.[18] Although utterances might be spontaneous and unscripted, they always have an intended audience, because they are constructed between two socially organized persons whom, for the purpose of this study, I will term the private and public persons. Since each individual's inner world has its stabilized social audience that comprises the environment in which reasons, motives, and values are fashioned, the "private" person is the individual offender, engaged in a dialogue with the "public" person. The public person referenced in an offender's self-narrative is presupposed to be a representative of the various constituencies addressed by the offender, including law enforcement officials, politicians, counselors, victims, and society at large. In the process of conducting these interviews, I symbolized the material presence of the "public person." As the offenders related their narratives to me, they expressed a variety of emotions, such as remorse, defiance, anger, and apprehension, since they clearly perceived me to represent various potential audiences.

The social constraints that narrators experience when fashioning their accounts can be explored via a postmodernist perspective, in which relations of power, dominance, submission, and confession are embedded in social discourse. Michel Foucault, the brilliant French historian, offers perhaps the most influential perspective on discursive reality. In many of his books, such as *Discipline and Punish: The Birth of the Prison* and *The History of Sexuality, Volume 1: An Introduction*, Foucault focuses on the institutionalized forms of talk and writing and the various forms of power that these institutions embody. Foucault's argument is that once individuals subscribe to a particular discourse, such as religious discourse, they promote certain definitions about which persons or what topics have legitimacy. However, they themselves are often not aware of these embedded definitions. Foucault's description of the disciplinary use of the "confessional" is perhaps most applicable to the way in which convicted sex offenders are permitted to tell their stories.[19] In the Catholic practice of confession, the penitent is persuaded that he or she possesses some damning secret (usually sexual) that has been hidden. By confessing to the proper authority within the proper setting and context, the subject can then receive absolution, or at the very least, a list of what can be done to erase and atone for the original sin. The powerful institutional pull of Catholicism means that the confessor believes he or she is purging the darkest recesses of the soul, and once the idea is believed, the idea continues to exert its power of subjugation. A postmodernist interpretation of "confessional" implies that the narrator is enacting a discursively produced reality, yet remains in a submissive state. The narrator's ability to speak, and indeed, the narrator's willingness to speak, is constrained most potently not by external mechanisms of power but by the narrator's own participation within these mechanisms. We view expressing accounts as a means of justifying our behavior, and perhaps absolving our sins, yet the means by which we are able to confess—and the rewards or punishments we receive as a result—are controlled by the audience to the narrative (or rather, by the control we give to the audience). Shades of Jeremy Bentham's Panopticon, we are ever aware of being watched and measured, and this self-consciousness dictates the way in which we express our understanding of ourselves and our place in the world.

At this point, it should become clear that the social constructionist approach to uncovering identity and motives through self-narratives potentially makes it difficult to formulate well-ordered predictions about behavior, since it ignores the pull to establish broad criteria that form patterns of dialogue. The social constructionist approach seems to demand a paradoxical vision: that we embrace the unique, spontaneous nature of the conventions and utterances of individual self-narratives, yet simultaneously maintain their connection to the social sphere. This is a break from the traditional assumption in the social sciences that we can only understand things by discovering underlying patterns and order, the hidden laws and principles that determine their nature. The idea that the most important aspects of a phenomenon are what make it novel means we need to relinquish our hold on the familiar drive to categorize and organize. However, I do not think we can interpret the individual narratives of convicted child molesters and draw useful conclusions for treating sexual offenders and combating the crime of sexual abuse without distinguishing some broad patterns of motive and behavior. Indeed, our legal system requires that we classify and categorize crime and criminals, as does our approach to corrections. Yet the rhetorical dynamics of child sexual abuse seem to bear out the idea that the communication surrounding such an event works within a material background of the unsaid and unsayable, the relationship between speaking and silence that characterizes the workings of stigma and taboo. Ultimately, our psychic life manifests itself in our practical activities as we express them, dialogically, with the social world beyond. Our inner dialogue, and the ways in which we share this dialogue with others, is regulated and constituted by the way in which we understand our place in the world. Self-identity does not exist within a vacuum; it is created, defined, expressed, and potentially altered through our dialogic interactions. So it can be helpful to distinguish some similarities and broad patterns within these offender self-narratives. Showing how each individual's self-narrative connects with the narratives of other offenders, and then pondering the ways in which these narratives reflect a socially driven understanding of the world, can shed light on the social construction of the crime and its perpetrators.

In addition, a particularly appealing aspect of a social constructionist perspective is that self-identity is never static, continuously in the process of being constructed through social interaction. The concept of "self" is not fixed, but open to change as we interact in different contexts, with different persons, and for different purposes. The essential facts of an event may be indisputable. However, the impact of the event will be determined by the manner in which the event is perceived, defined, and interpreted within the greater social context. This is not to imply that meaning is also relative; all claims to knowledge are not necessarily as good as another. The moral and ethical content of action is not ambiguous, although it may be dictated differently depending on the cultural context, and such concerns will constrain the ways in which we justify our behavior. These concerns are embedded in self-narratives, yet ultimately our "selves" are beholden only to the constant process of revision.

This assumption has far-reaching implications when applied to the social construction of our concepts of crime, punishment, and rehabilitation. Although recent rhetoric may belie this, the American prison system has its roots in the Quaker philosophy of reflection and redemption. The American penal structure was intended to be in sharp contrast to the hellish conditions historically found in other societies; it was to be a noble model of a humane institution that focused on rehabilitation rather than vengeance. Yet gradually, this philosophy gave way to more practical, cost-effective means of addressing the rising rates of criminal behavior. Today, prisons are often viewed as warehouses for criminals. The overcrowded conditions and ever-increasing costs of incarceration provide justification for claiming that the majority of criminals, particularly sex offenders, cannot be rehabilitated, even though evidence exists to bear out the idea that in-prison therapeutic intervention can reduce recidivism rates. The result is a widely disseminated belief that most criminals are beyond redemption, and this belief is especially easy to construct and maintain for child molesters since their crimes are violations of such a deep-seated taboo. Yet if the self is constantly in the process of construction, then it follows that an offender's identity potentially can be altered. By understanding and challenging his perceptions, and determining a method for encouraging him to do the same, we can possibly show him a means of controlling his behavior. Note, however, that I am not suggesting it might be possible to change an offender's fantasies or desires, although certainly the attempt is worth the effort. Yet perhaps if we can identify the source of an offender's impulse to molest, we can teach him to control it so at least he can prevent himself from acting on his desires.

My goal with this study is to contribute to developing a sociology of offender self-narratives or, as Ken Plummer defines them in his excellent book *Telling Sexual Stories: Power, Change and Social Worlds* (1995), "the personal experience narratives of the intimate."[20] Telling a story is inevitably shaped by political constraints. For years, child sexual abuse was kept secret; it occurred, perhaps at the same rates it does now, but was rarely voiced. The political and social atmosphere of the time restrained victims from speaking out, since they were afraid (with good cause) that their stories would not be believed or legitimated by the public, even family members, the police, or the courts. After the women's movement exhorted victims to break the silence that shrouded rape and other forms of sexual assault, there was a context for these stories. Today, victims have been empowered by a political atmosphere that accepts the plausibility of sexual abuse. The dominant patriarchies of the past have subtly shifted to permit a forum for these narratives. The rhetoric helps to legitimate the experience of sexual assault for the survivors as well as the general public. Social, legal, and political responses to sexual abuse have further legitimated its existence. Yet these responses to sexual abuse are based on the narratives of victims, which shore up the perspective of the offender as "Other." From this perspective, the mass-mediated stereotype of the sexual offender evokes superficial assumptions of an offender's motivation. Public perception of child molesters seems to be that they are grotesque comic-book creatures, as devoid of free will as any cartoon character. Consequently, the most effective means of dealing with these creatures is to lock them up, castrate them, or put them under constant surveillance—in short, take reactive, punitive measures on an individual basis rather than approaching them as examples of a greater social issue.

My interest is in viewing how these narratives function within the wider frameworks of power by showing how these narratives reflect a socially constructed drama. The storytelling process is the sensible result of the narrator's experience of politically driven, socially located, and individually enacted states of domination, hierarchy, marginalization, and inequality. Each self-narrative is embedded within the assumptions gleaned from the broader social structure. Our lives are shaped through the storying of experience and through the performance of these stories. Therefore, our self-identities are constituted through the process of interpretation within the context of the stories we enter into and those that other people perceive for us.[21] Ultimately, the ways in which individuals define themselves through self-narratives are constrained by cognitive capacities in addition to familial and political-cultural roles. A popular interpretation of child sexual abuse maintains that it is an offshoot of the sort of power processes valued within a patriarchal political order. If we begin with that assumption, then deductively we may assume that victims and offenders define themselves against the backdrop of that political order, in which sexuality and sexual practices are means of offenders achieving empowerment through disempowering others.

From this perspective, sex and power are inextricably connected in the social narrative of child sexual abuse and, hence, are embodied within the self-narratives of offenders. Since the transformative effects of storytelling require performance, relating their "sexual autobiography"[22] is a way for these men to come to terms with the experiences of their lives, particularly the events that led them to prison. My purpose was to give these offenders a forum and a context in which to perform their self-narratives. Therefore, as I conducted these interviews, my goal was to provide an atmosphere that encouraged spontaneous utterances, but I also formulated a broad set of questions to help guide the narrative along (these questions can be found in the appendix). Overwhelmingly, I found that there was little need to refer to the guidelines, since each offender's narrative seemed to travel along a similar path. In reminiscing, they began their stories at the beginning of their lives, taking pains to paint a clear picture for me of how they perceived their childhood environments and their gradual descent into committing their offenses. The narrative form they naturally chose was familiar and paradigmatic, which lent credence to the expectation that their understanding of their experiences was framed by socially constructed conventions.

Certainly, since all of the men I interviewed had received some measure of counseling by that point and had volunteered to speak with me, their stories were undoubtedly well rehearsed. By the time they spoke to me, they had told aspects of their stories over and over again, to police officers, lawyers, probation officials, judges, counselors, family members, and sometimes fellow inmates. This relates to the prospect of retrospective interpretation by the men I interviewed. As Douglas Pryor describes in *Unspeakable Acts: Why Men Sexually Abuse Children* (1996), retrospective interpretation is the idea that a person's perception of an event changes over time, as past behavior is reinterpreted in light of new information and experiences.[23] The time the study subjects spent in mental health treatment and prison contributed to and may even have inspired them to refashion their self-narratives on the basis of how various audiences reacted to their stories. After all, this is actually the goal of some in-prison therapeutic and training programs: to encourage participants to become self-reflective. Thus, the longer that time had elapsed between their offenses and my interview with them, the greater the possibility that their accounts were "contaminated." In the interim years, they probably altered their interpretation of events with newly minted knowledge of psychological jargon, jailhouse religion, and any number of other confounding factors. In addition, the fact that they voluntarily permitted me to interview them, out of whatever motive, whether boredom, curiosity, honest efforts at rehabilitation, or the opportunity to capture a woman's undivided attention, also stacked the deck in terms of objective recall. However, as previously mentioned, the concept of discerning objective truth—or even how their recollections might have softened over the years—was not the point of this study. The focus was on the way they talked about their lives—how they envisioned themselves and the circumstances that led to the offenses—and how this was a product of ongoing social processes and experiences.

Although I've spent the greater part of this chapter building a rationale for approaching each self-narrative as a unique utterance and not viewing it as merely part of a pattern, I invite the reader to keep in mind the following four levels of analysis, inspired by Ken Plummer's work:

1. The *personal* level, which concerns the motives the offenders have for telling their stories. This focuses on *description*, in which offenders relate the events of their lives. Clearly, these offenders have a vested interest in making sense of their life stories, since they led to prison, in order to determine how to avoid reoffending (or at the very least, getting caught reoffending) once they are released. In general, people tell their personal narratives for a variety of reasons, including relieving

tension; as part of a therapeutic intervention; for understanding, forgiveness, and redemption; or out of a desire to contribute to science. Or they might just want to focus attention on themselves. In any case, telling their stories is an attempt to express some innate truth about themselves and their lives.

2. The *situational* level, which examines the processes through which people transform themselves into social objects by becoming "mythmakers, storytellers, dreamers, definers of situations, scriptwriters, [and] world-makers."[24] This is the point where the narrators offer potential sources of *attribution, motivation,* and *accountability* for their crimes by discussing the impact of significant others and the community upon their lives.

3. The *organizational* level, which focuses on the organizational elements that shape a story, such as narratization. The patterns given to their stories reflect the dialectical tension between speaking and silence that shapes the social construction of child sexual abuse. How the offenders structure their stories, including the potential similarities and themes that emerge, reflects the power of political processes on what can be said and what can be legitimated within the *social expectations and constraints* experienced by the offenders.

4. The *cultural/historical* level, which highlights the historical moment of public reception. This concerns the timing of these narratives and how key social worlds can use and benefit from listening to them. This level presents the *social context* of the stories and how they enter into the public discourse. A significant issue at this level is the struggle between secrecy and disclosure that has traditionally influenced sexual stories such as those of rape and sexual abuse.

Fundamentally, four primary assumptions of self-narrative guide this analysis:

- First, an individual's life is shaped through the storying of experience and through the performance of these stories.
- Second, self-narratives are constitutive frames, not truth-telling.[25] Self-narratives furnish rational grounds or justification for conduct.
- Third, an individual's self-narrative is embedded within the assumptions gleaned from the broader social structure.
- Fourth, a person's self-narrative acts to create, sustain, or change social interchange. These self-narratives provide a vehicle for persons to interact with their environment.

When we enter into these offender self-narratives, we are not passive observers but active participants. Two crucial processes occur simultaneously. First, we encounter their stories with a presumption that these offenders represent the "Other." The "Other" is separate from "Us," which constitutes the image we have of the social system and our places within it. This knowledge of the "Other" comes from a variety of potent sources, not the least of which are mass-mediated images of child sexual abuse, sexual abuse victims, and sexual offenders. Given this presumption, we have specific expectations of what the offenders' narratives will reveal, and these expectations influence the ways in which we can understand the discursive strategies employed and the transformative effects upon their object. Second, the offenders define themselves, their actions, and the roles they play in the greater social system through similar assumptions about the way the world should be. This is why I maintain it is crucial to recognize that these types of child molesters are not born; they are made, and are the inevitable offshoot of our particular form of social organization. It is important to know their life stories, because the desires they experienced, and the offenses they committed, were the result of their knowledge of the world around them and their place in it. These knowledges of "Self" and "Other" are socially constructed, as is our perception of "Truth."

In summary, viewing the self-narratives of individual offenders through a social constructionist framework allows us to recognize the ways in which their stories reflect social expectations and how our personal experiences inevitably color the ways in which we understand the motivations behind their crimes. The social construction of child sexual abuse dictates our assumptions about the offenders. I'm hoping that these individual narratives may challenge, or at least rattle, a few of these assumptions. The majority of child molesters are not the inexplicable result of some nightmare made flesh. They are not spawned; they are created, in part by the social structures that dictate a system of ongoing power relationships. As a result, or perhaps as an inevitable consequence, child sexual abuse has been cyclical and self-perpetuating. Although individual offenders have unique characteristics that contribute to their offenses, ultimately the social construction of the crime and the perpetrators dictates their actions and our reactions to them.

Notes

1. Jack Kay, "Ethical Considerations in Studying Communities of Hate: Using Ethnography to Explore and Critique the White Separatist Movement in the United States" (paper presented at the Fourth National Communication Ethics Conference, Kalamazoo, MI, May 1996).

2. Kay, "Ethical Considerations."

3. Lois Presser, "Stories of Violent Men" (Ph.D. diss., University of Cincinnati, 2002), 4.

4. Presser, "Stories of Violent Men," 7.

5. See, for example, Judith A. Cook and Mary Margaret Fonow, "Knowledge and Women's Interest: Issues of Epistemology and Methodology in Feminist Sociological Research," *Sociological Inquiry* 56 (1986): 2–27; Shulamit Reinharz, *Feminist Methods in Social Research* (New York: Oxford University Press, 1992).

6. See, for example, James A. Holstein and Jaber F. Gubrium, *The Self We Live By: Narrative Identity in a Postmodern World* (New York: Oxford University Press, 2000); Steinar Kvale, *InterViews: An Introduction to Qualitative Research Interviewing* (Thousand Oaks, CA: Sage, 1996); Claire M. Renzetti and Raymond M. Lee, eds., *Researching Sensitive Topics* (Newbury Park, CA: Sage, 1993); Kathryn Anderson, Susan Armitage, Dana Jack, and Judith Wittner, "Beginning Where We Are: Feminist Methodology in Oral History," *Oral History Review* 15 (1987): 103–127.

7. Ken Plummer, *Telling Sexual Stories: Power, Change and Social Worlds* (London: Routledge, 1995), 87.

8. Catherine Kohler Riessman, "Analysis of Personal Narratives," April 20, 2000, at www.xenia.media.mit.edu/%brooks/storybiz/riessman.pdf (accessed March 6, 2004), 19.

9. Peter L. Berger and Thomas Luckmann, *The Social Construction of Reality: A Treatise in the Sociology of Knowledge* (New York: Anchor, 1967), 86.

10. Theodore R. Sarbin, "The Narrative as Root Metaphor for Psychology," in *Narrative Psychology: The Storied Nature of Human Conduct*, ed. Theodore R. Sarbin (New York: Praeger, 1986), 8.

11. Kenneth Gergen, *Toward Transformation in Social Knowledge* (London: Sage, 1994), 187.

12. Marvin B. Scott and Stanford M. Lyman, "Accounts," *American Sociological Review* 33 (1968): 47.

13. Barry R. Schlenker, Michael F. Weigold, and Kevin Doherty, "Coping with Accountability: Self-Identification and Evaluative Reckonings," in *Handbook of Social and Clinical Psychology: The Health Perspective*, ed. C. R. Snyder and Donelson R. Forsyth (New York: Pergamon, 1991), 110.

14. See, for example, Erving Goffman, *The Presentation of Self in Everyday Life* (New York: Penguin, 1969); Erving Goffman, *Forms of Talk* (Oxford: Blackwell, 1981).

15. Riessman, "Analysis of Personal Narratives," 11.

16. V. N. Volosinov, *Marxism and the Philosophy of Language* (Cambridge, MA: Harvard University Press, 1975), 85.

17. Walter R. Fisher, *Human Communication as Narration: Toward a Philosophy of Reason, Value, and Action* (Columbia: University of South Carolina Press, 1987), 17.

18. See, for example, Volosinov, *Marxism and the Philosophy of Language*; Bakhtin, *Speech Genres and Other Late Essays*, trans. Vern W. McGee, ed. Caryl Emerson and

Michael Holquist (Austin: University of Texas Press, 1987); John Shotter, "The Social Construction of Our Inner Selves," *Journal of Constructivist Psychology* 10 (1997): 7–24.

19. Michel Foucault, *The History of Sexuality, Volume 1: An Introduction*, trans. Robert Hurley (New York: Penguin, 1981), 65–67.

20. Plummer, *Telling Sexual Stories*, 19.

21. David Epston, Michael White, and Kevin Murray, "A Proposal for Re-authoring Therapy: Rose's Revisioning of Her Life and a Commentary," in *Therapy as Social Construction*, ed. Sheila McNamee and Kenneth J. Gergen (Newbury Park, CA: Sage, 1992), 98.

22. Plummer, *Telling Sexual Stories*, 33.

23. Douglas W. Pryor, *Unspeakable Acts: Why Men Sexually Abuse Children* (New York: New York University Press, 1996), 300.

24. Plummer, *Telling Sexual Stories*, 35.

25. Kenneth Gergen and John Kaye, "Beyond Narrative in the Negotiation of Therapeutic Meaning," in *Therapy as Social Construction*, ed. Sheila McNamee and Kenneth J. Gergen (Newbury Park, CA: Sage, 1992), 173.

CHAPTER THREE

~

Tony—The Actor

The first perpetrator I interviewed was Tony, an articulate, passionate man whose poor health muted his naturally forceful personality. I had met Tony a few months earlier when I sat in on a few of the groups. Tony seemed to take special pride in his role of peer leader, but that pride in no way diminished his seemingly sincere desire to grapple with the crime of sexual abuse. He was quick to admit his own faults, although he often presented them in such a way as to minimize the depth of the offense. Interestingly, Tony also had moments of clarity in which he recognized his tendency to rationalize his actions. At such times, he would openly break down and even begin to cry, his frustration evident. He was also openly emotional in response to the other men's stories. He truly seemed committed to getting them to face the enormity of their crimes so that they had a chance to succeed without reoffending once they were released. Only later did I learn why Tony was so passionate about getting the others to work on their issues. Tony was serving a four-years-to-life sentence for first and second degree sodomy. Already incarcerated for eight years, it seemed inevitable his bids for parole would continue being denied. Now nearing seventy years old, he feared he would die in prison. His failing health, brought on by diabetes, heart troubles, anxiety attacks, and a host of other minor ailments, intensified this fear.

Oddly, immediately upon meeting Tony, I felt both completely comfortable and slightly uneasy. Initially, I dismissed this unease as a natural manifestation of the circumstances—after all, when we met, it was my first time sitting in on the group and there I was, a lone woman surrounded by male sex offenders, shut in a tiny windowless room in a prison. Yet as the interview progressed, I began to realize why I was both drawn to and repelled by Tony. Both in personality and physical appearance, Tony resembled my own abuser. He had the same overly dramatic gestures and gruff manner, one minute warm and the next harsh and demanding. This recognition hit me somewhere about midpoint in the interview, and it made my skin crawl for a second or two. Yet what made me so uncomfortable about the realization was not that he resembled my abuser. Rather, it was acknowledging that it didn't bother me as much as it should have. I still cared about John, and seeing him reflected in Tony's face even made me miss him a little. As a child, I had given that man my most precious possession: my open, innocent affection. And he repaid me for my gift by sexually objectifying me, using me, and manipulating me into protecting him. It would be easier to deal with John's betrayal if I could hate him. But I didn't, and I couldn't, and the fact that he was dead and buried meant I'd never be able to ask him for an explanation. So, listening to Tony tell his story, I wanted to imagine he was speaking for John. I wanted to believe that, given the opportunity, John would have felt remorse similar to Tony's. I wanted to believe that somehow, somewhere, John would have regretted his actions and wanted to change, if not for himself, then maybe for me.

Tony's Story

My father was an uneducated man who left school when he was in the fourth or fifth grade. He worked in the poultry industry that was in New York City at the time, delivering chickens to butcher stores. Mama played the piano and graduated high school, which was a big achievement in those days. She came from a more cultured, educated family than my father did, and it caused a lot of problems because her brothers always felt she had married beneath her. That was the sort of lifelong relationship my mother and father had with her brothers. They would meet often and go to each other's homes and so forth, but my father was always the butt of their humor. While it was all kind of light, there was an edge of hurt beneath the laughing. Even when I was nine or ten years old, I could spot it, and I wondered why they went along with it.

This left my father frustrated. He took out his frustrations on people who were weaker than he was. My father wasn't a violent man—he wasn't a physical person—but I was his favorite target. At an early age, I stammered and stuttered. His way of approaching it was to be mean and make fun of me, especially in front of a lot of people. "Look at that, he can't even get two words out," he'd say. I'd burst into tears and he would sneer, "And now he's crying."

My father knew he had some very serious limitations himself; he knew he'd have to take kidding from his relatives, so he would find victims of his own, like his small son. He was a terrible tease. Even to this day, when I'm under some emotional strain, sometimes I'll stammer and stutter. It took me a long time to work my way out of it. I wanted to speak well. I knew that you had to be a good communicator if you wanted to do anything in life. I found a teacher who was sympathetic, who empathized with my problem, and she gave me special attention. She encouraged me to read parts of plays, and this blossomed into my interest in theater later on.

In my family, I was the oldest. I had one sister, who was six-and-a-half years younger. My father had four or five sisters, and they all lived nearby. They visited us a lot. I remember that on at least two occasions, they cornered my mother and confronted her about her obvious favoritism toward her daughter over her son. She'd dress my sister like Shirley Temple, who was the child icon of the day. My mother was always trying to appear like things were okay, and that they were financially well off, although this was the middle of the Depression and people were selling apples on the streets. My father may have been the butt of the family's jokes, but at least he was working all during the Depression. Here we were with four people in the family—my father, mother, sister, and myself—all living in three rooms. My mother liked to cook and have people over to eat, so instead of having a living room, she had a dining room. In the middle of the room was this enormous mahogany table, surrounded by massive chairs and a huge china closet in one corner. Then there was the kitchen and one bedroom. At the end of the kitchen was a pullout couch that I slept on at night, and my sister slept in my parent's room in a crib. Yet my mother still had a fur coat. They had twisted values. She had a fur coat, and my father had a car. That was their idea of status— to be able to walk out of their three-room apartment on Sunday, with my mother in her fur coat, and step into my father's car.

I'm sure other people had it worse, but I didn't know what it was like to have any privacy. I lived in the kitchen. Because my father got up at 5 a.m. for work, he'd go to bed at 8 p.m. He'd leave the bedroom door open, and everything had to stop. But he wouldn't close the door. He'd lay in bed with the door open and his ears cocked to see if anyone was disrespecting him by making noise. I was alone a lot because my mother was a club member. At seven or eight in the evening, she would get dressed in her fur coat, douse herself with perfume, and go off to the Ladies' Lions. She had a lot of friends and was always on the phone or doing things, like going to movies. So I was usually alone at night, sitting in the kitchen, with my father listening inside his bedroom, waiting for me to annoy him.

That was the good part of my childhood. By the time I was thirteen or fourteen and my sister was like seven or eight, we moved to a place with four rooms. My sister and I shared a room. That created an awkward situation. I had already had sexual fantasies about her. When I was eleven or twelve, I had already exposed myself to her. It began when I became interested in one of her girlfriends. An opportunity came when I was home from school with a stomachache, and my sister and her friend were playing. My mother wasn't there—she was out to a meeting or something. I allowed my bathrobe to open accidentally on purpose and left it wide open. I continued to expose myself to my sister's friend for some time after that. I exposed myself to my sister, too, since she was usually there at the time. This went on for a few weeks. My sister's interest in looking at my penis provoked me. I wanted it to continue, but on the other hand I felt like the dirtiest, filthiest person in the world. I couldn't believe I could think that way about my own sister, and I never touched her, but the potential was there. She knew that I knew, and I knew that she knew, but we didn't do much about it. And we stayed in that room together until I went into the navy.

My interest in sex really started with the girl who lived next door. When my parents would go out on the weekends, they'd have the neighbor girl stay with my sister and I. I was about eleven or twelve, and this girl was only about two or three years older than me. She was more there for my sister. We'd play Monopoly and cards together. Since she'd go home and right to bed when my parents got back, she used to get into her pajamas at our place. One night while we were playing cards in our pajamas, she told me she had heard my friends and I using bad words, and she asked me what the word "fuck" meant. This gave me an erection. Then she said something along the lines of I'll show you mine if you'll show me yours. Here she is, fourteen years old, and she's getting into my bed with me and massaging my penis and extolling its size. Finally, she says, "Do you want to touch me?" and that did it. I had heard about sex on the street, but this was acting it out. I loved it. Our counselor here says that I was abused by that girl. I don't believe it. It was such a fantastic experience for me that I never thought of it as abuse. It did seem that I got so much pleasure from this girl, I became obsessed with finding somebody else. But I didn't know how to ask anybody to do it. That's what exhibitionists do. Exhibitionists stand around like nothing's happening, waiting for somebody who is more aggressive than they are to make the first move. Exhibitionists are so passive, they expose themselves because they can't take the prospect of being rejected. I expose myself so that somebody might say to me that they want me. Or on the other hand, maybe they'll tell on me, and I'll get caught. Maybe that's what I always wanted.

I've tried to figure out why it began that way. When I was exposing myself, I felt like a freak. I was eleven or twelve, already had the makings of a beard, and a penis that was like a cat growing into his tail. Here I was, with a full-size penis at eleven or twelve years old, short, with hair on my face, and I felt freakish and unattractive. I ended up paying attention to younger girls since I didn't feel confident enough to pursue my peers. But after a couple of years, I grew to my full height and became a good athlete. Lo and behold, girls started to show some interest in me. That's when my interest in exposing myself to younger girls stopped. It stopped with my sister as well. But the fantasies about her—the sexual tension—remained. And she created a lot of it, too. I overheard her talking one time about me, but I never approached her. She wanted me to be the aggressor, and I couldn't do it. So at age seventeen, I joined the navy. World War II was going on, and I signed up to get the hell out of there, out of that little room. I was in San Francisco, then Japan for six months, and during the occupation, sex was anywhere you wanted it. After I got a lot of experience with women in Japan, I felt okay about my ability to be with women.

When I came back from the navy in 1946, I immediately went to college. I was a very poor high school student because I had no place to study. I just wanted to get out of that house. So I didn't get into a great college, but I worked hard and ended up graduating *cum laude*. There was a theater club, and I wanted to meet some girls, so I joined up and found I was a pretty good actor. I could sing, and got cast in feature roles in musicals. The whole thing made me feel better about myself. When I finished school, I went back to New York and auditioned for some things, but the timing wasn't right. Eventually, I ended up in Ohio and went to work for a big engineering firm out there. I also worked in a repertory theater. Then, at the age of twenty-four, I met my first wife. She was enormously attractive, so pretty, with red hair and a good body. She was so vulnerable, so wanting to be in love, wanting to have somebody to take care of and somebody to take care of her. So we went back to New York to get married and had my parents arrange the wedding for us according to Jewish tradition. This was absurd, since my Jewish faith was nothing. My father made fun of people who were religious, although my mother would have liked to keep a kosher home. My father had the idea that if you did something, you did it 100 percent or you didn't do it all. He left no room for compromise, no room for growth. And since my mother couldn't keep our home 100 percent kosher, my father demeaned her for it.

Still, as a dutiful son, I let them plan a Jewish wedding. Soon afterward, my wife got pregnant and got extremely sick to the point where she had to be hospitalized and fed intravenously. I was worried sick about her, so my mother convinced us to move back to New York. My mother was a natural healer—that was her role. My sister had married and moved out by that time, so my wife and I moved back into my childhood room until we could find our own apartment. After our son was born, we ended up buying a house in New Jersey. I was a GI, and could get a GI mortgage with no down payment. You couldn't afford not to buy a house, it was such a good deal. And we were happy for a time. But somewhere along the way, I began to fantasize about exposing myself again, and I didn't have a clue why. I would go out of our neighborhood and stand around, with my pants open, just stand around like I didn't know what was happening. Waiting for someone to make a move or something.

It was crazy. I had a terrific job as the chief engineer of an architectural firm. I was making good money. We lived in a lovely little house, but all of a sudden my wife felt that our house was too small. She became ashamed of our little house, although it was well furnished and cozy, with a picture window looking out into the woods and a little patio. The pressure was on. And that's when my troubles really began. Through therapy, I have an insight that at that time, I began exposing myself again because somewhere deep in my sub-conscious, I felt that my wife was unhappy. Since she was unhappy with me, I came to believe she was unhappy with sex—that I wasn't providing for her financially or in the bedroom, either. I had entered adulthood with lots of bag-gage from my childhood, and I began to feel that maybe I was inadequate—maybe I was unable to take care of this woman the way she deserved. Little girls became attractive to me because they had no basis of comparison. Any-thing I showed them and anything I did with them was okay, because they didn't know any better. When I was young and that baby-sitter had sex with me, she made me feel warm, liked, even attractive. My parents were never demonstrative—I never got hugged or kissed or told I was okay. But that fourteen-year-old girl made me feel loved. So now I'm drawn to young girls again. The dick and feeling okay went together—so, ipso facto, if I show the girls my penis, they are going to like me, and if they like me, then they'll hug me and I'm going to feel okay. You know, this wasn't conscious knowledge, although I often consciously told myself, "I shouldn't be doing this."

I also used to consciously say to myself that I shouldn't have this great job, I shouldn't be looked up to—just wait till they find out who and what I re-ally am. I'm that nonachiever from the Bronx, with that demeaning father, who didn't do well in high school. All this is fakery and fronting. When they really see me, I'm going to lose all of this, anyway, since I don't deserve any of it. I took into my adulthood feelings of inferiority that I covered up with a lot of bravado. But I can't say that exposing myself to little girls made me feel more adequate—it actually made me feel disgusting. I felt compelled to do it, but that didn't make me feel good. There was self-hatred in it. What am I doing exposing myself to somebody's daughter? Somebody's little girl? I knew it was wrong, but it was an obsession. There was really very little reinforcement from my victims. Once in a while, I will admit, I told myself I got a positive reaction from one of them when they looked at me. This was all the encouragement I needed to carry me over to the next time.

I got caught. I got caught a lot. But since I wasn't touching anybody, and had a job and a family and a nice house, the police didn't do anything. They would arrest me, and I would get probation with the promise I'd see a psychiatrist. The lack of serious repercussions also reinforced the behavior because I always had the idea in the back of my mind that I could talk my way out of it. I was arrested seven times, and each time got probation. Then, finally, I got arrested and it got into the papers, and my boss found out about it. I pulled into the parking lot one day, and they came out with a box of my personal goods and said, "Hey, you're gone." My sentence was to spend a term of up to three years in a psychiatric hospital. I was released after about fifteen months and went back to work for another firm I was friendly with. I was good at what I did, so they gave me a chance. My wife didn't. She divorced me while I was in the hospital. She had supported me for a while because she thought it was a sickness, but finally couldn't take it anymore and left.

That sent me into a spiral. I began to stretch the limits. I began to think up little routines to get the girls' attention, and then masturbate in front of them. I would approach the girls on the street. I'd say I had a flat tire and needed to change my pants so they wouldn't get dirty. I'd tell them I was going to go over to that pole over there, and if they'd warn me about anyone coming, I'd give them a dollar. "Now, don't be embarrassed if you see something," I'd say. The girls would usually titter and giggle, "Oh yeah, I don't want to see THAT." And I'd say, "Well, then, that's fine, I'll just find somebody else." The prospect of making a dollar generally made them change their minds. Lots of times, they'd say, "No, that's okay, I've seen it before." Once they agreed, I'd ask them again if they'd be embarrassed, and they'd assure me they wouldn't be. So I'd position them in front of me so they'd be blocking the street, and then I'd take my pants off. "Is that what it looked like when you saw it before?" I'd ask. "Well, it's smaller." "I can make it bigger," I'd say, and then I'd go as far as they would let me go. I became less and less inhibited, to the point where I'd actually ask them to touch me.

When I was doing this, it got to be on a daily basis. I was accumulating arrests like crazy. But I kept getting bailed out. So I felt like I could always get into trouble because someone would bail me out in the end. Then I'd get a grip on myself and stop, for months and even sometimes years. It depended on the kind of emotional state I was in at the time. It got to the point when I stopped feeling it was horrible. I had desensitized myself. What I discovered was that the girls who accepted my invitation were very curious, and I preyed upon their curiosity. My biggest fantasy was that I could get one of them to participate. That thought would turn me on for days, and then some potential victim would show their disgust, and this would bring me back to reality. But I rationalized, and I have to stress the word *rationalized*. I rationalized because in my mind, I'm a decent, moral person, and the only way I could stay sane about what I was doing was to believe it was okay. I wasn't forcing them, they weren't running away, I wasn't hurting them, and so forth. I could rationalize that I wasn't doing anything wrong. Of course, I was doing hideous things. Getting young girls used to accepting money for sexual acts—that's a terrible thing to do. But I didn't want to accept my actions as being terrible, because I saw myself as giving the girls choices. They could go away, or not. They could participate, or not.

What many people don't seem to realize is that pedophiles get their victims to participate. They often give the children choices, and lots of times the kids end up liking their abusers. So we tell ourselves, how can we really have done anything wrong if the kids like us, and sometimes even their parents like us? The most difficult thing for us to do is realize that, even though our victims may not have been physically harmed, we have affected their lives in a negative way. The biggest turn on for a pedophile is to be involved with a boy or girl who seems to enjoy what is going on, and even comes back for more. That justifies our rationalization that we're not doing anything wrong.

Me, I'm great at rationalizing. I can make myself look good for my own benefit. Being the type of person who doesn't want to hurt anyone or do anything wrong, I could rationalize in a million different ways. "This is something they've done before"—that's a good rationalization. I was an addict; I had to find some excuse to allow myself to continue my behavior. So I kidded myself. The only one I kidded was myself. And I ended up exposing myself to maybe a hundred girls over a five-year period. I never had intercourse with a victim, although there were opportunities. That was the barrier I never bent. Even with my last offense, which was with a fourteen-year-old girl—it was all oral sex. She had been having sex since she was twelve, so there was no question I had the opportunity, but I never penetrated her. I couldn't do it.

Funny thing is, all this time there was nothing wrong with me sexually. I had a lot of experience with age mates. I even got married again in the early seventies to a woman who was sixteen years younger than I was at the time. I was doing very, very well. My first wife moved to California, and my two kids came to stay with me. So I had my family back together again. But then I blew it in the same way. After I was married for two or three years, I began to question my success, to question my relationship with my wife, to question whether she was happy with me, and question everything about my life. The feelings of inadequacy came up again, and I destroyed my perfectly wonderful world. I had a lovely young wife and a lovely home. I mean, it was perfect. But Tessie was the kind of girl who never seemed to be really happy. We had a nice relationship. But we'd go out to dinner on the weekends, and then she'd drink too much and some kind of anger would overtake her. She'd get angry as hell and lash out at me, then later claim she didn't remember what happened. Once she even came at me with a knife and then laughed at me. I never got to the bottom of her pathology. I had enough to worry about.

So her unhappiness made me unhappy. Even though I was doing very well, I didn't feel like I deserved any of my success. I began racking up arrests for exposing myself, and then I'd get a good lawyer so I'd get probation by promising to pursue treatment. My wife eventually had enough. I didn't blame her at all. She was Catholic, and it made her feel better to have the marriage annulled rather than divorce me. I didn't challenge her. At this time, my son was already out on the West Coast and my daughter was away from home in college, so they weren't really aware of all my arrests as far as I know. They didn't find out until after my marriage broke up and I was finally sent to a facility for treatment.

It was the late seventies. I got arrested for two cases of open lewdness and this time couldn't get out of the charges. I was sent to a diagnostic center in New Jersey, which turned out to be a terrific program. At that time, you got three years for each case of open lewdness, so I was given a maximum of six years. I ended up spending four years there out of six because I was such a difficult case. I was so intelligent and able to defend myself that they couldn't make any progress with me. The people operating the group there were very confrontative, but the more they confronted me, the more argumentative I became. So it took a long time for them to beat me down, since that was what they had to do. When I finally got paroled from that facility, I was in really good shape. I had an insight into the crime and I had insight into myself, and I had made certain personality changes to lessen the stress I had always experienced. I understood my tendency to have self-pity and my ability to be arrogant and try to push people away with my arrogance. I recognized that I had to take full responsibility for my actions.

I remember earlier on—before I was sent to the diagnostic center—one time I got arrested and my wife came to bail me out. On the way home, we stopped on the turnpike to have a cup of coffee. She said, "Tony, why do you do this? What's the matter? Why can't you stop?" And I said to her, "I do it because apparently I get some positive reaction that I need." I said I liked doing it because I liked the connection with the kids, I liked their response. I had never told anybody that before. I said, "You don't keep on doing this because you must like it—you must like it because you keep on doing it." That's all I knew at the time. When I told Tessie that, what I was really saying to her was, "I can't help it and nobody is going to be able to help me." And then I went to the diagnostic center and, for the first time in my life, I realized that I could help myself. I wasn't insane—I had control over the things I did. To tell somebody that this is a compulsion is ridiculous. If I don't want to do something, then I don't have to do it. If I don't want to smoke a cigarette, then I just don't smoke it. If I don't want to have that drink, then I don't drink it. It's as simple as that.

If I got anything out of the facility, that was it. I realized I didn't have to do it anymore. If I found it distasteful and it was fucking up my life, then I didn't have to continue. That was a revelation. A pedophile can be stopped. Pedophiles do it because the only relationships they feel comfortable with are with young children. If they can learn how to have relationships with other adults, for example, or they can learn to feel comfortable with aging or whatever dynamic leads them to commit the crime, then they can stop the behavior. Do I make myself clear? You take away the thing that's making you feel good about this aberrant behavior and then you can change. Yes, a pedophile can be helped. But the problem is, many times they don't want to be helped. They reach some kind of comfort zone and it's scary to move out of that zone. The majority are not out of contact with reality. My time in the diagnostic facility made me take stock of what my actions had done to my life, and then I wanted to make that change. After a few years of the counselors beating me down, I just opened up my eyes and ears and my soul and took in what I needed to stop my crime.

When I came out, for a long time I didn't reoffend. I went to support groups, and I was okay. Then one day I had a tennis date with a woman who worked at a local shopping mall. We met there, and then she sent me off to wait while she got ready for our date. I ran into this teenage girl in front of the mall. She was eating a pastry and licking her fingers. I initiated the conversation, I admit that. "Geez," I said, "I never saw anybody enjoy a piece of pastry as much as you are enjoying that." Then she looked me dead in the eyes and said, "I wish I had some money to buy some more." You're talking to a guy who has been involved with little girls for a long time. The old light bulb went on—she's asking me for money, in a way that says she'd do anything for it. At that particular time, I didn't bother to get hold of myself since it seemed as though she was offering it up. I'm not the victim here, though—she is the victim, I'll admit that. So I said to her, "Well, ah, you want to run errands together?" Something like that. So the crash you heard that day was me falling off the wagon. This was comparable to taking an alcoholic who has been on the wagon for several years and giving him the keys to a bar, then asking him to baby-sit the place until the owner gets back. Yes, I had choices, just as that drunk has choices. But it would be kind of difficult not to baby-sit that bar and then baby-sit that one drink, and then another, for old times' sake. I was being offered the keys to that barroom, and I knew it. So I asked her, "What would you do for the money? I've got some money." "Whatever." Without another word, she followed me behind this church across the way, and I had her masturbate me and fondled her in return. Then I gave her a couple of dollars.

She ended up telling me where she lived, where I could find her. And that is what I did. For the next seven months, I went out there a couple of times a month. Since I knew where she lived, I'd intercept her on her way home from school or went over on the weekends, knowing she would be somewhere in the neighborhood. She'd see me and tell her friends, "Oh, I got to go some-place with my uncle. I'll be right back." So she cooperated. What we did be-came more intense, to the point where I was doing oral sex on her and she was masturbating me. Then finally one time I went to see her, and it was cold, and she took me to a place where kids hang around in the basement and smoked pot. The building superintendent was apparently setting himself up for a situation similar to mine. But he saw me, and I got arrested. Because she had to protect herself, the girl said she had just met me that day. The police went ba-nanas when they saw my history. I copped out and took a plea bargain.

Now, here I am in prison, years later, working in these groups, trying to find out what I had perhaps missed in my previous group experiences. At first, I tried to get the group facilitators here to understand that what I did this time was different than what I did before. But that wasn't true. I thought that because I wasn't exposing myself and had done okay for years before meeting that girl, I should have still had the ability to make the right choice, but I wasn't aware of the addictive part to this behavior. So I've been trying to work on the addictive aspect of this thing while I've been here, and also the effects I had on my victims. I never really looked at that before. Even the girl who cooperated—who seemed to offer it and so forth—even that girl was negatively affected by my actions. I always kind of glossed over the negative effects because I kept telling myself I never hurt anybody—all those ration-alizations. I think that I've finally dealt with it here, but then I wonder. I know I've looked at the effects on the intellectual level, but I don't know if I've connected with the feeling level. I'm still trying to cope with that aspect.

I've considered what should be done with us, with pedophiles. I think the first thing they should do is put us all into one facility to standardize the treatment. In this state, they have different groups in different facilities, but they're not all run the same way. I think the most important issue in dealing with any sex offenders is that they should be given different sentence instruction. What I mean is that, sure, they should be given parole, but based on their ability to do the work in treatment groups. Hold out that carrot to them; hold out the hope that if they do well, they will be rewarded in some way. They're usually sick people who don't understand the need to be introspective for their own benefit, so they're not going to help themselves just to help themselves; but if you give them a carrot, they'll work because they'll have a goal. Why not give them that carrot and guarantee that everyone who does it right has a chance to redeem themselves?

I know I'm going to sound opinionated and pushy. But I've had a lot of time to think about this. There should be a facility where pedophiles are all in one place, where there is no stigma about being in that particular place and they can be open about their crimes. They should feel free to talk about their problems with other group members when they walk around the facility. You should have a facility of about four hundred to five hundred beds, where the inmates go to therapy every day and have groups a couple of times a week with professionals, then groups run by paraprofessionals—their peers—the rest of the time. Everything should be fair game in the groups, then nobody could be considered a snitch. I don't think pedophiles should get sentences that are more severe than [those for] any other crime. I think that the sentences should be structured in such a way that you know you've got them there for a while to do the work. In order for the pedophile to be released, the facilitator or therapist who works with him should recommend him to the other professionals in the facility, and they should do a report on him. Then, when they are satisfied he's completed the work, they should move him up to an independent panel with people who have sociological or psychological backgrounds, and maybe somebody from the corrections field. Let him go before this panel, made up of experts, and prove that he's ready to be released. Have them judge him not by what he's done in the past, like a parole board does, but take into account where he is right then in his psychological development. "His facilitators have sent him to us; they've passed him. Now it's up to us to find out if he's really made the changes, if he has insights and if he's ready to go back into the world and not reoffend." If he isn't ready, then send him back and say, "We'll see you in another six months."

Okay, so my plan isn't perfect, but at least this way you'd have people from the community with expert credentials evaluating him. Tell him what things he needs to do specifically before he goes back before the panel. To just throw pedophiles on the dump heap of life and say that we don't have any help for you is really saying that we don't want to help you. We despise this crime with such passion, we don't care about helping you change. Whatever the recidivism rate is, don't you think it would improve if guys like me were put in treatment programs and had to prove they've changed? People complain the recidivism rate of sex offenders is so high—well, hell, what percentage of those reoffenders were ever in treatment programs? How about breaking those figures down into the ones who have had treatment versus the guys who haven't? And what kind of pedophile are you talking about anyway? Do people really understand the definition? Is the guy who kidnaps a kid and then buries her in the Adirondacks a pedophile? No, he's not a pedophile. He's a kidnapper and murderer. A pedophile is somebody who is inadequate, who wants his victim to enjoy the sex. It's warped, but there it is. We have to tell ourselves that our victims are really getting pleasure from us. If we really thought we were hurting the kids, we wouldn't do it.

As for notification policies, they simply aren't fair. You can't take one segment of the criminal population and say that we are going to notify everybody when they come out of prison, but not notify people about other criminals. Once a pedophile gets out of prison and moves into a neighborhood, he's usually more scared than everybody else is anyway, so he's not going to do anything. How in heaven's name is a pedophile going to stand a chance to change if when he gets out, everyone is notified about him? How can he get a job? How is he going to find a place to live? How is he going to get into any kind of rehabilitative program if he's not allowed to work, not left alone? Take me, for instance. My daughter has two children, so it would be inappropriate for me to move nearby when I got out of prison. My daughter would know that I would never do anything to my grandkids, but I couldn't move into her neighborhood because my granddaughter might come home from school with my picture on a piece of paper, showing me as a pedophile. So, now, instead of being close to my family, having the security of my family around me—which would be very helpful—I couldn't do it. I'd have to get the hell away, move down someplace into a metropolitan area where I'm more anonymous. So I'd be all alone. I'd make it, but that's not the way to start me off on the right track. Where will I go? What will I do? How am I going to live? I've done the work. I deserve a chance to go out and make amends for myself—to make up for what I've done. I've done a great many things to address my problem, to be the person I'm capable of being. But people only see the person on my rap sheet, the 20 percent of me who has done these terrible things. What about the person I was 80 percent of the time? The father, the husband, the loyal employee and businessman? Doesn't that count for anything?

Today, the way society treats pedophiles is to lock us up and throw away the keys. This is hysteria. I heard somebody say, "You know, I'd rather live next to a murderer than someone who might fondle my little girl." That's ridiculous. I wouldn't want my little girl fondled either, but I'd rather live next to a pedophile than Jack the Ripper.

Summary

The major theme in Tony's self-narrative is his need for attention, which he sublimated in a positive way through his acting experiences and in a negative way by exposing himself to young girls. As he describes his life experiences, it becomes apparent that a few events helped mold his personality into that of a man whose superficial confidence is undermined by a nagging sense of inadequacy. First, his parents undermined his confidence as a child. His mother obviously preferred his sister to Tony, and his father took every opportunity to prey on Tony's weaknesses. Tony was strong enough to use his father's merciless teasing as an impetus to improve his own ability to communicate, which blossomed into a lifelong interest in theater, yet even the accolades he could receive as an actor did little to stem his insecurities.

Second, another constant source of stress in his youth was the sexual tension between Tony and his sister, since they were forced to share a bedroom. This is when Tony began exposing himself "accidentally on purpose" to his sister and his sister's friend. The thrill he got from exposing himself later grew into an obsession.

Third, Tony's early physical maturation didn't help his lack of confidence. Although he views an early sexual encounter with a baby-sitter as a positive experience, he admits that it might have contributed to his exhibitionism. About the time his baby-sitter molested him, he began exposing himself to his sister and his sister's friend.

These three experiences helped shape Tony into a man who craved attention as a means of overcoming his sense of inadequacy. Tony even tried to pursue a career in acting, but eventually settled into a more financially secure profession. At various points in his life, he possessed all the attributes that should have constituted self-satisfaction and success: lovely wives, nice homes, and children. Yet when this suburban oasis was invaded by potential sources of stress, Tony's innate feelings of inadequacy undermined his confidence, and he turned to exhibitionism for relief. Unfortunately, although

Tony had kept up his participation in the theater, the applause and attention he received while on stage was not as potent as the surreptitious thrill he got from exposing himself to young girls. In addition, he views his exhibitionism as a form of "self-hatred," since this excitement was mixed with disgust. Yet the more he did it, the more obsessed he became.

Ultimately, Tony views his life as a roller coaster of middle-class contentment and seedy addiction, and he could never seem to reconcile the two radically different sides of his personality. The plot twists of his own life—which he precipitated by the dichotomy within his own character—continue to perplex him. Tony shows disgust at his actions, but tries to mediate it by insisting that he is a "decent, moral person" who always gave his victims choices.

Tony, the actor, appears to be a man caught between feeding the demands of an outsize ego and a sense of inadequacy every bit as gluttonous. As long as the people in his life were uncritically offering up applause for his achievements, he felt secure. When he wasn't receiving the positive reviews he craved, he turned to another means of getting attention. Although he was often filled with disgust after he offended, any slight sign of interest on his victim's part was enough motivation to do it again. Even if he didn't get rave reviews for his performance, at least his naïve young victims were an uncritical audience.

~

CHAPTER FOUR

Red—The Martyr

First impressions

✓

When I first met Red, he found it difficult to meet my eyes. Red was an unremarkable man in every way, of medium height and build, with a pleasant yet undistinguished face and a manner that vacillated between wariness and bravado. He seemed determined to charm me, yet his obvious discomfort made his awkward efforts more desperate than disarming. I later discovered why I made Red so uncomfortable. He finally confessed that I reminded him of his stepdaughter, whom he had molested. Seeing her image flicker in my eyes raised painful memories of what he had done to her, and what his actions had done to his own opportunities in life.

Red's salvation was religion. Although he claimed to have been always interested in spiritual issues, while in prison he had embraced Christianity as a means to an end—namely, as a perspective he could use in trying to make sense of his crimes. Unfortunately, Red wore his conversion like a hair shirt, using God to alternately excuse and excoriate himself. He was prone to peppering his dialogue with awkwardly stilted terms such as "my sick lust," which worked oddly as a means of making his crimes seem even more salacious. If Red could convince himself that lust overtook him and that his godlessness had led him to offend, and then indulge in dramatic bouts of self-loathing, he could pretend he was less accountable for his actions. It was a precarious defense at best, and I suspected at some level he knew it wasn't working.

Red's Story

My childhood was rough. I lived in an abusive family. My father ruled us with his fists. At the time, I didn't know my family was unusual because it was so common. I just thought it was a normal thing to live in fear. I loved my father, and yet when I grew older and understood the things he did, I realized he was definitely abusive. I got an older brother, and he went through the same sort of beatings. We were never sexually abused by my father or mother, but we'd get beaten by any object our father could get his hands on. I'm not saying my father was a bad man. Well, in a way, I guess he was. He'd just beat the crap out of us. My mother was more like myself, very kind, more the mediator between us. We preferred going to her for our punishment. Dad would never do anything to my mother, just us boys. We came from a middle-class background because we had our own house and all that. But we were still poor in terms of our family life.

At the age of ten, I went to work for a friend of my brother's ex-boss. I was supposed to rake this guy's driveway, which had gravel on it. When it got late, he didn't want to drive me home, and I was shocked to find out my father had agreed for me to spend the night there. The guy would take me to school the next day. While I was cleaning myself up, he entered the shower and forced himself on me. I pushed him away then, but later when I was asleep he came in and raped me. It was oral sex. I was ten. He was in his forties, and there was nothing I could do—he just overpowered me. That was the beginning of everything. The rape brought lust into my life. The next day, the guy drove me to school and he told me not to say anything. He was a very rich man, and he tried to buy my silence. He bought me new clothes and other stuff, and paid me very well for raking his gravel. He didn't want me to say anything, so I didn't. I didn't tell my parents because I knew what would happen. If I told my father I had been abused, I would have gotten another beating. I didn't want to tell my mother because she would have had a stroke. My mother was a heart patient for most of her life, and it wouldn't take much to set her off. She was only in her fifties when she had to have a bypass operation. So, anyway, I just squashed it. I buried it. I didn't talk to nobody about it, and I kept it bottled up inside.

When I was eleven years old, I got involved in the church. A church family asked my parents if I could go to church with them. My father was an atheist and didn't believe in nothing, but I wanted to go. I didn't have a social life because we lived way out in the country and my parents were very strict about letting me go anywhere, so I thought going to church could get me some friends. I started going to church, and that helped me to feel better about myself. I still didn't tell nobody about the rape, but at least I had other people I could talk to who wouldn't beat me. But I kept thinking about what that man did to me, and even though I hadn't liked it at the time, it brought up a lot of sexual feelings. I thought about sex a lot.

A few years later, I got involved with another guy who was about two years older than me. I was fourteen and he was about sixteen. He came over a lot to our house to visit us, and since we only had two beds, one for my brother and one for me, he slept in my bed with me. We had oral sex. I let him do to me what the guy did when he raped me at the age of ten. I kind of enjoyed it and it went on from there. I didn't stop him from doing what he wanted as long as he didn't physically hurt me. This went on for the next four years.

I graduated from high school with a pretty decent average. My father beat me if my grades were too bad, so it was kind of forced education. He would sit at the table while I did my homework, and if I stopped at any time, he would whack me. My homework always had to be done in front of him. While I was in school, I kept everyone, even girls, at a distance. It's not that I thought there was anything wrong with women—I just didn't feel like I could reach out to anybody. I kept to myself.

After I graduated from high school, there was about two years before I joined the service. I worked on a farm, and all the money I made I had to lay out on the table for my parents. I didn't mind. My parents loved me, even though my dad beat me. Or so I kept on thinking. Years later, when my dad died, I went back home and spit on his grave. I lay down and cried on my mother's grave, but I spit on my father's. I just never had the opportunity or the strength to tell him how I really felt. The one nightmare that keeps running through my head is from the first grade. I was sitting in class when blood came pouring out of the back of my shirt and they sent me home. The person sitting behind me wanted to know what I did to get whipped so bad. But I just went home and sat down next to my father with a bowl of cereal and didn't leave his side. He said I deserved what I got.

I also got marks on my arms from playing with matches. I was six years old, and my father would turn on the burners on the stove and put my brother's and my arms on the stove and burn us. "If you play with matches, that is what can happen," he would say. The scars never left. Most of the time I was in school, I wore long-sleeved shirts to try to hide the scars. I guess I hid the scars to protect my father. Or maybe to protect my mom. I didn't want the family to break up or other people to think bad things about my father.

When I joined the service, I was twenty years old. In my second year on a carrier, I got raped by two guys. The first day I arrived on a new ship, they jumped me while I was coming up the gangplank. They threw a blanket over my head, and even though I kept on swinging, they just attacked me. I probably would have been dead, but they heard someone coming and took off. I didn't say anything about the rape. It is kind of embarrassing for a man to admit he has been raped or abused. I just said somebody jumped me, then I went on duty. I felt ashamed afterwards, but I took a long shower and cried and got it out of my system. I must have been an easy target then or something. I guarantee they wouldn't do it today. Those guys didn't know me. They probably thought, "Here's a guy—let's take his money and his virtue and go." It was my virtue, too, because I was a virgin then. I had oral sex before, but nothing else. Afterwards, I thought about the attack a lot. They have these balconies on the carriers where you can walk and look at the water, and many times out there in the middle of the ocean I wanted to disappear. "Just jump," I'd say to myself, "just do it." I thought I wouldn't get hurt anymore if I left home, but it didn't happen that way.

To deal with all my pain, I did a lot of drugs. The harder the drug, the better I liked it. It didn't matter what I took—there was really no purpose to my life. There was no foundation other than working. I did have a few friends while I was in the service. I'm not a social person, although I've been trying to become more sociable. I need to crawl out of my security blanket and step outside, but I'm afraid to show people who I really am. If I keep on hiding, then maybe people can see what I want them to see, which is who I was before I was damaged. I did get involved with some prostitutes while I was in the service, although I hadn't had relationships with any women before that time. I was somewhat scared to be with a female. It was better than being with men, though, and my attraction became more female in orientation. I just couldn't face opening up to a man. I'd be afraid he'd hurt me. I'm trying to get over this by working in these groups while I'm in prison. When I first got into prison, if a male counselor wanted to talk to me, I'd just leave the room. I couldn't stand being alone with a guy.

When I got out of the service, I got married to a girl that lived in a trailer park. I finally had a straight sexual relationship with a woman, which to me was wonderful. I didn't have to pay for her company. I really loved her. She already had a child, a boy who loved me to death, and I just loved him to death in return. But it lasted only about a year. My father died, so I went home to take care of my mother. My brother called me—we hadn't communicated in a long time—and told me that Dad had died. I was freshly married—we were newlyweds—and we didn't really have anything to give up yet, so we were the ones to take care of my mom. At that time, I was on top of the world. But there is always something that pulls the rug out from under you. I kind of felt that my father, and then later on my mother, died on pur-

Attraction loosely defined
Attraction to sex

pose. I had just gotten away from all that crap, and then they expected me to go running back home and leave everything I had worked so hard for.

So my wife and me packed up everything and left. About a year after we went back home, my wife left me. My mother got between us. My wife said that my mother had pushed my father to death. I didn't really care about my father's death because of what he did to me, but I was really protective of my mother. So I ended up divorcing my wife because of my family. My wife got real bad at the end, getting into arguments with my mother and all that. When she started taking drugs, I just pushed her out of my life. If she hadn't started taking drugs, I might have kept her. But it didn't happen that way.

When I moved back home, I didn't have no job. After my mother died, I didn't know where to go, so I just bounced from relative to relative. Then I started to get sexually involved with some female relatives, like my cousins. You could call them kissing cousins, I guess. They were about the same age as I was or younger. I was twenty-five at the time, and they were like twenty-four or twenty-five. One was seventeen. They were sexually attracted to me, so it was more like mutual affairs. One cousin even wanted to take off with me to another world where we could get married. In fact, a couple of years down the road she did have some sons, and she swears none of them are mine, but one of them looks exactly like me. Every time I would go over to their house, this one would always come up to me and attach himself to me. I can't say if he's mine or not.

Finally, I got involved with a very heavyset lady who had four kids. We were friends with her family, and she was stranded down in another state, so I volunteered to drive down and bring the family back. While we were on the road, I kind of got attached to them. The lady was obese, but I was alone at the time so I got involved with her. We had sex and she had my son. We got married, but it was like blind love—the blind leading the blind. I had jumped into another relationship and a marriage just because I didn't want to be alone. I'm actually still married to her after eleven years, but we've been away from each other for quite a while now.

That's when it all started. I was drunk one night when she was in the hospital having my son. I had the kids all to myself since I had to baby-sit them while she was in the hospital. At that time, the oldest boy was almost twelve and the oldest girl was almost eleven. Then there were five-year-old twins, a boy and a girl. In the middle of the night, the younger girl jumped into bed with me, although I was too drunk to know it. I guess the oldest daughter came into the room to find out where her sister had gone, and saw the younger girl doing oral sex on me. She had seen her mother doing it to me when she came into the room one day, and I had kicked her out of there. I

Annotations in margins: "talks to her as a object" (left margin); "blame Alcohol, got caught" (right margin)

didn't know what she was doing, though, because I was dead to the world. I didn't feel too good when I found out what happened. I was kind of ashamed, because she was just reenacting what she had seen. I had never been physical with the kids. Even after that point, when I started having sex with them, it was all oral sex and their choice, not mine.

I had oral sex with the oldest boy. I don't know how it started other than him asking questions about girls. I had never had a real family life and I didn't know what to do. I started explaining it to him, and then it went into showing him, too. It only happened once. I didn't force him. It didn't go on for very long. Afterwards, I sat with him and told him that it was not right for a daddy to do that and that he wouldn't have that problem with me again. And he never did. He wasn't too happy with me afterwards, though, and I had a lot of rough times with him. He was very bitter. It did happen a few other times with the girls, though. My wife found out about it and we got into a big argument. I told her it had happened once or twice and that I was just sick about what I did. I figured she would dump me then and there, but she didn't.

My wife was angry for a little while after that, but I guess she really didn't want to lose another husband since I was her third one. I was also a role model to her kids. They had never had a father figure in their lives; they were all just abandoned. So she and I stuck together. I worked a lot, and then I would come home and nothing would be done, so I'd have to clean house, pick up after the kids, make supper, and wash the dishes. She would just sit there and leave the house a mess. I put up with that for about three years. She was just one of those types that raised kids and lived on welfare. She had always done that. So our relationship was not very stable. I stayed with them because I didn't have anybody else and they got attached to me. I kind of did her family a favor by taking care of her. I thought I was pleasing them, but I wasn't pleasing myself. I put myself aside a lot and did things for other people instead of for me.

Our sexual relationship wasn't very good. The first time we slept together, I was drunk and that's when our son was conceived. After that, my eyes were opened up more and more. She wouldn't take care of herself, and I didn't force anything. I never raised a hand to her, and I tried not to argue with her. I'd just tell her she had to take care of herself. I had to take care of myself, too. I was a hundred pounds overweight because I was so unhappy. My wife must have weighed something like 350 pounds. "I had twins," she'd say, "that's why I kept the fat." And many times I'd blow up at her because she kept blaming the kids for her weight. I said that a lot of women are skinny and have kids, then after they are done they go back to the way they used to be. All that fat made my wife less attractive to me. I tried a bunch of different things to satisfy me. For example, the wife of a neighbor attached herself to me. She would ask me over, and one thing led to another and we got involved. And, of course, I molested my kids. It was a ridiculous life. None of my life really makes sense at all. I guess it was good that I finally got locked up. It all started with rebellion with my oldest daughter. I had never even really touched her. What happened was that one day she was in the shower with the younger girl. I had to go to the bathroom, and I said to close them curtains so I could go. Mind you, I never had kids before. I had never raised them, but ended up with this instant family, so I was kind of dumb when it came to raising girls. Boys are easier because they take care of themselves. Anyhow, I opened the curtain to make sure that they weren't horseplaying around and not getting their shower done. I noticed that the oldest girl had some white stuff around her private area, and I pointed it out to her. Well, I actually showed her. I touched her where the white stuff was and told her to clean herself better. I never physically hurt her. I just pointed out where it was and then I left.

Some time later, she ran away from home. I spent nine hours searching for this girl. I walked around streets talking to cops. When I got her home, I ended up almost like my father, I was so tired and pissed. It got physical between us. I whacked her on the butt and told her to chill out, and she started fighting back. She bit me and I slapped her. I should have waited until the next day before confronting her instead of doing it while I was angry. So I took off and squashed my anger and gathered my thoughts. When you are all tired and frustrated and don't know what to do after looking for this girl for nine hours, it can just overtake you. And she had never fought back before, so it escalated.

A few days after that, we were in the midst of moving to another place, and she wanted to ride with me to pick up some stuff. Her mother said no. So I gave her a hug and said, "Your mother has known you longer than I have and I am not going to cross her. You just can't go this time." I wanted to take her, too, but to keep the peace I just hugged her and took off. Apparently, she then went to school and told them she was ticked off with us, so she was going to tell all. She told the school counselor about the incident in the shower, and one thing led to another. They started an investigation. They talked to the kids and they told their stories, then they came to me and I told them mine. I said, "I ain't got nothing to hide—yeah, I was guilty of that." I went to court and they said, "Do you want to plead guilty or not guilty?" I said, "Well, I am guilty, so I don't need no lawyer or nothing—do what you got to do."

My wife was speechless, she was so mad. And the rest of the family was kind of mad at the oldest daughter because the whole family was close. We had sat down and discussed it, so they all knew about it. I didn't hide nothing from them. Anyhow, I got sent to prison. I got one-to-four years. I was scared to death. I figured I'd face all kinds of hatred. When I was in the county jail for six months, they were more supportive than in prison, trying to get me not to do anything stupid. Then I ended up going downstate. At first, I was quite open about what I did, quite honest with people. They'd tell me what they were in prison for and I'd tell them—I don't care what you think, this is my crime. So I got beat up several times. I had a guy punch me in the mouth for no reason at all. The other guys ran over to him and told him to leave me alone. But he didn't. I said I'm not going to put myself in more risk, so I signed into protective custody. And from there, I went to a different correctional facility and didn't talk to nobody anymore about my crime, not even any counselors. There was never really any therapy available while I was in prison the first time.

My family did come visit me. But I wouldn't see them. I was kind of angry. What had happened was supposed to be a family issue, but my daughter turned it into a public issue. But none of them hated me. I couldn't hate them, either, not even the daughter who told on me. When I finally was ready to talk to them, I said to my daughter, "You really didn't have to put us through all this. You could have squashed it in the family." I asked her why she told, but she wouldn't answer. Everyone came to see me, even the oldest boy. And the twins, too. I had never physically raped or abused them. I just did sexual acts in front of them, which is abuse, yeah, I know it is. I ain't going to say it isn't, but I never did touch them.

All in all, I was incarcerated for about a year; then I made my first parole. I made parole early because a religious family took me in. I was very religious, then. I tried to walk the Christian way, and this family took me into their home. I never went back to my family after that. I went to court for visitation rights, and that's when the war started between my wife and myself. She was supposed to show up with my son, but she wouldn't do it. I tried to get a court order and the judge demanded her to get my son down to see me, but she never did. I never pushed the issue, so I haven't seen my son since he was three. He's going on twelve now, so he's confused and probably hates me.

My divorce is still not finalized, because I just detached myself from everybody except my brother. He had tried to find me for a long time. When he did finally find me, I was in here in prison for a second time. He found out about my charges and he kind of backed off. My aunt wrote to me for a while, but I cut her off, too. I cut them all off. I'm in prison now for something I did not do. I'm spending a seven-to-fourteen-year sentence for something I did not do. I never laid a hand on a child after I served my first bid. And now I plan to max out my time in prison because when I do get out, I don't want my name announced all over for people to think that I am still what I used to be in my past.

But I'm getting ahead of myself. When I was on parole for my first offense, I lived in the basement of a church. I took care of the church—I was like a maintenance man. When I got away from the religious family, I went to visit some old acquaintances. I was by myself, and they pushed another lady on me because they knew about the incident with my wife. I got involved with this woman sexually, and we had a child together. I wasn't allowed to live with anybody who had children, as a condition of my parole, so I had my own place. I got a new apartment and a different job at a supermarket, and everything was going good. I would go to visit her, do what I had to do, and then go back to my apartment for the night.

Anyhow, it got me back into trouble. One day, I went over to my friends' house and I watched the kids while they went to get food. They were on welfare and needed to use their food stamps. The parents were very challenged. They would send their kids into the neighborhood for money for milk and stuff, and then go spend that money on beer and cigarettes. Anyway, when I was there, the youngest daughter, who was eleven years old, came down the stairs wrapped in a blanket with a long nightgown on that went all the way to her ankles. She came over and sat on my lap. Her older sister came down and said the girl didn't have no underwear on. I slipped my hand up on the side of her and, sure enough, she didn't. So I said, "I can't have you sitting on me when you ain't got nothing on underneath you. Go get proper before you come sit on my lap." She got really mad at that, but I told her that she knew my rules.

language suggests he entered not touched

That was one of the incidents that was brought up in court. She said that I put my finger into her privates, which I didn't. No way in the world could I put my finger up in her privates when she was wrapped up in a blanket with a long nightgown all the way to her ankles. And there was another incident. She was fighting with my stepson, so I took her into the bathroom and locked the door to talk with her privately. When it came up in court, I said, "Yes, it happened, but I did not make no sexual advances to her at all." I didn't tell her to take her pants down or whip her or nothing. I sat on the end of the bathtub and explained to her that she should knock it off or I'd tell her mother and father and then she'd really be in trouble. She started bawling, and we left. The older sister was on the stairs, and since the walls were paper-thin, she never heard anything happen like sexual advances. She was more on my side than her sister's side. But seeing that the door was locked and we were alone gave off a bad impression, because everybody knew

fighting could spark sexual tensions

what I was in for the first time. The court was not going to believe my story over that of a child. So I lost.

When the girl made a statement that all this had happened, I decided to fight it in court because I knew I wasn't guilty. But I got seven-to-fourteen years on the charges of being in the bathroom. It seemed like a pretty stiff sentence. I wasn't a happy camper with that. I was going to throw out another appeal, but I left it alone. I said to myself, well, this must be karma from the first one. I must not have done enough time for the first crime, I thought, so I treated it as such because the first crime was legit. That was serious. A year after I arrived in prison, I got a newspaper clipping from a friend of mine who knew the family. The clipping said the father of the family was charged with molesting his boys. I was furious. I knew he was on probation for child abuse when I was hanging out with his family. I'm not putting the blame on him for my sentence, but it seems kind of funny. I was on probation for the same crime he was on probation for. Then I get nailed for something I didn't do, and a year later he gets charged for abusing his boys.

I think that was partly why the family dragged me into court over the daughter's charges. I had pulled away from them. They got pissed because I said, "I can't be around this environment and keep helping you out. It puts me at risk." But it was too late for me. While I've been in prison, I have really been trying to forgive my enemies. My friend included a letter with the newspaper clipping in which he said that the wife had been lying all along for the husband and she was tired of it. Before I was arrested, the father took the girl into a clinic and had her checked for AIDS. Guess why? Because he has AIDS, so he took the child to the clinic to get checked for something I was accused of doing to her. I didn't do nothing to her. The only reason he blamed me is because they knew what I was in for the first time and they were mad at me for pulling away from them. I pick poor friends. There could be the lowliest family in the world and if they look like they are in dire need, I will step in and try to be a hero. And then I will get stomped on. I don't know why I do it. Maybe because I hate to see people going through garbage when they don't need to be. I figure that all that needs to be done is to show them a little care and train them to do better.

I tend to take care of everybody else but not myself. But it doesn't matter anymore. Right now, I am in here for something I didn't do. The first time, I think it happened because of my sick state of living. I spent all this time taking care of everybody else, and what have I done for myself? Where has it gotten me? I got myself in prison. When I first got in, I wanted to die. I got along with everybody, though. If I thought somebody needed something, I gave it to them. That way, I'd know I had somebody watching my back. I went right to church; I stuck to doing things for God. I was involved in the choir and Bible studies. I worked sixteen hours in the metal shop there. I kept myself so busy, Red wasn't thinking about Red. And I am still doing that. But I'm trying to stop by taking groups. It's forcing me to stop and think of all the crap done in my life and how to sort it all out and get it away from me, so Red can be Red—so people can accept me for being who I am. I'm wounded, but I am still a human being that needs—well, I don't know what the heck I need. I know I need time. A lot of time.

The first group I was involved in got me communicating about being raped when I was ten and being abused all the time I was growing up by my father. I didn't add my brother into it. I left him out of it. I was going to leave him out of this, too, but what the heck. My brother was abusive toward me sexually. He made me orally masturbate him. It happened a number of times during my childhood. I know that is a big thing, really significant actually, but I don't like to think about it, so I don't talk about it much. When I first started opening up about these things, I did a lot of crying. It felt good to get it out, to dig out old wounds. And believe me, that was the hardest thing for me to ever do, to sit in a room of guys doing what I swore I would never do: to talk about my sexuality and my past life. I felt they would never understand, but there are guys who have been abused themselves. And it's not just physical abuse, but there is a lot of verbal abuse, too. They lose their self-esteem because their parents say that they are stupid, they're dumb. They don't ever put in a positive word, but instead are negative all the time. It sticks in kids' heads—kids hear that and it sticks with them. They say, "Well, I am stupid, so why try to learn anything?"

That's one thing that I done right. Of all the kids I ever had around me, I never told them they were stupid or that there was something wrong with them. I always gave them positive messages. I even went back to the ones I abused and explained to them that Daddy was sick and that things happened to him in the past that made him do bad things and that I would never hurt them again. My whole family wanted to take me back, even the ones I abused, even the oldest daughter, who put me in jail. She wrote to tell me she lost her first child to crib death and I could have said, well, that's what you get for putting me in here, but I couldn't go and do that. I just wrote to her and told her I was sorry for her loss. "There's always other ones," I said, "and you just have to learn and prepare yourself for the next one. Know your mistakes." I have always been supportive of everybody else. I can always give everybody the greatest advice for them, but the hardest one to give advice to is myself.

The worst thing I have to deal with is the forgiveness aspect of my religion. That is the hardest thing in the world. Me and God have gone through that for a long time. I ask, why have you forgiven me? I mean, your son didn't come down to die on a cross because he was a child abuser. Or a molester. I hate that word. The more I hear that molestation word, the more I don't want to exist. Being branded with knowing that I was one of those who grew up to hurt other people—it's so painful. The one thing I never wanted to do in my life was be like my father or the guys that hurt me. I don't want to hurt no one, but love them and to do for them as much as I can. It's not easy to dump the past and to be forgiven. There is no such thing as being rehabilitated.

I wonder what I would say to my father if he was alive. I probably wouldn't say much—I'd probably hit him with a chair. I would probably give him the same treatment he gave me. But then again, the person that I am, I'd probably hug him and forgive him and walk away. It's hard to forgive and forget. You can forgive, but you can never forget. My brother thinks I ought to just forget what he done to me and forgive him. He wants me to forget what he done to me, but he won't forget about all this stuff he sees on TV and in the news—all that garbage—and look at me as a brother in need of somebody's support instead of as a child abuser. Just last week, I told him, "You got your life to live and I got mine—I don't plan on coming to see you when I get out. Maybe down in the future I might, but right now all I got is me and God." I don't know if all that stuff with Dad affected my brother or not. All I know is that he is working hard, has a new baby on the way, got a new nephew. And all I've got is me.

Since I don't got too many people to talk to, I think about what happens in society a lot. I don't blame society for being scared of abusers, but they got to look at the other side of the coin also. The one who is doing the abusing may have been abused himself, and just didn't get counseling. I can't acknowledge anybody other than myself, but I regret I never opened my mouth after I was raped the first time. I wish I had gone back to kill that guy. I still remember the man's name after thirty years, point blank. I know what he looks like, where his house is. I don't know if he's still living there, but the man's name still rings in the back of my head.

This notification thing that society has now, this Megan's Law—to me it sucks, but it is understandable. I understand people's fears because I have children of my own and I wouldn't want them in danger of being abused, either. I think people need to be careful, but I also think that society should know that some guys aren't what they used to be. Give us a chance to prove that we ain't that way anymore. And tell the kids about us. If I had the chance—if I was strong enough to put myself out there and speak up—I'd tell a child to watch himself. Be careful about everybody else, even your relatives.

Your private parts are your own—don't let anybody mess with you. It's not just a matter of saying no. It's saying no and then getting away from the person and telling the person to get help before it is too late. Get abused kids to a counselor while they are young so they don't hold it in like I did. If they don't talk to somebody, later on down the road it will fester.

If I had the chance, I'd also want to tell people that for me, incarceration wasn't the answer. People who are abusing children need to be in mental institutions where they have one-on-one counseling and psychiatrists who know how to get things out of people's heads. That would be the most beneficial. You need to find out where the pain comes from. Putting us in prison means we are not going to get nothing except getting hurt by other guys who don't like us. We can't talk to nobody here because nobody wants to listen to us. Guys like me need to be able to speak about what's really in our hearts with people who are willing to listen and understand what is real and what is phony.

I'm just tired. Tired of being sick, tired of being hurt. And I walk very softly, now. Sometimes I feel like a keg of dynamite ready to explode. To keep it from going off, I hold onto my spirituality. My religious side keeps me alive and keeps me going. I want to get into the mission field when I get out because I am always wanting to do something for others. I figure that the mission field would be a good spot for me since I'd be doing what I love to do: helping people. But I really can't go out and try to help others if I can't help myself. So I got to keep talking about it. I got to keep pondering all this garbage, although the more I think about it, the more it makes me sick. But I got to verbalize it, because otherwise I'll never heal. And I would never really know what my pain has caused others. That hurts the most—knowing I was in that same category. Every time I see something on TV about a child being kidnapped and later found dead, I want to go find that person and just do away with them. Then I want to do away with myself for being in that category, because it is a sick way to live. If I had a choice between telling the world about what I was or taking a shot to the head, I'd take the shot. But I'd like to leave something to let people know about me. I got a journal that I write everything down in. I keep it very secure so no one else can read it but me, but someday I'd like people to see it. I'd like people to know how I felt, after I'm gone.

Summary

Red views himself as a long-suffering saint, a man whose paramount desire is to help other people and show them the path to salvation, yet who is cruelly exploited by the very people he seeks to save. Red wants to be a hero; he wants to rescue the downtrodden and raise them up to his level of spiritual awareness. Fundamentally, for all his self-loathing now that he is in prison, Red has an ego that requires frequent feeding. He desperately wants to believe that he is a better person than his life's circumstances would seem to imply.

Two major themes characterize Red's self-narrative. The first is the importance he places on the concept of family. As he comments, his own family wasn't poor in monetary terms, but rather poor in the emotional support the family structure is supposed to provide. His father was physically and emotionally abusive, and Red lived in constant fear.

Red was tormented by the tension between the family he wanted so desperately to have and the family he got. He even ended up with a ready-made family with his second wife, who seemed to symbolize the same sort of impoverished circumstances of his childhood. He set himself up as a surrogate father to her children and seems to view himself as their rescuer, although he ended up translating his desire for paternalism into sexual molestation.

The second major theme in Red's story is his own molestation, once in childhood and once when he was an adult and was raped by two men. His brother also sexually abused him. His molestation at ten years old by a friend of his brother's former boss "was the beginning of everything. The rape brought lust into my life."

The result of Red's abusive childhood and violent sexual attacks was to leave him "damaged," in his words. Red passively accepted his victimization, and seems to consider that the rest of his life was a series of events thrust upon him, but he uses that image of passivity to advantage. Red claims he would never have initiated sex with the children, but that they wanted it, so he went along with their wishes. Even while he was sexually molesting his stepchildren, Red believed he was their "role model." Because Red was religious and "tried to walk the Christian way," he made parole early for his first offense. His second bid occurred when he magnanimously got involved with another impoverished family and was punished for his efforts to improve their station in life.

Red presents himself as an extraordinarily giving person who selflessly sacrifices his own needs for others. Although I don't want to go so far as to claim he considers himself "Christ-like," certainly he uses religion as a means of empowering his own self-image. Red feels that his efforts to save others were exploited. He had no control over his "lust" and the situations other people put him in; he was merely a victim of circumstance and his own good intentions. If he can believe that God forgives him, then he expects the rest of the world to forgive him as well. That this forgiveness doesn't seem forthcoming is the source of his continued self-flagellation and pain.

CHAPTER FIVE

~

Billy—The Monstrous Child

Billy was an imposing man, not unusually tall, but husky, muscles rippling beneath a layer of fat. He peered at the world from beneath shaggy brows, which lent his potentially affable, pleasant face a threatening appearance. His forearms were covered with ballpoint tattoos. On his left arm, the names of his wife and children—including one of his victims' names—were surrounded by a heart, providing a constant reminder of why he was in prison. Billy was missing three front teeth, a souvenir of the night his wife hit him in the mouth with a paddle when she caught him sodomizing his stepdaughter. Obviously slow and uneducated, Billy struggled with his words, taking long pauses to carefully think out his responses.

When I first met Billy, he was sullen and unresponsive. His consuming concern appeared to be maintaining a macho image, stern and unapproachable, perhaps as a defense mechanism. Yet this distant demeanor could not completely hide his insecurity. He seemed to lap up any attention paid to him, positive or negative. The childish hankering for attention was at odds with his forbidding exterior.

Months later, during our interview, his attitude seemed to take a drastic turn. He gestured wildly with his hands when he spoke and constantly fidgeted. In contrast to his glowering, aggressive attitude of months previous, Billy now acted like a grotesquely overgrown adolescent. Although he was well into his thirties, his intellectual and emotional I.Q. probably approximated that of his youthful victims. It was a bizarre, ironic, bitter realization—that this hulking bear of a man harbored the soul of a child. He was acting out his affinity for children, but in the most profoundly adult of ways.

Billy's Story

When I was young, my dad kept moving from place to place. He left us when I was six years old. He got a job driving a truck for some milk company and told my mom and us that he wouldn't be back. I more or less decided that I was going to be a tough guy after that. I was the second oldest—I have one sister older than me and a younger brother and sister—and I always stuck up for my brothers and sisters. I was the troublemaker in the family.

Before my dad left and [when] I was a real little kid, we had an old white-faced Hereford bull. When my dad would go to work in the morning, he'd take me with him and sit me on the back of this bull, and we'd just ride around the pasture all day. So instead of a little kid having a dog for a pet, I had this big old two-ton bull. I still got a picture of it. He ended up hamburger, though. I wouldn't eat none of it, either. After that, I was always bringing home cats and dogs, whatever animal I found. I used to get in trouble for it. My folks told me we ain't no dog pound. But I was always taking off and picking up strays, so they decided to start tying me to the porch. I was just three or four years old. I remember how pissed off I was because I couldn't get loose. I loved to roam around. I was always getting into stuff.

I used to run over to my grandpa's house a lot. He lived up the road. Me and my grandpa was always real close, even up to the day he died. Later on, my grandpa tried to take us kids from my mom because my stepfather was so mean, but the courts said nope. So he told my real dad what was going on, but for some reason the courts wouldn't let him have us, either. I have a lot of good memories of my grandpa. Then he had cancer, but the only thing that killed him was when they took away his beer. They took away his beer and cigars, and two months after that, he died.

My stepfather was an idiot and a drinker. If you didn't do something the way it should have been done, you got throwed around the room. He would hold your hand up and burn your fingers with a cigarette lighter. And if you decided to do something like steal, then your fingers got smashed. He mostly did it to my mom and me. I took the part, if you're going to hit somebody, hit me. That way, my brother and sisters didn't get it.

My mother never stuck up for me with my stepfather. I guess she loved him. That was my interpretation. My one uncle that I lived with for quite a while, he was going to do something about it, but my mom told him not to. I got that scar there from my stepfather, and that's where I got my broken nose. He told me to clean the dishes one night, and instead of walking around the table to pick up a glass, I just reached across the table for it. He said to put it down and walk around there. I took the glass and slammed it down on the table, and it went all over. So we had a fight. I was twelve or thirteen and I was having none of him. He went to hit me, but I was a little too quick and took off. When I figured he was gone for the night, I came back home. It was two o'clock in the morning, but he was still there. That's how I got the broken nose, the busted eye. My mom didn't do nothing about it.

When I got up off the floor, I took off again. I was gone for three days. I had two black eyes and my nose was bleeding all over. I stayed in the woods for a while and then hung out by the laundromat. If I got thirsty, I'd go into some farmland and grab a cow's tit so I had my milk, and I'd steal donuts from behind the grocery store. But I got tired of being by myself. I finally made a collect call from the laundromat to my uncle and told him I was hiding there. What a mistake that was. He made me go back home. Back then, in order to get the cops to do something, there had to be a dead body. There was no such thing as domestic quarrels, and nobody wanted to get involved.

Soon after, I got in trouble all over again. This time, I got in trouble with my aunt. She was living with us at the time, and in the morning when you'd go out through the living room, she'd always be laying on the couch. That's when I started learning about sex. I just went over one day and started playing with her. I went right down to her vagina and she goes, "What are you doing?" "Looking for a yo-yo," I said. I don't know why I said that. She started laughing and made me quit, and I think that if I had gotten yelled at right then and there, I wouldn't be here now. That's just what I'm thinking. If they had put me in a home or something when I started to become a problem to everybody, maybe I'd have straightened out.

Of course, I had been about five years old when I first had sex. It was with my cousin underneath the old horse barn. She showed me what to do. She was only about five—about the same age as me—but she still knew about sex. Years later, I found out my uncle had molested all my cousins. After my cousin and I did it, there was a neighbor girl. We were like seven or eight years old and did everything, except I could never figure out how to get my penis into her so I always used my fingers. And then, later on, the incident with my aunt happened. After that, I just kept on messing around with all my cousins and the neighbor girls. I figured if they ain't yelling, then it must be all right. I've taken all these courses while I've been in prison and they keep telling me that those girls didn't want it, but none of those girls hollered like it was bothering them. I know it was wrong because I was older than them, but they didn't fight me about it.

This went on for a long time, until I was just turned twenty and got married to my first wife. Then I just wasn't interested in sex no more. I tried to get it from my wife, but that was fighting a losing battle. All the time we was married, I think we only slept together maybe eight times. I tried to have sex with her before we got married, but it didn't work. I think that was why I married her—to say at least I finally got you. We had been going out for two years before we got married. I tried to get her attention for the longest time. I think it was the hard-to-get thing. I thought I was doing all the right things—you know, being polite and a gentleman. I'd get her roses and stuff. It took me two years before she finally says okay, we can get married. But the marriage didn't work too well. Even though she was my wife, she was never home. She was always out with her family and friends and whatever. That bugged me for a while—that every time I came home from work there was nobody there. I cleaned the house, I did all the laundry, I tried to make things pretty to get her attention. But I couldn't figure out what I was doing wrong. It didn't dawn on me that it was my attitude and the way I treated her like garbage. When I did come home and she was there, I'd get really jealous and hit her. Damn, I think I'd spend the next two hours trying to apologize, and I'd clean up the house again and do the dishes. She'd finally come downstairs and I'd try to make it up to her, and we'd start making out, and then she'd go, "I'm going out." That would make me mad and I'd hit her again. I'd say to her, "This ain't worth it—one of us has got to go." She says, "Well, what's in it for me?" "I don't know," I say. "Okay, then I'll stay," she says. This way at least she'd have a roof over her head.

Around the time my marriage started to fall apart, my cousins started bringing my niece over, and for some reason, that is when I crossed the line. I don't know if it was because I was getting back at everybody or what. In my group here at the prison, the guys were all asking me why I done what I did with my niece, and I couldn't face it. So I quit going to the group. I kept thinking, damn, why am I thinking about this garbage? But finally I realized how deep this thing got with me and figured out that if I had gotten help when I first crossed the line, maybe I might not be here today. So I been trying to think why I did stuff with my niece. Maybe it was because I was angry or just horny, I don't know. I came right out and asked her, "Cindy, play with me." I just kept talking to her about it and she finally said okay.

Cindy was my cousin's daughter, the cousin I had played with when we was kids. I just had her fondle me and we kissed, but for some reason I felt guilty about it. Nothing was said about it until the next time she came over to baby-sit—my wife and me had one kid at the time and she was pregnant with our second. Anyhow, I kept saying to myself, nope, nope, don't do this, but there was something in my brain that kept saying, well, you did it once and it was all right, so go ahead. So I did. I'd play with Cindy, make her stand upside down or give me blow jobs. If I ever went someplace, she'd want to go with me, so I guess she felt okay about it. I was so angry at everything at that time. I think if I had had a gun, I'd have shot everybody in sight. I was always trying to do the right thing, but I couldn't stop the voice in my head that kept telling me to do it to her again. The only time me and my wife had sex was when she wanted to get pregnant. So I don't know, I guess I just was pretty crazy.

The thing with my niece went on for like two years. Whenever she came over, it was like she knew what I wanted, you know. She'd come up to me and start grabbing, and I'd say, oh, she's ready for me, without realizing that was the picture I put in her brain. I just figured, she likes it. This is where the group showed me that I was the one who had her doing that, going along with me. She was just a little girl, and I put into her head that she should play with me and that it was all right. I never said nothing to her about not telling nobody. I just said to her the first time, it won't hurt, I promise, and I was nice to her. After that, it seemed just normal. Even I got to thinking it was normal. Cindy didn't seem to care. When she didn't tell anybody and nobody said nothing to me about it, I figured it was all right. I wasn't hurting her or being mean to her, and she was more or less making me happy because I was getting some attention. She thought I loved her. That's where I crossed the line. Instead of respecting her, I made her grown up before she really was.

The day I left my wife, I came home from work and peeked into my neighbor's window and thought I saw him on the couch with her on top of him. So I ripped my coat off and came running through his back door. By that time, she was coming down from upstairs and he was laying on the couch. I decked her and left. My neighbor didn't do nothing. He was afraid of me, anyway. I told my wife, "That's it, we can't do this no more. You go your way and I'll go my way." I went to live in a small town a ways away for about six months. A friend of mine had a log cabin there, and he gave me a gun and shells. When I was hungry, I went out and shot rabbits or something and just stayed there by myself like an old hermit. I didn't have no job—just lived off the land. If I needed money, I took the animal hides down and my friend took them into town and sold them. Then he'd give me more shotgun shells. I was having a grand old time until I got homesick.

I moved back to my hometown and stayed by myself. About a year later, I met the woman who became my second wife. I was doing work on an apartment house and forty feet up in the air redoing a chimney. I wanted a cigarette, and the guy that was working with me wouldn't walk up the ladder. So

I heard this woman down there getting a cigarette out of my truck. She walks all the way up the ladder to me and says here. Not bad, I thought. "Do you want to go out?" "Someday," she says. Hmm, I thought—I found another one that's hard to get. I would like it if a woman would just say yes, right then and there. Then I wouldn't have to go through all this work.

I tried to get her to go out with me for about three months. I'd see her down on the ground while I was working up on the roof. She'd be taking her kids to the school bus, and I'd be going, "Kibbles and bits, your ground is shaking." I guess I made her mad. The more I said that, the more she'd yell at me. But at least she was paying attention to me. Instead of climbing down the ladder, I had this habit of grabbing the sides and putting my feet on it and sliding down to the ground. I liked to show off for the neighbors. One day, when I was about halfway down, the ladder went thump and I fell. Everybody comes over to ask me if I was all right. She was there, and that was when I asked her again if she wanted to go out. "When I can get a baby-sitter," she says. I pointed to a lady who was standing there and said, "You got one right there." So we started going out.

Her name was Elaine. Things started off a little rocky because even though she was seeing me, when I'd go to work during the day, she'd go down the street to her boyfriend's house. I don't know why I stayed with her. But later on, I was putting up a picket fence, and she comes over and gives me a rose. "Here," she says. "What the heck do I want with a flower?" I says. "You aren't supposed to give a man a flower." "Yes, I can," she says. "Well, I'm not taking it," I told her. She put it on the dashboard of my truck. It smelled pretty. And we worked things out and were together ever since.

After I left my first wife, I didn't have no more contact with Cindy. I'd go over and see her and her family, but that was it. It was like she didn't exist for me anymore. She'd ask me if we were going somewhere or if I'd spend some time with her, and I'd say, "Not today, I'm busy." I guess she hated me for a while, especially later on after I first went to prison, but she got over it. After I came to prison, I talked to Cindy and told her that it wasn't her fault what I did. I made her into something she wasn't because my wife and I were having problems. Cindy paid attention to me, and she never told me no. I never pushed her. I think she loved me in a way. She was paying attention to me, and I was paying attention to her. But then I began to ignore her when my life got going okay again, and that really hurt her for a while.

Anyhow, back to Elaine. After she gave me that rose, things were going really good between us. Elaine had two kids, a little boy and a girl named Annie. When we were first going together, I did anything for those kids. I'd take them to the park and baby-sit them after I got home from work. Elaine lived next to a bar, and when she worked nights, I'd put the kids to bed and then go next door to the bar. I'd sit there and drink until it was time for Elaine to come home, and then I'd go back upstairs to wait for her. That was when things started between Annie and me. The first time Annie came into the bathroom when I was in there, I didn't know if she saw me or not. She just stood there when she realized I was in there. She was looking at me so hard, I thought, well, maybe she likes me, so I started trying to get her to have sex with me. She always said no, so I backed off.

I didn't do anything with Annie until her mom and I had been together for five or six years. Elaine and me eventually got married, but it wasn't till after I was in the county jail, something like eight or nine years after we met. When things started with Annie, she was nine years old. I was always trying to be like a dad to her, but it was hard. She'd walk around the house and do little things that reminded me of sex. Why do little girls do that, you know? Swing their hips when they walk around and wear nightgowns or something that you can see through? It didn't dawn on me to tell Annie to go put her clothes on. I just ignored it. But really I didn't ignore it. I just let her do it because I thought, what the heck. Then one night Annie got messed up with poison ivy and her mother wouldn't touch it. So I had to be the one to put calamine lotion on Annie. I rubbed the stuff all over her body and when I got to her vagina, she didn't say no. Well, she didn't scream and yell at me, anyway, so I thought that maybe it was all right. So I tried playing with her. She got mad and said no. Then I got mad and I said, "You're going to let me do it or I'm going to beat you up." So she let me because I scared her.

For the next four months or so, things didn't go good for me and Elaine. I decided I wanted out. Every time I wanted to leave, though, I didn't have no money, so I just got to the point where I didn't care. I mean, I'm usually trying to do my best like cleaning up the house, but I just snapped. I was like an animal. If you left something lying around, I'd take it, or if you left your car unlocked, I'd get into it. I was stealing tools, food, you name it. I'd go into a store and take cigarettes right in front of the clerks. And they never said nothing to me. Damn, I thought, I'm going to keep doing this because I wasn't getting caught. I don't know if I wanted somebody to stop me or not. I figured I'd just see how far I could go. I tried to break into people's cars, but I ain't never got the hang of that, yet. I couldn't ever get the cars open. And I tried to get into pop machines, but that didn't work. I just didn't care if I lived or died. I was in one of those—what do you call them?—depression states. That's where I was.

This went on for a while, and then one day Annie made me mad as hell. I can't remember why she made me mad, but I said, "Okay, I'll fix you." I was so mad, I went out and got drunk so then I wouldn't have to worry about it. I thought when I got back home, everything would be all right. But it didn't work that way. Annie said to me, "You're not my dad and you can't tell me nothing." I told her to give me a kiss. She said, "No, I hate you." So I took all her clothes off and I slung her over the bed and I said, "Now I'm going to give you something." And that is when I sodomized her. I think I was bent out of shape because I was trying to compare Annie with Cindy. I just asked Cindy and it was always all right. But when I'd ask Annie the same thing, she was like, no, get away from me. I'd think, you know, you're supposed to say yes. I crossed the line. I made both of those girls grow up before it was their time. I guess I needed all their attention, but I went too far, especially with Annie. Annie was a good girl. But I screwed up her life.

When I was sodomizing Annie, she started crying and screaming, and I held her mouth so she couldn't make a sound. I was just being downright mean to her. I was like a great big ape. I didn't care if I was hurting her or not. But Elaine came home and caught us. I didn't see her at first, but I guess she just stood there for a minute. She says, "What are you doing?" "What do you think I'm doing?" I say back. I didn't care if she saw me or not. That should have clicked right there, you know. Hey, there's somebody watching. But it didn't click. I was just like a great big animal. Afterwards, I felt relieved a little bit because I had let all the anger out. I didn't think nothing about Annie. I didn't care about her. I didn't feel sorry for her. It had nothing to do with sex or love. It was just like, all right, you got the hole and I'm taking it. Annie just stood there. She wasn't crying and she didn't look like she was in pain, but if she had a gun, I'd be dead. Maybe she should have had a gun. Elaine asked her if that was the first time it happened, and she said yes. I had always been trying to grab Annie's butt or pinch her boobs, but she never said anything about that. Elaine told me she was going to call the cops. I yanked the phone off the wall and said, "I'm not going to do it again." She said okay.

For the next month, it was like everything got back to normal. I thought, wow, this is decent. I never tried to play with Annie or grab her. I was more or less finally becoming a grown-up. Annie's attitude toward me was like, don't come near me, but I'll still talk to you. I helped her with her homework and I helped her with the dishes. For about a month, we were a regular family. There was no fighting, no quarrels. But Elaine told her friend Linda about what happened, and Linda didn't like me because I cracked her husband one night. So Linda called the cops and they came to get me. The cops asked me if I knew why they was there. I said, "Yeah." "Why?" "Because I sodomized my stepdaughter." I decided then that if I can go off the wall and do that to somebody without caring, then there is something really wrong with me. I was charged with sodomy first and endangering the welfare of a minor. I admitted to all of it, all but the sodomy part, that is. So we went to trial, and I was so mad and bent out of shape that I told the judge, the lawyer, the DA, and the jury to kiss my ass and go to hell. I just didn't care.

Just before I was sentenced, Elaine came up to me and goes, "Are we still getting married?" Now, why is she asking me this after what I just did? But everybody was saying to go for the trailer visits, so I said, "Yeah, let's get married." Elaine was standing by me. I didn't have the common sense to know that even though I hurt her and her daughter, she was trying to make amends. "Why don't you go find somebody better than me?" I'd say. But she didn't want nobody but me. When I first got to prison, they said, "Well, what do you want?" I said, "I need help and I want to work in the shop." So I was making money. I'd send Elaine half and I'd keep half. It was pretty decent for a while. She'd come to visit me every weekend and bring her son, and once she brought my real boys from my first marriage. I was still on okay terms with my first wife for a long time. Even though she hated the hell I put her through, we kept talking for a while. But I haven't talked to her or my boys for the past four years. I sent the boys each a birthday card, and she sent them back, stating that I hope you appreciate my feelings and don't contact us again. So I wrote her a letter back saying that's fine, when the boys turn of age if they want to see me they know where I'm at. And that's where I left it. You know, I just don't need any of it. I got to get myself straightened out before I can think about any of those people.

Once, Elaine brought Annie to see me. That was an all right visit, but I felt awkward after the way I treated her. Now I was supposed to expect her to be nice to me. It don't work that way. Annie had to testify at my trial. Everybody said to take the cop-out, but I said no, I did this, and we'll go to trial so everybody will know. It was hard for Annie to testify, but she had to do it. At least her and I could talk civil to each other. But then there came a time when I wasn't getting no letters, no visits. Every time I tried to call Elaine, I'd get the answering machine. It made me nuts. Finally, she came up to see me. She goes, "I got something to tell you." I said, "What, you're pregnant?" "How do you know?" she asks. Because it wasn't hard to see—I mean, she was sticking out to there. She told me she didn't like the father and wanted to give the baby my name. I couldn't believe it. Now she's had the baby and is with another guy. I wrote to her and told her that it seemed to me she was happy and that was fine. I wish you all the love in the world, but I got to move on. So if you want a divorce, let me know and I'll be glad to give it to you. That was twelve months ago, and I still ain't heard no answer.

I was in prison for six years and four months before I really started to deal with what I done. I never even started touching any of this until two weeks before my first parole board, when I got sick. I was working up in the welding shop as a teacher's aide. I took a coat hanger and was trying to get some grease up off the floor when there was an accident. I woke up two days later and my neck was out to there—I couldn't talk and I couldn't eat. So I went to the hospital and they said I burned the glands on each side of my throat. That's when I had all these flashes and I said to myself, you've screwed up enough, now start helping people. But before you help people, you got to help yourself. And when I went to the parole board and I said, "I don't care if you believe me or not, but I'm not ready to go home," this one lady says, "You have no idea what you've done?" "No, ma'am," I said, "but I'm going to start really working on it." I told her I planned to face up to who I am and what I am.

People said you couldn't play games in groups, but I did. I did it for six years and four months, until I got sick and made my realization. The counselors would ask me questions like, "Well, how did you get your stepdaughter to go along with you?" And I'd say, "I told her to do it, or I'd beat the shit out of her." That's all I'd say. I'd shock them, and then they'd back off. Or I'd just sit there and say, "I don't care if you don't like what I'm saying or not—that's just the way I am." And that has been me all my life. If I come out with something negative, I know I'm going to keep you way out there. I don't know why I don't want people to get close to me. I think it might be because whenever I've loved something or somebody, it's either died or taken off. Instead of me going through that hurt again, I can just keep you away from me. I think that is why I took those two little girls and made them bigger before their time—because somehow they got to me. They got too close. I didn't think of them as little girls. I made them grown up, but they weren't grown up—only in my mind. And now those two are going to go through the rest of their lives wondering if it was their fault. They might think, what is my boyfriend going to be like? What is my husband going to be like? Is he going to hurt me like Billy did? I chewed up a lot of lives.

This last group I been in here, I screwed up and left. I was getting aggravated because I wasn't ready to share anything about myself. The more aggravated I got, the more I was swearing and cussing and stuff. I figured, well, instead of getting so aggravated, I'm just going to quit. I ain't going to go. But then I got this counselor who changed me around. He is one of the few people that for some reason has gotten past that barrier I put up. I lied to him over and over, but he didn't do nothing. He just kept talking to me, and somehow he got me to trust him. I've done everything in my power to get that man to hate me, but he's still coming back. Now, even though he is a counselor here in prison and I could hate him for that, if I ever had to watch his back and give my life for him, I would do it. So now I'm trying to get back into that group, as soon as I come to grips with myself and stop playing games. I owe all the guys an apology for the way I treated them.

I know I'm not ready to go home. I don't think I'll be ready to go home, even in another two more years, because I've got thirty-six years to make up for. And I could take another forty just trying to figure out who I am. So I'm trying to take that first step. You have to want to be helped. If you say that you don't have a problem, then nothing in the world is going to help you. The only thing that made me wake up was when I got so sick. I don't know if the man upstairs is looking out for me, but he seems to be doing pretty good. So I'm working on myself. Since I've been in prison, I've gotten my GED, and I've been certified as a welder. I've become more of a man here than I ever was on the streets. I'm sorry for what I did, but I'm not sorry for coming to prison, because I've done quite a bit since I've been here. And I'm not ready to leave yet. I want to keep learning while I'm here. If I can pick up what they're trying to teach me, learn how to revamp my thinking, then it'll keep me out of trouble.

The other thing I got to work on is not to masturbate. I used to do that a lot. There was no problem with me masturbating twenty times a day. The one thing I've realized is that even though you've got the thoughts, you can change them. That's the big thing my last group taught me—how to think different. After the thing with Cindy, I used to just sit there and look at pictures of Cindy and masturbate. Same thing with my stepdaughter. Other than that, little girls didn't bother me. Most guys, they go out after many little kids, but for me it was just Cindy and Annie. Maybe it was because I really loved them as girlfriends or whatever.

I'm working on breaking down that barrier I got around me. I'm trying not to be such a tough guy. Even when I was a kid, I never let nobody see me cry, because if you cry, you are not a man. I got some screwed-up lessons when I was a kid. I should have been sent to prison long ago. When I do get out, I'm going to start going to churches and schools and tell them like it is. I got a dream that I tell the little kids that it's all right to tell somebody. If it will help get guys from hurting any more of you kids, then go ahead and say something, because it's only going to help you and it's only going to help us. It took me a long time to come to this way of thinking.

About this sex offender notification stuff—I think it is a good thing. If I get out and I'm trying to hide who I am, what's to say that I am not going to do this to some other little girl. If people know who I am and what I used to be, then they are helping me because now they are going to put their kids in check. Before, if a sex offender got out, nobody knew it. The minute he got out, he could go around the corner and do it again, because there were no programs to help him. We need programs to help us and for communities to be aware of the problem. We need that help and support, because if we don't get it, we are just going to keep doing it. Sure, I'm afraid that some people might come after me, but on the other hand, if I'm not hiding something, maybe they will leave me alone.

To keep from ever doing this again, I got to take one day at a time and keep talking. If I can keep my frustration down and not let myself get so hot-headed and angry all the time, then I can make it. I still got this little bit of the male macho-ness, you know, but I'm getting rid of it as much as I can. Now that I do have the help and the counseling, I'm going to take advantage of it. I should have been in prison a long time ago, but now I've changed my life around.

Summary

Billy's self-narrative paints an occasionally poignant and often frightening picture of a physically powerful man who possesses the soul—and self-control—of a child, or as he refers to himself, an "animal." The lack of security and looming possibility of violence he experienced in his childhood worked to shape him into a person who has always functioned on instinct. Three primary motivations seem at the heart of Billy's crimes. The first is the warped value system that dominated his childhood. Billy's birth father left him when he was very young. The man who became his stepfather was frequently drunk and physically violent. Billy was often the source of this violence, and Billy's mother was either too passive or too frightened to protect Billy from her husband's rage since she, too, endured physical abuse. There is evidence of intrafamilial sexual abuse as well, since Billy claims that his uncle molested all his cousins and then Billy had sex with them, too. When he was young, Billy prowled the neighborhood, looking for sexual partners. He began to masturbate obsessively.

The second motivation is the desire to possess what seems to be unattainable. The women he became sexually involved with, and the second girl he victimized, initially intrigued him because they seemed "hard to get." Unfortunately for the child he eventually sodomized, the more she resisted his advances, the angrier he became, until he finally exploded into violence.

The third motivation behind his crimes is his anger, and the way in which he used sex as a way to release this pent-up violence. At the time he molested his niece, he was angry enough to have "shot everybody in sight." When Billy began to make sexual advances toward his nine-year-old stepdaughter, Annie initially resisted him. When Billy finally attempted to fondle her vagina, Annie protested, but he threatened to beat her up. One day, Billy lashed out at Annie with his pent-up anger and violently sodomized her, then yanked the phone off the wall when Elaine threatened to call the police.

So Annie and her mother kept silent out of fear. If one of Elaine's friends hadn't reported his behavior to the police, they might still be trapped in his version of family life. Finally, after six years in prison, Billy claims to have had an epiphany. Billy seems to believe that prison has finally shaken him loose from the thoughtlessness and excesses of childhood. Prison has provided a stable, paternalistic, and ultimately artificial environment for Billy. Whether this has truly forced Billy to grow up remains to be seen, since the true test will be when he is released back into society. Billy's instincts and brute physical strength seem to override any sense of control. Perhaps, as he says, notification laws will help keep a tight leash on Billy once he is released from the cage that has contained him. Or perhaps cognitive therapies and the strong role models provided by the prison's male counselors will teach Billy the lessons of manhood that his own fathers failed to deliver.

~

CHAPTER SIX

Darrell—The Altar Boy

Confused on, before early admitting homosexuality

Darrell was a slender, rather fragile-looking man in his late thirties who greeted me with a shy smile. With his slight frame and tousled (albeit thinning) hair, he could have passed for a man ten or even fifteen years younger. Although he began his story haltingly, once he warmed up he was articulate, even passionate, in the telling. He seemed childishly proud when he admitted to being homosexual. It took him a long time to come to terms with his sexuality, and he acted like an adolescent in the throes of early dating as he described the experience of finding romance with adult males. Darrell openly admitted to his crimes, but was squeamish in offering details. He would begin to downplay the severity of the offenses, then catch himself and say something along the lines of, "Well, of course, it was serious." He had trouble referring to the boys he molested as "victims." Despite the ten-year age difference, he still described his first offense as "being in love" with the boy. Although Darrell hadn't had much solid counseling, he had pursued help on his own and seemed genuinely determined to avoid future offenses. He was willing to take steps to make certain he wouldn't reoffend, although he seemed to put inordinate store in maintaining an adult gay relationship as the primary deterrent.

Darrell's Story

My crime was committed because I am a homosexual. Not because of the homosexuality, but because I denied my homosexuality. All through my childhood, I was afraid of homosexuals, but I was really afraid of myself. My victims

95

multiple
victims

were children. There were six of them between the ages of twelve and thirteen. The youngest boy I molested was eight, but that was only one time. The boys were all friends of the family or family members. I'm in prison because I molested my nephew—I attempted to molest him, that is. He was the eight-year-old.

So, anyway, you want to know my story. My father divorced my mom, moved away, then I was the man of the house. Even though I was the middle child, I took care of my mom and I took care of the other two kids. All the while, I was denying my homosexuality. Mom was the very strict type, and my religious beliefs didn't allow homosexuality. There was this turmoil inside me all the time. It wasn't until after I came to prison that I accepted who I was. I'm not sure if I can explain this turmoil that I experienced; it was like being pulled in two different directions at the same time. I had to hide my true self. I could not act out the way I wanted to act out sexually. So I thought of alternate routes. Unfortunately, the alternate route I chose was sex with boys under the age of consent.

I did get molested myself by a priest when I was eleven. The gentleman who molested me wasn't a parish priest, but a very close friend of the family. He was also a special education teacher in high school, and I spent a lot of time in his classroom helping his students. I spent a lot of time with him outside the classroom, too. I was a religious kid, and since my dad had left us, I needed somebody to talk to about stuff. This man was around for me, and he became my father figure. That's why I'm in here. I turned this priest in, which consequently revealed something I did five years prior to that. So when I turned him in to the police, I was really turning myself in as well. But I'm glad I'm doing my time as long as he's doing his.

I wish I could articulate clearly what this priest did to me. I know I was molested by him, but I have put a lot of it back in my memory. I didn't even know I was molested by him until after I was in the prison system talking with the counselors. I suppose the molestation happened because of all the changes in my life at the time. I was hitting puberty right about the time my father left us, and that's about the time I got molested. So I don't know if my life change occurred because of the molestation or because my father left.

I had been really close to my dad, but I was even closer to my mom. When Dad left, I took on the manly roles of shoveling snow and taking care of outside the house. If anything needed to be done, I was there to do it. There were times I was pulled out of school to help out at home. Mom leaned heavily on me. This was part of her responsibility in my crime. She never gave me the opportunity to express my true self. The only thing she ever said to me about sexuality was no sex before you're married. She threw that comment to

me so casually. Afterwards, I didn't feel like I could say anything about what I really felt.

You've got to know how hard it was for me. I had homosexual feelings for so long. I can remember feeling that way when I was just four or five years old. Feeling homosexual has always been a conflict for me. When you get up the courage to talk to somebody about it, and they say, "Oh no, that's wrong, you shouldn't feel that way," what do you do? There was this big confusion within me, and I could never express it. I grew up in the sixties and seventies, when homosexuality wasn't really accepted yet. It made my life very difficult. I ended up being a total loner in school, so that gave me the opportunity to spend time down in the special ed classroom, which ended up causing other problems.

I fooled everyone for years and years. I even dated a couple of girls, and I thought that meant I was really okay, but there was no real connection. It's like I was playing a role—yeah, I've got a girlfriend, so I guess I must be normal. Most of the time, I did feel normal, except when the feelings would arise, and then I knew I wasn't really one of the crowd. It was just another lie I had to maintain. I didn't know any other homosexuals to hang out with. I did hear of a few guys who were called queer at my school, but I didn't want to get labeled that way, so I never sought them out.

It's not like I could share any of my feelings with my family. I took care of everybody. When my mom remarried, I denied any real relationship between my mother and stepfather, even though I was close to my mom. Me being in prison has helped them. Mom and my stepdad have a better relationship, and my sister and brother have grown up some. So a lot of positives have come out of my incarceration.

I don't know why I ended up being in charge of the family. I know that most of my adult life, I've been in some sort of leadership position, so maybe I have a natural instinct to lead. This is strange, considering my role as a loner in school. I tried to avoid being in leadership positions but at the same time was drawn to them. For instance, look at the jobs I had. I started in as a clerk at a convenience store and worked my way up to management. Then I was a foreman for a print shop. I went back to college to get a computer degree and was supervisor of the college computer lab. I had all these leadership roles, but I kept to myself. I seemed to be one thing, but was really drawn to be another.

I was fourteen or fifteen when I had my first sexual experience with another boy. I was at Boy Scouts. A lot of teasing was going on toward another individual. We talked, and then I had sex with him. This was a mutual thing. But that's where I got introduced to younger boys, and I never really grew out of that age group. I felt satisfied because I found somebody that I could do something with. They weren't going to say anything, and therefore all the secrets of my homosexuality weren't in danger. Actually, it wasn't a homosexual experience in my mind at that particular point, because neither of us was able to ejaculate. It was oral sex, so it didn't count as much in my mind.

This only happened once or twice, even though there was this available person who was a willing partner. So it was frustrating. My whole life has been frustrating. During my time in the Boy Scouts, there were actually several experiences with different people similar in age to me. After I turned eighteen, I said, "Wait a minute, this is wrong. Now I'm more into religion, and this behavior is really stupid. I can't do this. It's against the law." So it was a moral issue for me, and the law issue on top of it. And I'm saying, "That's it." So there were very few experiences with guys my own age after I turned eighteen. I was afraid of having sex with guys my own age. I felt that if I enjoyed it, then I really was a homosexual and I couldn't deal with it. Anyone prior to the age of eighteen was okay, since having sex with younger boys didn't mean I was a homosexual. It doesn't seem to make sense now, but that was my mode of thinking. After age eighteen, I went out with a couple of girls once or twice, and I masturbated a lot. I wasn't attracted to the girls, so my only release was masturbation and frustration.

At the age of twenty-three, I got transferred to another store to be a manager in training, which gave me my first experience of being totally away from my family. I was still in denial. I was still going to church. I wasn't necessarily looking for anyone in particular but attracted to twelve, thirteen, and fourteen year olds, although not pursuing it actively. I did experiment with homosexual magazines. One of the magazines was like a *Playboy* only focused on schoolboys. I enjoyed looking at the magazines but was scared to death. I was scared to do anything with anybody of my own age, although I was attracted to a few people.

Then I met an individual who stole some things from the store I worked at. I told him not to steal anymore and let him go. We ended up becoming friends. He was twelve or thirteen. I moved into their house because his parents had a room to rent, and this twelve-year-old and I ended up doing something like falling in love. It was a mutual approach since he was curious. So this boy ended up having oral sex with me. We did end up doing quite a bit, but it never went beyond oral sex. Shortly afterward, I found out his brother went to prison for molesting somebody. Kind of ironic. Anyway, I believe it was love between this boy and me. Now that I look back at it— that was twelve years ago—it wasn't really love. But at that time, it felt like love.

This boy's mother and father were alcoholics. I spent a lot of time with him, helped him with his schoolwork, went to his school for open houses. So I took on the role of father to this boy, sort of like the priest who molested me was more like a father. I never really made this connection till I got to prison. This went on for about six months, then I got arrested. I've only been arrested twice, and this was the first time. Basically, his father was raping his mother. I didn't have to call the police, but I did. The father got mad at me because I called the police, so he decided that there was something wrong between me and his son and turned me in. But the father wasn't the only one who thought something was going on. As I learned later, apparently the school was concerned because I was spending all this time with this kid. So they had already investigated me once and had even talked to his parents. The police told them to let them know if they noticed anything. So, apparently, the father did. I know that they ended up talking to the boy. The boy had told them nothing. In fact, he even used the word "lover" in his statement, and they asked him to clarify that.

I was really upset. But I always felt guilty. I knew it was wrong because I was over eighteen and he was under eighteen, but it was just easier to go ahead and do what I wanted. The guilt for me was always right after. But the guilt wasn't enough to stop the next time from happening. So I was arrested and they pressed charges. I ended up doing 120 days in the county jail and probation for second-degree sodomy. Getting a prison sentence for this made me feel terrible. I did try talking to the priest, and my mom and stepdad, to tell them that I had a problem, but everybody sort of ignored it till I got arrested. Nobody had wanted to ask questions, and most still didn't after I was in jail. But I got the priest's attention all right. He was still a very close friend of mine. He became my counselor and my probation officer, too. For the next couple of years, when the priest was doing counseling with me, he brought up sex quite a bit. He did institute some very good rules, such as I wasn't allowed to be alone with any boy under the age of eighteen, that there always had to be an adult around. We talked about fantasies a lot, and I talked about my fantasies about him. He would literally put me into situations where I would basically be forced to fantasize. Then, after a couple of years, other things in his own life started to fall apart. Without revealing too much about him or his crime, I can say that he ended up wanting to hold my hand.

This was when I was in college, working in the computer lab. Then, after I graduated from college, I stayed in the printing shop and ended up being print supervisor. The priest would say to me, "Why don't you stop by before you go to school?" Or, "Why don't you stop by before you go to work?" "Okay," I'd say, "I'll stop by. Why do you want me to come over?" "Oh, just to chat," he'd say. Then he'd move a little too close and laugh. He was flirting with me, really flirting. Because of me offering corroborating evidence, he ended up with ninety-seven counts against him. When I had gotten arrested, he was afraid I'd say something about how he had molested me. I found out later that he wanted to be my counselor because he was afraid that I would reveal him. So you can guess how good the counseling went.

The next victim, the one that I'm in here for, was my nephew. I take the blame for the whole thing. I will never pass the blame to anyone else. However, I will put part of the blame on my sister. My sister told my nephew all the details of my crime, and I don't think she should have ever done that. He was eight, going on nine. That type of age shouldn't know about sex. I allowed certain things to transpire. One time, we were working in the garage at a family gathering, and he asked me why I had been in jail. He said, "Mommy said you sucked on somebody's dick." And I said, "What? You shouldn't know about that." He said, "How was it?" After that, I should have never been alone with him. But because I knew he was curious, the next time at a family gathering I made sure that he would find me when I was alone, which he did. He sure had piqued my interest.

This was only a couple of months after my release. I should have said, "Whoa, Mom and Dad, you got a problem here with your son." But I didn't. I had no oral sex with him. I did see him nude several times, but I didn't touch his penis once. He undressed himself. He asked me to touch him, and I said I'd do it, but I chickened out. I just couldn't go back to jail. It's listed on my record that I supposedly saw him naked on three occasions. I know of two. Then, for almost a year, I deliberately avoided him. I wouldn't be alone with him. But at the end of that year, I ended up saying okay. I couldn't hold it in anymore, the need and desire to be with somebody. For that whole time since I had been released from jail, I had been basically celibate, other than masturbation. I couldn't even look at magazines anymore, not when I was back living with my parents.

All the time I was living at home, I kept telling my mom and sister that I couldn't baby-sit, I didn't want to baby-sit the kids, but they kept putting me in positions where I'd have to baby-sit. I don't think they really understood the problem. I was already arrested once, but I don't think that reality hit them. My family was sort of naïve and religious, so they didn't really connect with the idea that I could do this thing. My nephew eventually ended up saying something to his mother that she got suspicious about. We assured her that nothing happened, but I guess my nephew was apparently feeling guilty, which was perfectly fine. I'm glad he finally came forward and said something. So we all agreed at that point that they would finally listen to the counselor about my situation. I said, "I've been telling you for years about not wanting to baby-sit, Mom. Now you know why you needed to listen." So we kept it in the family at that point, and I didn't actually get arrested until two years later. As long as I was in counseling, no charges were filed. In fact, my family never filed any charges at all. My sister never signed the arrest warrant. I mean, she was a little upset at the beginning, but she understood that nothing happened. She did come up and say, "Gee, I should never have said anything to him while you were in jail."

So, finally, I got Mom and Dad and the other people in my life to listen, and then I could make some progress. The rule was that if I went anywhere— if I was going to be with anyone younger than eighteen—I had to go with another adult. If I needed to go to a public bathroom, an older male went with me. I don't use those urinals because urinals are dangerous for pedophiles, especially pedophiles who go after younger boys. And as for grocery shopping— that's a danger, too. A pedophile shouldn't go grocery shopping alone unless he absolutely, positively has to. These are the rules I came up with on my own, along with the priest. We did a little bit of research. But the priest wasn't following these rules.

What basically happened is that the priest who was in charge of the priest who was counseling me died. This priest who was counseling me was the only priest left, so he was in charge while the church looked to replace the priest who died. Since this priest had to spend more time at the church, he started doing some of his counseling with me in the basement of the church. Since I was involved in this church, I would help to fix stuff up. Once or twice, I'd go down to the basement to fix this or that, and he would be there for a counseling session with another boy. I can't swear to it, but once or twice I saw something going on. It was just that I know the signs too well. There were quick movements, like the boy would jump off the priest's lap. I kept all that from everybody. I should have said something, but I didn't. The priest did approach me one time, and we talked about my homosexuality. I agreed that what I did was wrong, but he said he was having the same feelings and he was attracted to me. I told him to get away from me, since he's a heavier type gentleman and he wasn't attractive to me. I was totally upset. He told me several things he shouldn't have said. I'm not a confessor, you know. The church ended up hiring him full time, so he became the head priest in charge of the church.

Soon after, the boy I saw him with finally turned him in. But they didn't turn him in to the police; they turned him in to the church, and the bishop made sure no charges would be pressed. The church thought everybody would be happy with their solution, but not everybody was. Some people turned to me and said, "We know that you know something." The priest's wife wrote me a letter and said, "I know about these incidents and I'm going to turn you in." I got all panicky. She knew about my past crime, too. So I told my parents, got an attorney, and he said he couldn't be my lawyer because his son was a member of the church. So I was scared. This lady was going to make trouble for me because she was mad at her husband. They didn't have a good marriage, and her whole motive was to make things worse for him.

I went down to the police station and called the investigator, shared the priest's wife's letter with them, and my former rap sheet. Until that point, they hadn't heard anything about this priest molesting any boys. The bishop had made the story go away. So we talked for several hours, and I shared some bits of information, but I didn't give them the whole story. Then they said, "Well, we want to get this on tape." And they pressed me about my own fantasies, and later on I ended up telling to the court system in two different counties how the priest took my fantasies and lived them out. I did admit to the police that the only thing I had done since the last time I was arrested was to see my nephew naked. Then they released me. A month later, they tried to set me up with counseling, but when I went to the center for counseling, it ended up being an interrogation that went on and on. They said that I molested twenty-five people in my adult life, which I know is bogus. Altogether from that point, I can name twenty-five people from the time I was ten, but not since I've been eighteen or nineteen. You know, there is a difference. Then they used this term "love addict" and said we won't press charges against you as long as you give testimony against the priest. No problem.

The trouble was, I was a county client, and the priest hired the assistant district attorney to represent him. The assistant district attorney said point-blank, "If you testify against the priest, we're going to get you five-to-sixteen years in prison." So I panicked and tried to get something out of my lawyer, and they ended up getting me four-to-eight years. I testified in two different courts against the priest. It really was very comforting because they took the information that I gave them and went to the people involved, and the people confirmed my story. Everything I gave them to go on was everything that had happened during the five years of counseling I had with him. He had manipulated me by asking me, "What do you think of this boy?" Then he would get me to fantasize and drill me on what kind of fantasy I had. He used me.

As for the twenty-five victims they said I had, I explained it all to them. I said that during those years, there were several different people that weren't the same age, but I don't see how there is a victim when you're both the same age and the feeling is mutual. If we're both under age eighteen and we're having mutual sex, I don't see how that is a crime. But it didn't matter much, anyway. It might have if there had been a trial, but since I didn't have one, it didn't matter. So now I've been in prison for five years and four months. I've had professional counseling with a psychologist, and that has helped tremendously. Now I wonder what would have happened if I hadn't gone to the priest for counseling but had a real professional. But I was intimidated by him. I didn't know how to get away from him. Now in prison, I've had a chance to get away from the family, from this priest, and grow up. I finally accepted myself. I have had a boyfriend. We've had sex, I'll admit that, but he's no longer in the prison system and I'll probably never see him again. We were hoping to get together after we both got out, but unfortunately because of my crime, relocating from here is a little difficult. He finally admitted that reality. Then he dumped me.

I started counseling with the psychologist my first week of being in prison. I have been pushing ever since to get into a sex offenders program, but I've been denied all the way through. I did my homework, trying to get to a place that has groups, but the court system said no, the parole department said no. Counselors say they can't give you the transfer. The state says, "We can't move you." "Why can't you move me?" I ask, "I'm a sex offender. I want to go through a sex offender program." When I was on probation the first time, I did get a set of programs from the National Council of Churches, but the group I got into wasn't for sex offenders, it was for people who got molested. That one wouldn't work. Then, finally, when I was transferred to this prison, I found a combination group for sex offenders who were molested as kids. It was a very, very good group. It helped me to deal with the main issue, which was my homosexuality. I was able to finally accept that, and I have no problem with it, although now and then I'm still a little afraid.

After I was in the group for about a year, the counselor said she got a promotion and was going to be leaving, so she couldn't do the group anymore. During her last group session, she went around the room and pointed out what each of us needed to do to stay on the street when we got out of prison. She told me that the only way I was going to stay out of prison was to have a boyfriend, that without a boyfriend I'd end up doing what I did to repress the desires and find alternative ways to have sex. So accepting myself was an important step. That boyfriend may have dumped me, but I have a new boyfriend, now. He gets out in a few months, and we are planning on getting married.

I actually initiated contact with the two boyfriends I've had. When my first boyfriend and I became lovers, I felt so much more fulfilled with him than I did with the boys. I used to be afraid to be with men my own age, primarily due to the semen. As long as nobody ejaculated, then it wasn't really sex. The first time I had sex with my boyfriend and there was semen, I'll admit it was terrifying. But I managed to go through with it. The whole thing was rather fulfilling. I just wish we could have made the parole board at the same time. We both went to the boards at the same time, but I didn't make it, so my first boyfriend left without me. So that relationship didn't work out. But my homosexuality has actually caused me more problems in prison than my crime. Security represses people from having sex.

I actually had a problem with my sexuality back at the other prison. Somebody wanted to stab me because I wouldn't have sex with them. It's funny. I was always scared of being teased and picked on for being a homosexual, but in prison, being a homosexual can be fantastic if the person wants to be open about it. I can now accept myself under certain circumstances. I still believe homosexuality is perfectly fine, even in a biblical context, if I only have one lover. But in prison that is kind of hard, only in the respect that everyone you know wants sex. I'm not going to give it, which has caused me a lot of problems.

I believe that as long as I have an adult relationship, I should be able to have no trouble staying on the street. The public is naïve. They are paranoid because of media stories and because of some fruitcake cases. Some offenses are hideous; some people are really sick. The priest took my fantasies and lived them out, and he has over ninety-seven counts against him—you know he's got problems. Sure, I've got problems, but he has a bigger problem because his victims came from the general population. Mine were people I knew up close. As for these community notification laws, I agree with them 100 percent. But, unfortunately, this puts my family at great risk. They've already been stopped by the police three or four times, and I'm not even out of prison yet. Why were they stopped by the police? Because they had children in the car—nieces and nephews—and the police wanted to see their identification. I'm not even released yet, but the police are looking at my family. Because of these notification laws, they are doing their job by harassing my family. I'm the one that's guilty, not my family. I'm the one you should be watching out for.

I know that when I get out, I'm not going to see my nephews. I'm not going to see my nieces. I don't want to see them. I certainly don't want to see my victim, my nephew. At this point, he is going to be eighteen next month. But I don't care if he's twenty-five. I know that I cowered in front of the priest who molested me, even though I was in my twenties and early thirties. I cowered to him, and I'm sure that I would still cower, even though a couple of years ago, I would have blown his brains apart, I was so angry with him. But that is a normal reaction, I guess.

So I agree with some aspects of community notification, but I also think that it goes too far. I need to be responsible for myself; I need to protect me. I can't drive by schools. I don't plan on it. I don't want to be around children. If I have to be in a position where I might be near kids, then I have to have an adult with me at all times. On the street, I won't be going anywhere unless I'm going to work, and then Dad is driving me there and picking me up. If I'm offered employment and there's a park nearby, I can't accept that job. I don't care what parole says, I won't accept it. I don't want to be in a position where I can even be slightly tempted.

Yes, I should be registered, and [if] you want to point me out, point me out. I don't particularly care. You want me to hang up a sign on my front door saying I'm a child molester? Fine, I'll do that, but if I'm going to do this, then you've got to do something: leave me the hell alone. That's it. Don't talk to me, don't come anywhere near me. If there's a notification law, which I agree with completely, then the community has got to do its part, too. Stay the hell away from me. Don't point out the child molester. But people are doing just that. Three people I know that are sex offenders who got out are back in prison. They haven't done any crimes, but they are on parole violations. Why? Because some individual walked into an apartment house with a friend and some lady who knew his friend opened the door and said, "Hello, why don't you come in for a cup of coffee?" They went in for a cup of coffee and there was a child in the house. This guy wasn't even arrested for being with a child, but he was a sex offender, so his parole was violated.

I'm not a tree jumper. I don't hide behind trees or bushes or expose myself to anybody. I didn't run up and kidnap somebody and take them away and molest them and choke them. There are those people, but most child molesters aren't like that. I think about 99 percent of child molestation is done with either a relative or a close family member. Therefore, you better be looking at the husbands or wives or your good buddy who comes over drinking. You better not be wasting time looking at those people out there who don't know you, because those people are never going to get close enough to you to do anything to your kids. Most child molesters are not going to kidnap kids, rape them, and then kill them. They wouldn't ever think of doing that. In prison, I've run across a few guys who could do that. I mean, they really scared me. But that's the exception. Most child molesters don't really think about hurting their victims. They want to believe the victims enjoy it or at least are curious about it.

I think that child molesters need to have a program provided for them. Most child molesters are in self-denial, and they don't think they committed a crime. They are low self-esteem individuals. They usually have something

speaking on behalf of other offenders ?, but really himself

that causes them to commit the crime. There is usually something in [their] relationships that is askew; that is the reason why they turn to molesting younger children. They prey on children for three reasons. One, younger children are naïve. Two, they are curious and it can be experimental for them at the time. And three, they are easy to fool. They are not going to tell on you, because you're older and intimidate them. I don't think I ever tried to intimidate them. I just said, "Please don't say anything because you are going to get me in trouble if you do." Now, in one respect, in my timidness I ended up intimidating, and I understand that. My intimidation was a different sort. I'm scared to death of violence, so I would never threaten to beat anybody up. I'd just say, "Don't tell anybody I saw you naked." Junior isn't going to say anything, anyway, because Junior knows he's the one who asked me in the first place. So I don't see that as violence, not in the respect of seeing someone put a gun to anybody else's head. I see a lot of violence in this place. I see other people cut and stabbed, and blood all over the place, and that's violence. But I don't see that kind of violence going on [in] the sexual abuse of younger children. I mean, I understand that it's hurtful, but I don't necessarily agree it is violent.

As for longer prison sentences for sex offenders, that isn't going to do shit. Eventually, they are going to get out of prison and they are going to commit offenses again unless they get mandatory counseling. The whole crime is built on lies and secrets. You can't keep any secrets. I can't keep any secrets. The people in my life need to know everything that is going on, because if I start keeping secrets, then I'm going back into my crime. Not necessarily doing my crime, but I'm falling back into the mode. Maybe everybody has secrets, but I can't have any. Don't tell me a secret, because I can't keep it. I'm a homosexual, but I'm also a child molester. If I just accept that I'm a homosexual but not that I'm a pedophile, then I'm in danger. I can't keep secrets anymore.

NOTE: *The priest Darrell referred to was convicted on two counts of second degree sodomy and one count of first degree sexual abuse. He received a seven- to twenty-one-year sentence.*

Summary

Primarily, Darrell blames his crimes on his conflicted feelings concerning his own homosexuality. A number of factors played into the course of his life that led him to prison, where at last he came to terms with his identity as a homosexual. The first major influence on Darrell's destructive plummet into molesting young boys was a priest, a family friend, who molested Darrell when he was young and then took advantage of his vulnerability when he was an adult. The second major factor was the value system he gleaned from his mother and the church, which forced him to negate his innate homosexuality.

Darrell considers the priest's molestation to be a watershed moment in his life: "I was hitting puberty right about the time my father left us, and that's about the time I got molested." The most pressing conflict at that time was Darrell's budding realization that he was gay. Since his mother made it clear she didn't approve of homosexuality, he kept his feelings to himself. He seems to believe that if he had reached out to other homosexuals when he was young, he wouldn't have ended up committing his crimes.

Darrell claims to have been "in love" with his first victim. Since the boy's older brother had already molested him, the boy was primed for Darrell's sexual advances. Even after Darrell was arrested, he maintained the belief that the boy and he were engaged in a love affair. When Darrell was arrested, his probation required that he have a counselor and, ironically, the priest who had molested Darrell when he was young arranged to take on that role. The priest apparently took advantage of his power over Darrell by encouraging Darrell to fantasize in their counseling sessions. This certainly did little to curb Darrell's sexual attraction to boys. His next victim was his nephew. Darrell perceived the boy's curiosity as sexual interest. Since his family showed an odd tendency to disbelieve there was anything amiss with Darrell and encouraged him to baby-sit, Darrell had plenty of opportunities to draw the boy into his fantasies.

While in prison, Darrell has been able to express his "true self," and he believes it has freed him of pedophilia. The counseling and the opportunities he has had for sex with other men have provided the salvation that religion failed to give him. When he was struggling with his own demons, abandoned by his father and confused about his homosexuality, he turned to his religious faith for guidance, but instead was abused by the priest from whom he sought solace. From Darrell's perspective, the faith he viewed as a source of morality actually sent him down a path of depravity. Rather than relying on faith to save him, Darrell considers that he has saved himself. He has convinced himself that, as long as he is sexually involved with adult males, he won't be attracted to boys. Ultimately, in Darrell's view, pedophilia was—oddly enough—a more acceptable means of sexual fulfillment than homosexuality.

Religion a cause for behavior by denying him the to be his true self

CHAPTER SEVEN

~

Abe—The Family Man

Although the knock on the door was halting, even tentative, my first impression when Abe entered the room was that he was caught up in a whirlwind of intensity and enthusiasm. He swept in, eyes bright and eager, no trace of nerves. He was tall and slender, and the missing front tooth was a surprise when he smiled. Yet as I spent more time with Abe, it gradually dawned on me that all the staccato energy was mostly born of anxiety. Abe was articulate, loquacious, self-absorbed but struggling to be introspective, and deeply, passionately angry—angry at his parents, angry over his life, angry at the society he felt failed him in some potent, damaging way. Perhaps his state of perpetual motion was his way of running from his past and his problems, and the only way he could run while trapped behind prison walls. As he talked, Abe tried to reframe his crimes as a form of worship in a desperate attempt to bolster his ego and perhaps capture my sympathy as well. Although Abe exhibited little empathy for his victims, which he claimed numbered over seventy boys and girls, he maintained that he venerated the children. When I pointed out that pilgrims generally don't rape their deities, he shuddered and convulsively thrust out his hands, as though he wanted to push away the reality of my statement.

Abe's Story

I cannot remember a time of innocence in my life. My first initiation into sexuality was when I was three, going on four, so having a concept or understanding of innocence is something that I can't identify with. As I've come along in therapy, I've recognized that there must be something special about innocence, and now I sort of hold it in awe because I've never experienced it. My early introduction to sex was related to physical, verbal, and emotional abuse. For example, my potty training was to have feces rubbed into my face. My mother did that. I can remember her spanking me so hard her hands would split open and bleed. I can also remember spending very long periods in my crib, all alone. I really can remember that far back. One thing I don't remember, though, was that my mother was inclined to give me bottles so hot they burned my mouth. I don't recall that, but my stepmother has told me it happened a lot.

My mom came from a very abusive and dysfunctional home herself. To give you an idea, if you wanted to know about my grandfather on my mother's side, a good way to do it would be to look up his jail records. As another example, my uncle—my mom's brother—had the kind of mentality where he would take a horse and go out to plow. If the row he plowed was crooked, then he would come back in for lunch after he would hang the horse by its neck in a tree to teach it to plow in straight rows. It couldn't have been very pleasant in my mom's family's home. There was some bizarre thinking, and I seem to have a natural knack for the same kind of bizarre rationalizations.

By the time I went to kindergarten, I was already sexually active with my mother's best friend's daughter, who would later become my stepsister. She had been molested by a cousin of mine. She used to tell me that it was okay to mess around because my mom and dad did it, but not to tell anybody. I don't know if this was a line her own abuser had used and she repeated it verbatim, since she was only five when she was molested, but it taught me about privacy, about keeping quiet. It was a concept I couldn't put into words, but it told me that this was how it was done.

At that time, besides being sexually active with my future stepsister, I was also sexually active with my cousins down in South Carolina. My mom and I visited those cousins a lot. My mother was dying of cancer, although I didn't realize it at the time. I was just four or five when the doctors discovered she had cancer. It was shortly after my brother was born. But back to my cousins in South Carolina—I was always luring them away from the house out behind the barns to undress and things like that. It was my number one interest.

I can remember at some point that I even tried to molest my father. I was probably about four. He was changing clothes and I saw his genitals and I was just totally enthralled. I tried to touch him, and he did some wild hopping around to get away from me. I didn't know any better at the time, but I didn't grow out of this kind of mentality, either. Of course, my interest could have been construed as natural curiosity. But there were other things going on. Anytime I was confronted about what I was doing as a child, I was told not to tell my father. Whether it was my mom or my stepmother talking to me, they both emphasized not to tell my father. It was put to me as, "Don't tell your father because you don't want to give him a heart attack." I had such fear of my father dying.

My father hadn't had it easy as a child. He had an immense fear of his own father. His father beat him and abused him, not sexually but physically and verbally. So my father learned early on to avoid being at home any way he could. He kept this avoidance of home life with him even after he was married with a family of his own, and I learned my lessons about it from him. Dad didn't believe in me being spanked. I remember that, on a couple of occasions, he did grab me by the shoulder and shake me. I had this thing about money. I thought whoever had money was a big, important person, so I'd steal twenty-dollar bills out of my father's wallet and show them around. So my dad called the town policeman and had him talk to me about jail and stuff like that. But it didn't help. I was desperate to have something important, to do something important, to be someone important.

I was always lying. I don't know when I started lying, but I just never told the truth, even when there was no harm in telling the truth. I lied all the time, and I daydreamed. Every one of my report cards complained about my daydreaming. They didn't know what I was daydreaming about, but it was sex. So when people asked me what I was thinking about, I'd make up these terrible tall tales and I wouldn't back down from them—they could be the most absurd things and I'd keep insisting they were true. If anybody knew what I was really daydreaming about, I think they would have been more upset than at the lies I told instead.

Okay, so by the time I'm in school, I'm a holy terror. I used to joke that I was looking up girls' dresses before the girls knew they had anything under their dresses. I was into girlfriends right from the day I started kindergarten. I would invite them home, and then, with the girl who would later become my stepsister, get them into our sexual play. My big sister would take me to basketball games, and I would sneak up to cheerleaders and kiss them. Everybody thought it was so cute, since I was so young at the time, but I wasn't just playing around. I knew what I wanted to do with those girls, and it wasn't what little kids generally know how to do.

I hated living with my stepmother. I liked my stepsister, but I used to fantasize about killing my stepbrother. By the time I was seven, I used to imagine how I'd kill the people who hurt me. I wanted to be a hired killer when

I grew up, but there also came a point when I realized that if I killed the people I hated, then I'd lose the opportunity for sex. Those were my two choices: get even or keep doing what I thought was the most wonderful thing in the world. I chose the sex over murder, but as I got older, I obsessed a lot about guns. I studied marksmanship. I went hunting a lot. Initially, when I killed an animal, it crushed me. But I concentrated on learning not to feel anything when I killed an animal so that I wouldn't feel bad if I shot a person. I look back now and I can see I was expressing how bad I felt. I lived for guns. Apart from sex, it was the only important thing in my life.

So I wasn't getting along with my stepmom or my stepbrother. My stepbrother and I couldn't be in the same room for two seconds without wanting to kill each other. He tricked me into sodomizing him one time during a nap. He promised he would return the favor. Man, when I think back to all this, I realize that my whole family was into weird sexual practices. Like earlier on, when I was six, I had a teenage cousin spending the night with us. She kept after me that night to have sex with her. When I kept resisting, she seemed to think I was ignorant about what she wanted, and I can remember being frustrated with her because that wasn't the point. Finally, I gave in and went ahead to shut her up. But then I discovered she had pubic hair and freaked out. It was uncomfortable for me, even traumatic. I didn't want to do it anymore, but she wouldn't let me stop. So I vowed I'd never let it touch me again and developed a real phobia about pubic hair. There I was at six years old, vowing that I'd never let pubic hair touch me again. That is terrible. But much as that scared me, it didn't scare me off sex.

I remember that, in the third grade, I had a crush on my teacher. I used to think about having sex with her all the time. One day, I asked her if it was all right that I worked ahead in my homework. But she got it confused somehow and thought I was behind in my work, instead. She walked over and grabbed me by the hair, yanked me out of the chair, and started slapping me all over the head and face for being so slow. That just killed the crush I had on her. So here was another adult I learned I couldn't trust. I had enough troubles dealing with things at home, and that experience made school feel unsafe for me, too. That was how I was raised. I didn't realize I was abused until I was forty-one or forty-two years old and in prison. I thought I had led a normal life, and so when I became an adult, I treated kids the same way. I was brutal, absolutely brutal. I have terrible regrets over that, a lot of guilt and shame.

Anyhow, I didn't really mix well with the other kids at school because, until I got into seventh grade, I was still wetting my pants. I was petrified to use a restroom at school. I couldn't go if anyone was around. I still have that problem to this day. I have to wait until the restrooms are virtually empty before I'll go in. It's funny that I have a problem being naked or showing parts of my body around other adults, but not around children. That was always okay. My stepmother got so frustrated, she finally started putting me in diapers at age eleven. I guess she thought humiliation would work, but it only made me angrier and more hateful. I think it would have been more appropriate to get a psychiatrist or psychologist involved. Nowadays, when a kid is wetting himself at that age, you have to wonder what's going on with him.

By the time I got to eighth grade, I was making more friends. We also had a summer home on a lake. This was when I first fell in love. All the neighborhood collected at our summer home. We had one of the nicest swimming areas on the lake. One family had a daughter named Laurie. She started hanging out with us from the time she was about two years old and I was about ten. It was a long time before I had any feelings for her, but even when she was two, sometimes when she'd wrap up in her beach towel, she'd sit on my lap. All of the sudden, when I was around thirteen, the world rose and set on her. By the time I was about sixteen and she was eight, I just couldn't seem to exist without her. I can look back now and see that it was obsessive, because now I know about addiction and compulsion. Then I was beyond control. Although I got into some heavy kissing and petting with her, I treated her like a goddess. I put her on a pedestal.

Yeah, I'd have to say that the age difference made me uncomfortable. But this wasn't the first time I had engaged in this sort of thing with a little girl. Earlier on, when I was about fourteen, I was working for a family friend who owned a factory. The guy had married a woman who worked in his factory and was pregnant. After the baby was born, the woman split and left the kid behind. He couldn't run a factory and take care of a baby at the same time, so Teena starts growing up with us. Eventually, Teena's mother came back, but Teena still spent lots of time with us. When Teena was three and I was fourteen, I engaged her in sexual petting. Something clicked with me about the age of three—I've later learned that three was my age of choice. This went on for like two years. Then when I turned sixteen, I recognized that I had feelings for this other girl up at the lake. So I cruelly rejected Teena, who was about five at the time. It kills me to think about the pain I inflicted on her right from the beginning to the end. I used that child and then, when I thought I could move to someone else who captured my fancy, it was okay to just drop her. It was abominably cruel.

Later, when I was coming home from college one time on a Greyhound bus, who should I sit with but Teena's mother. She told me that Teena had gone on to become a juvenile delinquent, stealing cars, hanging out with the worst crowd in town, sexually promiscuous—so I've got no one to blame but me. I've tried to find Teena since. I just feel like I've got to find her. I would like her to understand that the things that happened to her were not her doing. I used her. Nothing I can do will ever make it right. But I am just really, really sorry. If there was ever anyone I really did love, it was Teena. And I'm not just talking about lust. She was important because, like a big brother, I can remember the first time she had the opportunity to lick the frosting off the spoon when we mixed up a cake. I remember all that.

I think I did it because I didn't know any better, and that's pure and simple and doesn't change things. Nobody was noticing the clues; nobody was responding to the messages I was sending out. I was virtually bombarded with sexual thoughts. Now I can see that I am a sex addict, even a love addict, and I can identify it, but back then sex was all I ever thought about. I remember before my stepmother married my father, there were some girls in the neighborhood and they came to visit one day. I was six or seven, and I actually had sex with every one of them. I remember having to take diapers off one of them. Where was the rationality there? There was no thought to what I was doing.

You ask me if there were any things my parents or other adults should have picked up on with all this shit. Well, there was a lot to see, if you really looked. I can spot those kids a mile away. Bizarre thinking—that's the only way I can describe it. It just looms right in front of you when you can see it. The isolation, the secretiveness—children are not naturally so secretive. I had migraines—terrible migraines—even as a kid, from the time I was six. They'd just wipe me out. All these things were there, but my parents never saw anything because no one ever taught them what to look for. Back then, nobody knew about this stuff. You didn't have training classes for people to identify these signs. Here's one instance. I molested my stepson. He was having all sorts of stomach cramps and we took him to a doctor. Now, with what I know about stress and anxiety, those were symptoms. But the doctor's solution was to give him popcorn to increase the fiber in his diet. If I hear that a kid is suffering symptoms like this, I would be looking for other symptoms to corroborate my suspicions. I'm going to look for trauma going on in that child's life. But that doctor didn't get it. I was terrified to take my stepson to the doctor's, too, for fear that somebody would discover our family secret. I was convinced at the time that I was the best thing that ever happened to that boy. I believed with all my heart that I wasn't doing my stepson any harm. If I ever thought I was hurting my victims, I wouldn't do it, you know? Or at least I'd find a way to convince myself that I was helping them, doing it all for their own good.

Anyhow, I became an expert at appearing normal. Image management took up a lot of my energy. Then I went off to college and lived in the YMCA. At the YMCA, they had nude swim nights. Kids would come there with their parents and swim nude. I hung out there, to the point where I even volunteered as a swim instructor. I taught swimming lessons for mentally and physically handicapped children. I found myself fascinated watching the little kids change in the locker room. I never did anything with them, but I thought about it all the time. I don't know exactly when my preference switched from girls to boys. My little brother was born a couple of years before I started college, and I'm pretty sure he was in diapers when I molested him. It's a real blur to me. But I continued molesting my baby brother right up to the time he was around ten or eleven and finally told on me. I was in the military at the time he told my stepmother, and she chooses every now and then to remind me that she hates me because of it.

I hung out at the pool until I finally quit college. I quit because of my migraine headaches. I wanted to be a policeman, and they said my headaches would interfere with my duties, so I couldn't get on the police force. I thank God every day that I never became a policeman, because just think what I would have done with my vulnerabilities and weaknesses in that position. So I joined the army—another place I could indulge my passion for guns.

When I went to Vietnam and discovered that the Vietnamese had very little pubic hair, I was home as far as I was concerned. I was really infatuated with their children, but I couldn't ever get close to them. While I was in Vietnam, I contacted a psychiatrist and told him about Teena and stuff like that. Here I am—I'm in the military, I've got a top secret clearance, and I realized that if someone ever would have traded me a child for information, I would have traded. I knew it. So I told this to the psychiatrist and he says, "We're not set up for that over here, so why don't you see somebody when you get back to the States?" Yeah, right.

When I finally got back to the States, I reenlisted. While I was waiting for my orders, I did my first hit of LSD. It took a while before it hit me, but then the sexual awareness was just awesome. So from this time on, there was nothing in my life more important than the drugs, not even sex. I did start dating a girl I had gone to school with and even asked her to marry me, but when I tried to have sex with her, there was nothing there. I just could not perform with an adult. And so I was left with nothing but my drugs and children. I got to the point where I was doing a hit of acid or two a day for better than a year and smoking lots of marijuana. I was working my military job, plus I worked another full-time job as a gas station attendant. I was constantly going seventy-two hours without sleep, and then I'd crash. The guys would take bets at night on whether I'd live to see morning. We'd laugh about it, but then we'd throw a couple pods of acid into the coffeepot at work and everybody would be tripping. I was still working in military intelligence, and man, we were a wasted bunch.

Then I got a chance to leave the States and go to Thailand. I hadn't seen any psychiatrist. I found my answer to my problem, and it was drugs. My real goal for going to Thailand was for the women. Over there you could buy human beings, so I bought myself a girl. I think I paid like $25 for Noi. She was fifteen years old. Soon after Noi and I set up house, I ran into a guy I used to hang out with, and he started pestering me to go to church. And so I finally went with him. When I got there, I started thinking about Teena and what I had done to my little brother and shed the biggest, saddest tears. I got down on my knees at the altar and said I was sorry. I wanted some relief, and I was expecting something from God, something immediate—you know, a cure. I started feeling self-conscious about living with this girl, so I ended up going to the people I bought her from and paid them the same amount to take her back. But my reformation lasted for maybe about a week.

We had this missionary outreach from the chapel, and contact with a lot of children. We also had adults coming in for these services we were doing in the Thai language. And I met these children. I realize now that my pattern is to meet the children and then fall in love with the mother because the children are there. So I met this woman who had these gorgeous children, and I moved in with her. I was infatuated with those children. I did try something with the little girl, and I think I tried something with the boy, too. Then I started having migraine headaches again. So I went to get help for the headaches and I ended up telling the doctor what I had been doing and that I needed help. Since I had this obsession with Christianity at that point, it was important to me that I changed my behavior. The doctor sent me to Bangkok for a psychiatric evaluation. They decided to medivac me back to the States, and I ended up in an army hospital psychiatric ward. I was open about my problem—I think I really was—but the doctors there didn't really talk to me about anything. I worked my way up the ward—it was a merit system, where you worked up to deserving more responsibility—and they finally said I was ready for work therapy. I was sent to a state school and hospital where I helped in the physical therapy department as an aide working with children. That's what the doctors thought I should be doing.

There, I fell in love with a little girl. I never molested her, but that doesn't mean it wasn't wrong. Her name was Elizabeth and she was eleven or twelve. She had cerebral palsy. I really took a shine to Elizabeth, but I took a shine to a lot of the other kids, too, like Missy. Missy was two and was blind because her parents had beaten her. Missy wouldn't smile for anyone but me. All I had to do was touch her cheek with my hand. I didn't want to leave there. Here again, I was reinforcing my comfort in children, in the child's world.

So finally the army decided I should be put on medical discharge, but I talked them out of it. I was put back on active duty and sent to North Carolina. I found a church group, and then I thought I belonged again. I realized that, even though I had thought I was saved in Thailand, I was actually just doing what everybody wanted me to do. So I decided I ought to get baptized. I became a strong member of the church and got involved in the bus ministry, which was going around taking children to Sunday school on a bus. Here, again, I was with children.

One day, an army buddy of mine was in town for training and I was driving him around on the bus route because I wanted to show him what I was doing, and here on a busy stretch of road was this kid walking. I recognized the girl as one of my bus kids. Her mother hadn't come home from her job at a grocery store, and this little girl was walking though a storm to find her. Her mother worked something like ten or twelve miles from where they lived, and this girl was only about eight years old, so we went to find her mother. I made a deal with the mother that I would pick her girl and boy up on Saturdays when she was working, and they'd stay with me until she was finished with work. Little did I know, this was a nutty family. The woman tried to commit suicide one day, and I ended up keeping these kids for three or four days while she was under observation. I molested the girl. It wasn't that I didn't want to molest the boy, but the opportunity never occurred.

I did this while I was seeing a doctor regularly. He had been a prison psychiatrist and he was giving me drugs to deal with my diagnosis. One of the problems they said I had was schizophrenia, but who knows. After I molested the girl, I raised the issue again. I really went official and had to fight to keep my security clearance because I had disclosed to my church. I was turned down on my appeal and reassigned to another state. One of my church friends told me to look up her brother as soon as I got there, and wouldn't you know, her brother had children. His wife had just left him. Since he was a full-time college student, and we really hit it off, he decided to go to take night classes so he could be home with his kids during the day, and then I could take care of the kids at night. I fondled those kids in their sleep. Finally, he and I had a falling-out and I left, but then I met another family through the church I joined. Turned out the church had a bus ministry, too, and no one to run it, so I stepped in. I was surrounded by children again. My obsession just grew to the point where all I could seem to think about was maybe kidnapping a child and killing the parents. I was always envious of people who had these wonderful families, so I wanted to steal theirs. I had a female caseworker at the time, and we got onto this subject through a discussion of fantasies. She was of the opinion that what you thought didn't matter as long as you didn't do it. I would tell her the exact details of these awful fantasies and then it would be, time's up, see you in two weeks. They really should have had me confined. Everything was there for them to see—all the clues—and they were professionals, too.

So anyway, finally I got out of the military and moved back home. My sister had cancer and I wanted to be near her. When my sister died, I needed to find some sort of meaning to life and suddenly thought that God wanted me to become a preacher; so I went off to Bible school. To put myself through it, I went back to working as a gas station attendant. I was so lonesome, and the only thing to solve my loneliness was a child, I was beginning to realize. I actually started to pray to Satan because I started feeling that God wasn't meeting my needs. I had been open and honest with Him when I knelt at that altar back in Thailand. I had a problem that was bigger than me, and I didn't know what to do about it, so I expected Him to take care of it. But I still had the problem. I was blaming God for it.

I kept seeing this one little girl, about three years old, always out on the street by herself. I started cruising, thinking maybe I could meet up with her. I was desperate. I don't think it was even a week later when I went out fishing and met some boys. I talked about how next weekend I was going to fish up at this other place, and they really wanted to go, too. I said that I didn't even know them, so they started telling me about themselves, and it ended up I had worked with their uncle before I went into the army. So I went over and met their mother. There were five kids in the family, three boys and two girls, and this was the family of that three-year-old girl. I seemed to meet them totally by accident, but then again, maybe it was the prayer I made to Satan. I really don't know, and thinking about it scares me. Anyhow, when I showed up the next week to pick up the kids, the woman's boyfriend had gone off the deep end and really beat her up. She was hollering down from the upstairs apartment to take the boys and don't come back. I took the boys home with me, all three of them. The next day, I went back and the guy was gone. I think the police had taken him away.

So all of a sudden this family is gathering around me. I nurtured the relationship. I thought that the kids were in danger and I had something to offer. At the same time, I got to date this really good-looking woman. She moved in with me shortly after that. I molested the boys. I tried to molest the three-year-old girl, but I sensed a resistance, and if there was any kind of reluctance, it was a no-go. I'd groom them by getting them used to my touch. I might start by giving them baths or asking if they wanted me to hold them. But if there was any resistance, I'd back off. I remember that with Teena there was one time when she was trying to say no and I went ahead anyway, but that is the only time I can remember. It's just that people have rights, too. I wanted the kids to think it was up to them.

When I was molesting those kids, I didn't want it to end. I was looking for one monogamous relationship that would be for the rest of my life. But then I realized that things weren't right and I was getting fed up with myself because I wanted to be normal. I went to my girlfriend and told her about what I was doing to her kids. I told her and some other people in the church, and they laid hands on me and prayed for me. They said they had sort of suspected, but if you suspect something like this, don't you think you should do something to protect your children? But when I told them, they weren't angry, so I felt safe for a while.

Then a situation I had with another kid blew up and I was arrested. It was with a little girl who was a friend of the family I was living with. She came down with venereal disease and I didn't have any, but I confessed anyway to taking liberties I shouldn't have taken. I don't know why I confessed—maybe because I didn't want the police to dig any deeper and find out more than I wanted them to find. I got five years' probation, then moved into the house of the church people who bailed me out. They had children. There was one boy who was like twelve, and I only molested him one time. But I was still really confused. Soon, the family moved and I got a place by myself. I was going to my mental-health clinic and seeing my probation officer. By that time, I'd made a connection with another family from the apartments I was living in. There were three boys and a girl. I just couldn't stand to be away from them. I ended up having a sexual relationship with three out of the four—fondling with the girl, oral sex with the boys.

After this situation fell apart, I tried really hard to stay sexually abstinent. I started hanging out with another woman who had some kids, but I didn't molest them. I even quit the drugs for a while, but then I picked it back up. I finally decided to try it big time with the church. I went back to church, and there in the row in front of me was this woman and she had this little boy. Lo and behold, one of the neighbors where I was living turned out to be her cousin. So we got to talking and visiting. I got so I really liked this woman, and then she started saying something about putting her kid up for adoption. I freaked out, and so I decided no, you're going to marry me instead. So we got married.

Before I got married, I went to the Christian education director in our church for a talk. He knew about my little deal with Teena. I said, "I'm concerned because one of the only things that has worked for me is to say no to sex, period. If I initiate a sexual life again, is it going to send me back toward the children?" He just said, "No, no, it will be good for you." So I went ahead with the marriage. On my wedding night, it was like I was being raped. She and I hadn't had sex before, and I just freaked. It wasn't a month after that when I went after Gregory, her boy, who was five or six years old.

It really bothered me that I was feeling such lust. I mean, here I was supposed to be a Christian, but I was into molesting kids. Finally, I turned myself in to the emergency room. I told them I was just overwhelmed with feelings of lust. It was with me twenty-four hours a day and didn't go away. So I was sent to a psychiatric center and I was there for maybe five days. Finally, I was sent home into my wife's care. I had three physicals while I was there, and other than that, I had no treatment. I was ready to go, though. I was bored, and I was afraid the past might catch up with me while I was there, so it was better for me to leave.

So my wife and I had a big heart-to-heart talk. I explained to her all about my problems. She was reluctantly supportive. I think it hurt her deeply, especially when I told her about Gregory. We came up with some guidelines, and I proceeded to earn her trust back. I don't know how long it took, maybe about a year. Then I started it up again with Gregory. I thought my relationship with my wife was good, but looking back on it now, I think our relationship must have been pretty horrendous, because I was dictatorial. I just couldn't stand being without Gregory. The thought of life without him was terrifying. I had to push away so I could take care of my family instead of just focus on the sex. So I decided to become a truck driver.

I worked myself to death in the hope that it would knock everything out of my system. In the meantime, my wife wanted to start doing day care in our home. We had to fill out this form for the background investigation for everybody in the home, and I filled it out truthfully. I told them all about the past because I didn't want my wife to do it. Well, even though the child-care counselor told us we didn't qualify, my wife brought in kids, anyway. So we had this whole bunch of kids, and I was really attracted to them, too. Supposedly, the deal was that I was going to be working all the time, and when I was home I would be sleeping, so there wouldn't be a problem. But I'd come home and it would be, "Honey, I've got to run an errand so you watch the kids." I'm working twelve to fourteen hours a day and I'm getting very little sleep, and now you want me to watch these kids? In the beginning, I'd load the kids right up in the car and head straight for a buddy's house where I felt safe. But sometimes, later on in my wife's baby-sitting career, I would take liberties—some touching, some fondling, some looking—before we got to my friend's house. At the same time, I was molesting another friend's kids and also a niece of mine. When I started working so heavily, everything just went downhill. There were my friend's kids, plus Gregory and a little girl my wife baby-sat. My whole life was way out of shape. I didn't like who I was and I didn't like what I'd done, but I didn't know how to be different.

One of the boys I was molesting finally said something, thank God, because I was looking for ways to talk about it, but I just couldn't do it. So I got arrested. Gregory refused to make a statement. I think it was probably because he felt guilty about something he had no control over. He was thirteen or fourteen at that point. I got Gregory hooked up with some counseling, and finally he got to the point where he could make a statement to the police. The cops lumped the two cases together and I was given a sentence at one time. But it took about eight months until Gregory was ready to talk, so in the meantime I was released on my own recognizance. I began to get insight on my problems.

I'm starting to realize I really messed up. After the police first called me in for questioning, the first thing I wanted when I left the police station was a child. That wasn't rational. I didn't know what to do, so I went into the library across the street. I ran across this book called *The Uncommon Secret* and I started reading it. I read it while I was on the road with my job. Since my truck was my livelihood, the police let me drive it. You don't know how hard it was to bring myself back to town after each job. I made every court appearance, but it was so tough not to run away. While I read that book, though, I realized that I had run all my life and running away was not the way to handle this problem. After I finished that book, I started buying all kinds of self-help books because I knew I'd be going to prison and wanted to set up my own library before I got there. I was starting to learn more about myself, and of course at the same time I had this mentality that, once I figured it out, I'd be all better. People were trying to tell me it would take time, but I kept saying no, no, I'm going to put all my effort into it and I'll get better tonight.

Once I realized that it would take a long time, I felt whipped. I was trying so hard to pretend I was normal. My wife had left me, and I wasn't supposed to go anywhere near her due to an order of protection. So I meet this girl, Diane. She's got a baby who is only about six months old, so I sort of feel safe with her. I told Diane everything, with more details than I ever gave my wife. Diane was shocked but decided to trust me, anyway. You've got to know Diane. She builds immature relationships just like I do. But I'm taking her trust as an affirmation. One day, I got home from work and there was this three-year-old little girl. "Who's that?" I asked. "Oh, that's my daughter," said Diane. I got along fine with Bonnie Sue, other than that I might have spanked her a little too hard one time. I realized I was creating a lifestyle that was not healthy for a three-year-old or even an adult, for that matter. I was expecting Bonnie Sue to fit into a rigid schedule. One day, I spanked Bonnie Sue because she wouldn't take a nap. I literally spanked her until she would lay down, keep her eyes closed, and go to sleep. If she opened her eyes, I would spank her again. That's the only mistake I can think of that I made with her.

In the meantime, Diane had a child caseworker from Child Protective Services who was having a fit about me. However, I was determined to do my best. Then I lost my job driving the truck, and the only thing I could find was working at a factory. I met this woman who worked at the factory. I was getting very disenchanted with Diane. Laura was different. I didn't know Laura had kids, but she invited me over to her house one time, and the kids and I hit it off right away. So that was a little different for me, in that I got interested in a woman and the kids came along later.

We pooled our resources and sort of moved in together. I wasn't sleeping with her or the kids or anything. I had a separate room. Before I moved in, the kids got to vote whether they wanted me there or not. It was a hands-down unanimous thing—they wanted me there. It was one of the happiest times in my life. We had family times when we'd sit down and read books together. I was getting so attached to Laura. Finally, the second charges came down and I was incarcerated. We had spent six months together.

It's now two years later, and we're still close, but it's changed, now. Now I can say goodbye and I don't feel like it's the end of the world, because Laura's got to learn to take responsibility for herself. I'm seeing that it's the same sick relationship I've always had, only with different faces. It doesn't mean that I don't care, but Laura's kids are on a collision course with disaster. I don't need to be a part of that. If they can't listen to me and they are just going to go their own way, then they can go it alone. Just because they jump into the cesspool doesn't mean I have to jump in with them. It doesn't mean that I don't care, but I just can't be tied to something like that.

Now that I'm in prison, I've had lots of time to think. I understand the way I worshipped those kids I molested. One of the things I used to like to do was to lay on my side and just look at their genitals. It was almost like a prayer for me. Looking at it from the standpoint of being worship saved me from killing people and doing more horrendous things. I didn't see the molesting as pleasure. It was God to me—it was actually God to me. In my thinking, the adult had always been contaminated. Adults are bad, you can't trust them. So you know this child is something pure, something perfect and safe. I didn't think I was contaminating the children with my worship because I thought I knew better than anybody else. I had already asked the question, "Well, what's wrong with this?" And nobody could tell me the reason, so I thought I knew best.

I was attracted to abused children. A child who was whole, who wasn't abused in some way, had no attraction for me at all. Basically, what I saw as beautiful and needy in them was actually symptoms of abuse. There's a child back home in our church I would have loved to get my hands on because he had all the symptoms of a battered and molested child. He was extraordinarily attractive to me, but he would never trust me, so nothing ever happened. It was only his lack of trust that stopped me, and that is another thing that really tears me up. I was misusing the trust and innocence of those kids. I never knew I was betraying them, but that is exactly what I did. I thought that I was giving them a reason to live by showing them that somebody loved them. I had an expectation, though, that they were supposed to appreciate me for loving them more than anybody else.

Essentially, I've had the emotional understanding of a three- or four-year-old. I discovered this when I was about forty-one. Since then, I'm above that three- to four-year mark, although the child is still inside of me and I have to talk to him sometimes. I would say that right now I'm in my teens. I wouldn't rate myself much higher than that, but I'm working on it. I've realized that one of the things I have to do to become mature is feeling my feelings. I used to have rage and passion but nothing in between. I either wanted to kill you or make love to you, and that was it.

Being in prison has helped me. Absolutely. First of all, I can work on my issues and I don't have to work on physically present relationships. That's been good. Just punishment for any crime or offense against people, I'm sorry to say, is death. We have what I would call grace demonstrated in society. They don't really punish you like you deserve. Maybe there is someone out there who understands that we weren't who we should have been when we did those things, because if I had the knowledge then that I have now, I wouldn't have done any of my crimes. I was definitely deprived of a lot of tools and knowledge to life. So I don't beat myself up about that; but the state has given me a safe place, and I have not been joking when I've told people that if they left the front gate open, I'd close it. I'm using that fence to keep the world out. I need time to catch up and this time has given me that. It's been safe time. Really safe time.

As far as if I'll be able to control my impulses to molest children in the future, I don't know. I still don't get it. It's sickening, and I'm very angry. My biggest concern is that I'm very pissed at the people who thought it was so cool to not give me the information I needed. I wanted help, and I don't appreciate all the bullshit I was given. I expect the state to be a little forgiving. Back when I had my parole, reports were supposed to be made to the state about what therapy had taken place. The therapy never occurred, and the court never enforced it. I'm the one who paid the price for that. Nobody else did. Well, wait a minute. My victims paid the price. They paid the biggest price because they lost their innocence when it didn't need to happen.

As for what I think should be done with pedophiles—well, incarceration is good for us. We can use that time, because after you face the big problem, you have all these little side issues you have to fine tune. I think incarcerated pedophiles need to be provided with a state-of-the-art library for looking into their problem. Sure, looking at the family situation is a start, but I need to know the pathology, where it all came from. I did some research from some friends who were taking college courses, and I was amazed to see all the dysfunction about sex in Western civilization, all the distorted thinking. I found places where pedophilia was being enforced and even encouraged. And now all of a sudden society says this is wrong. Well, granted, we shouldn't be doing this, but I needed some help to stop my behavior. Now that I have a safe place and information to help me understand, I can make some decisions for myself, do some goal setting. I have a tendency to live for the moment, and that's an addict's vision of the future. If you're saying my only problem is with sex, well, then I think you're off base. I think it has some spiritual, psychological, social, maybe even some intellectual ramifications. So we need to take a holistic approach and look at everything about that person. We need to take responsibility for ourselves, but if society is going to hold me responsible, then I have to hold society responsible for helping me. It's only fair.

When it comes to community notification policies, I'm absolutely against them. Basically, you are invading a person's privacy. He needs time to be alone, but not to go into hiding. Handling loneliness was a big issue for most of us in the past. When we can't handle loneliness, we turn to drugs, sex, or whatever made us feel good. So we might go back to that. People like us already have a history of overreacting to stress, and this registration thing might become too threatening. All you are going to do is ask for dead bodies. I will not register; I will not. Just because I've got this problem, people want to lock me up and see how bad they can make the story. The story is bad enough on it's own—it doesn't need any help. I'm pretty open about my problem now, and I don't want it to change when I'm out of prison. But not everyone can be trusted with this information. There are people who can handle it and people who can't, and I need to be able to choose whom I tell.

We need to get away from keeping secrets, but we have to be able to control how we express them. I have no problem with talking about this. There are people looking for answers, but if they speak up, they take such risks. Look at all the members of society who want to kill pedophiles if they confess. How are you going to expect people to be open and responsible if you overreact to what they tell you? In prison, it's the same thing. You need to shut up about this problem or else other guys get violent with you. By and large, when pedophiles are released from prison, society gets some very angry people who have not been given an opportunity to address their issues. So many people say this problem is untreatable. They really won't even try to treat us, or maybe they just don't want to do it. So if a pedophile is threatened because of community notification, let each community be willing to stand by to make some sort of compensation. You can have it one way or the other.

I'm extremely angry about the atmosphere out there. I get really pissed when I hear about people screaming over kids who are kidnapped and killed. Maybe you also ought to look at the person who was in charge of watching those kids but let them out unsupervised. This is not a rational or sane world. What reasonable person would let a three-year-old play outside unsupervised? I do understand what people are concerned about and their fears for their babies, for their little children, but they throw them into the molesters' hands—that's exactly what they do. We have to make our choice. If you want to keep your children safe, then watch your children. A lot of my victims came to me. I've had children throw themselves at me because what I had to offer was so much better than what they had to compare it with. That says we have some work to do out there. You talk about us exploiting children, but it seems to me that society trains us to use kids that way. Now, just because I'm invited, it doesn't mean that I have to partake.

Summary

Four major themes emerge from Abe's self-narrative. First, he claims that his childhood, in which he was physically and sexually abused, left him "definitely deprived of a lot of tools and knowledge to life." Second, Abe suggests that he spent most of his adult life—at least until he got into prison—with the emotional understanding of a three- or four-year-old child. Third, Abe's attraction to children stemmed from the way in which he worshipped them, particularly children who had been abused in some way; abused children were "extraordinarily attractive" to him. He believed he was helping these children: "If I ever thought I was hurting my victims, I wouldn't do it, you know?" Fourth, although he had asked for help a number of times, and even confessed his deviant desires to various authority figures in his life, nothing was done: "I wanted help, and I don't appreciate all the bullshit I was given."

Abe's description of his childhood focuses on the destructive patterns of abuse that appear to have been rampant in his environment. Abe observes that, had anyone cared to look closely enough, they would have seen that he was a profoundly troubled child. As Abe grew older, he became obsessed with sex and guns, constantly fantasizing about one or the other.

As he became a teenager, his sexual infatuation with younger children intensified. At fourteen, he began sexually molesting the three-year-old girl his stepmother and stepsister baby-sat. The age of three seems to be significant for Abe, since he claims that his own emotional development was stunted at that time, when he was first sexually abused. The age of three was also the age he preferred for his victims, although he seems to have been an equal opportunity child molester. Since he did not pursue sex with children if they seemed to put up any resistance, he tended to be opportunistic and took advantage of a potential victim, whatever the age. Ultimately, he took comfort in children, "in the child's world." Abe claims that he was most attracted to children who were vulnerable or had been abused in some way. He convinced himself that he was helping the children he molested, that he was "doing it all for their own good."

Prison pulled Abe out of this dysfunctional cycle and, hopefully, has offered an environment in which he can address his problems. No one helped to save Abe from himself, so now Abe is attempting to effect his own salvation. But he cannot shake his anger at the way in which his attempts to get professional help were rebuffed: "I'm the one who paid the price for that. Nobody else did. Well, wait a minute. My victims paid the price. They paid the biggest price because they lost their innocence when it didn't need to happen."

CHAPTER EIGHT

~

Greg—The Victim

Of all the men I spoke with, Greg was the most unassuming. Unremarkable in looks and mannerisms, on the surface Greg seemed like any other quiet, reserved, perfectly ordinary man, albeit with a noticeable air of timidity that warred with the underlying anger. As he told his story, his voice rarely changed inflection, but the tightly controlled monotone seemed stretched to the breaking point when he spoke of his own childhood molestation. Greg seemed deeply hurt and saddened by the string of circumstances that led him to prison. His anger appeared undirected, since he didn't seem to know who or what to blame for his crime. I suspected that he desperately wanted to be able to put the responsibility for sexually abusing his daughter on his own childhood victimization, since the image of himself as a child molester was too difficult to accept. He kept emphasizing what a warm, loving husband and father he was and what a good citizen he tried to be. Yet he couldn't escape the nagging knowledge that, in some dark and profound way, he had been tainted by the man who raped him as a child. From that pivotal moment, he felt silenced and tortured by that silence, believing that if he had been able to tell his parents—or if they had noticed his pain—his life would have been vastly different.

Greg's Story

I had a pretty normal childhood. I had two good parents, and there were six kids altogether in my family—three boys and three girls. I have a younger sister—she's the baby of the girls—and I'm the baby of the boys. My father worked and my mom stayed home. I was close to both parents. In fact, I just lost my mom about three years ago. She died while I was in prison, and that hurt. I did everything to help the family. When I was working for the summer, I helped to pay bills. It gave me responsibility. As a kid, I thought we were rich. It felt good. We were pretty comfortable.

Then something happened. A guy across the street—one of the neighbors we were friends with—molested me. I was twelve. I went over there to babysit for him, and his kids were crying outside. They said to me, "Daddy's got a gun." I thought he was going to kill himself, so I went into the house. He had a .357 Magnum in his hand and he said, "Close the door." What he did to me. . . . His wife was out working. That is why I was. . . . Somebody had to be with the kids, a little boy and a girl, maybe like four or five years old. Well, after that happened with me, he told me not to tell my parents or I'd never see them again.

He did everything to me—anal sex, the whole bit. He had me do it on him or he did it on me, and he had porno flicks on. I couldn't even move when I could get out of there. I went to our backyard and I fell asleep in my playhouse. I didn't go into the house until about midnight that night. The story I gave my parents was that I fell asleep in the playhouse and just woke up. Part of it was true. I was afraid to tell them the whole truth because the guy had said he would hurt them. Plus if I did tell them, I knew what my father and brother would have done. My brother was in Vietnam and my father was in World War II, and I know that they would have killed him. So I kept it to myself, and I isolated myself from my family.

The thing was, I had told the guy's wife. When she came home from work, she was in the garage washing clothes, and I went up to her and told her. She told me I was lying and said to stop saying things about stuff I didn't even know about. If she didn't believe me, who would? So in school, I had problems, and they thought it was because I had a problem at home. Part of it was true, but the problem wasn't in my household. I couldn't tell them. I went through counseling, I seen therapists. I didn't look for trouble, but if somebody came to me, I'd take care of it. I didn't care if it was a principal or a teacher, I'd take care of it right there and then. And I'd be out of control to where I couldn't even stop myself. There was anger about what he did to me, and anger because I couldn't go and tell no one because I was afraid for my family. To this day, I wasn't able to tell either parent. They never really saw how upset I was. I never showed it at home—I only did when I was in school.

Another reason that I couldn't tell no one was because my older sister moved in with the family of the man who molested me. We were good friends with the family, and she moved in with them when they moved to a bigger house where she could have her own room. Since they were right across the street from us, every time I'd seen him I would run and go into the house. When he came over, I went in the closet. I used to sleep in the closets, do my homework in closets. I felt safe there. The worst thing was trying to talk my mom out of getting me to go over there to baby-sit. She couldn't understand why I was giving that up. I told her I had a lot of homework. At night, I'd be with my mom because I didn't want nothing to happen to her. I wouldn't leave her side. They were part of the family; they were friends and everything. The man would ask my father to go someplace with him, and then my father would ask me to go. I'd try to think of everything I could to get out of it. But I had to go along with my father—talk about being frightened. He'd say, "There's nothing to be afraid of." I knew there was.

When my sister moved in with that family, I wanted so bad to tell what happened to me. Her son was about three when she moved in with them. Whenever I wanted to tell her about what that man did to me, he'd be somewhere in the house and I couldn't say anything. But my sister didn't stay too long with them. The man tried to do something to my nephew, and my sister walked in. Then she tried to tell his wife what had happened, and they got into a fight. My sister stayed with them about six or seven months and then found another place to live. I wanted to tell her because we were close. Now, since I've been in prison, I've wrote to her and got one letter back from her, but that was it. Her excuse is that she don't know what to say. When I get home, I'll talk to her. I have to talk to her. My nephew is nineteen or twenty years old now, and I'm planning to talk to him, too. I've tried to say something in a letter, but I just couldn't. I did explain things to my wife, but I didn't go into details. She asked me why I didn't ever tell her. I says, "Because I haven't told no one." Now it's been twenty-four or twenty-five years, and I'm finally going to.

When I turned thirteen, I began to go to Bible study. When I got on the bus to go to Bible study, my whole world changed. I knew where I was going: to church, where he wasn't around. It was a different world. I was safe. At that time, I started thinking about my sister and nephew and wondering if the same thing went on as with me. That was always on my mind, day and night. We would receive phone calls from her to hear how she was doing, and when we didn't hear from her, I cried at night. I was still having problems in school. I got decent grades—B's and C's—but I was slow in reading and stuff like that, so I was in some special classes.

When I was in high school, I met my girlfriend. She was in foster care and lived down the street from us, and that is how I met her. Because her mom was in the hospital and her foster father couldn't take her up to the hospital to visit her, I asked my father if he would do it. He said no problem, and he would take us up to see her mom. We'd come back home, and she used to spend nights at my house. We'd watch spooky movies. I was sixteen and she was two years younger. She also had a brother. Her brother was going with my sister, and I was going with her. Those two didn't make it, but Lori and I stayed together. When I was with Lori, I was able to be myself. I didn't know at the time she had told my sister that she was raped by one of the kids in another foster home. She kept that from me, and I could understand why. I did the same thing—kept a secret from her.

I was going on seventeen when my father died. He had a heart attack at work. I blamed myself because I wasn't there. I could have saved him. On that day, he woke me up to get ready for school and he was leaving for work. Sometimes, I would go to work with him instead of going to school, but today he told me to go to school. He told my mother to keep his watch running until it was lunchtime. Why would he keep his watch home instead of taking it with him? He knew. I should have gone to work with him. I was very close to my father, and that's why I was hurt because he left me, and I couldn't tell him what happened to his little boy. I wanted to get it off my chest, but I never told my mom. When I was with my dad at one of the two jobs he was working at, I could have taken him aside and told him what happened. But we still lived near those people, and I knew that if I told my father, he'd go and kill them. So I just kept it to myself. Then my girl left me. I guess I wasn't too good to be with then.

A couple of years later, Lori and I got back together. She already had two kids at the time, and I had a cottage all to myself. When I was working in security, I used to go over to their house and wait for her kids to come home from school. Then I'd take them with me to cash my check and ask them what they wanted to do—if they wanted pizza or [to] go to Burger King. They'd say, "Mommy is making dinner." "This ain't about your mother," I'd say. "I'm asking what you want to do." And they'd say, "Let's have a pizza." That's what I'd do with every paycheck. Her kids started calling me Dad. That helped her get to where she left the guy she was with and came with me. Whenever he bought her anything, she had to turn around and pay him back out of her welfare check. I couldn't see that. Finally, she left the guy because he didn't want anything to do with her or the kids. Now Lori has my daughter.

This was after I got out of the service. I went into the service the year I graduated high school. I was in for two years. I didn't go overseas. During that time, I had a lady friend, but my heart was set on Lori. I didn't have sex with any other women. Lori was my first. Lori and me didn't have sex until we got together the second time. She always thought I was kind of weird because I didn't push myself on her like other guys did. Since she had been through the same thing—been raped and all—I wanted it to be special and I wanted to be different. I didn't want it to be forced like it was on me. That is why I took my time.

It was funny how Lori and me met up again. I was in the city court with a friend. When they announced Lori's name, I looked and thought, "What is she doing here?" She had spent the night in county jail because she stole a small jar of something or other. I wanted her to leave the guy she was with. He didn't give Lori anything, and if he did, he'd want it back. When Lori had my daughter, she said it was his. So this other guy had to pay child support for my daughter, and when Lori got the check, she'd cash it and give some of the money back to pay his car payments. It was not right. It hurt me inside that she couldn't tell him the truth, that she was my daughter.

I first met the lady who became my wife just before I graduated high school. I was in a training program and we met there. Then we met again about ten years later, when I moved into an apartment building right across the hall from her. I was still seeing Lori then. I'd go over to Lori's and see my daughter, and I'd take my wife and two girls over there, too. My wife found out that Lori's daughter was my child after my son was born. I brought my son over there, too. When the girl stepped on my foot, my son said, "You stepped on my daddy's foot." The girl says, "Well, he's my daddy, too." This brings me up to what led to me being here in prison. When my wife was pregnant again and carrying twins, a lot of bad stuff happened. I had an accident on the way going to work. Then my wife tripped over the vacuum cleaner and miscarried one of the babies. Then I lost my job and we had to move out. I lost my job and house through my foster sister, who was jealous because we had a better home than she had and I was making more money than she was. I had a credit card, and she was denied. I had a car, and she was denied.

My foster sister called my boss and told him I was on sick leave because I didn't want to work. This was when I had my car accident and was on sick leave for a while. My boss told me to get into work and that if I came in late, don't come in at all. Well, my wife had the miscarriage then, and I was late into work. That night my boss came over to me and said, "Well, I see you were late." I said yes, and I explained to him why, but he didn't want to hear nothing. He said, "You are fired, and don't come in tomorrow." Now after all she's been through, how do I come home and tell my wife that I don't have a job anymore? When I got home, the first thing I did was I went to the fridge and pulled out a bottle of beer, opened it, and went down into the basement.

I stood in front of the fireplace and started talking to myself, then said, "I have to go upstairs and tell my wife what happened, that I don't have a job."

But my wife already knew because the company had called to verify I was not working there any longer. I looked for another job in security, since I have that background, and then I got hired that very same day. I called the bank and let them know I had found a new job. Well, I didn't have that job long, because they received a letter from my other employer saying that I'm lazy in doing my work, and they let me go. The bank told me to just get any job. That was proof for the car loan, and they were trying to help me out. But I had to lose the house, and I worked hard for that.

So now, this is leading up to my sin. We had to move and found another place. Then one day we had a fire in the kitchen, so we got the kids out and I went down in the basement to shut the power off so it don't spread through the rest of the house. I was thinking I'm doing a favor to the landlord, but he evicted us because we called the fire department. I saved his butt, but he didn't care about the house. That's why he evicted us. We had pictures of the whole house, inside and out, bare wires and everything, and we did have a case, but Legal Aid said it would be better to just move out. We moved out, put the stuff in storage, and stayed with my wife's mom.

We were at my brother's house when my wife's water broke, and I had to rush her to the hospital. She was in labor for two weeks. Two weeks. It was very painful for a woman. But I was feeling all the pain, too. I was going from the hospital to her mom's house to check on the kids, then back to my wife. They I'd go back to check on the kids and stay there overnight, then come back to [the] hospital and sleep there or in my car. I slept one night at my brother's house. I didn't feel comfortable staying there, though, 'cause I had to be somewhere where there was a phone in case something happened and I had to get to the hospital. My wife didn't want me sleeping in my car, so she asked the security guard at the hospital if he would go and check on me. Told them where I was in the parking lot—the only car there. He brought me coffee and asked me if I was all right. I says, "Yeah." Slept in my car, just to be close to her, and at the same time looking for a place for us to live. It was hard—it's hard on one person.

So my son was born premature—she had already miscarried the other twin before. He only weighed three pounds and eight-and-a-half ounces. He was in one of those rooms where they hook them up to a machine for breathing. He was doing all right. He knew who I was just by my voice, because I couldn't hold him until he started putting some weight on. In the meantime, I was visiting with my wife and bringing her down, then bringing her back up to her room so she could lay down, while I'd come back down and be with my son for a little while. Then off I go to the house to check on the kids, then go out looking for another place to live. When I found a place, I had to set up the house. I went to the hospital to see my wife, taking two or three loads of stuff to the house, then back to check on the kids. It was back and forth, back and forth. When I brought my wife home, my son was still in the hospital. Then my wife went back in because she had a blood clot where the nurse pulled the IV out. So we took her back in, and they put her on this medication where she had needles in her stomach at least three times a day. She had to learn it herself. She was doing it on an apple when I came into the room, and she asked the nurse if I could do it. The nurse said, "Do you have any experience with this?" I said, "Yeah, I gave insulin shots to my sister-in-law." Here's an orange, here's the bottle, and I showed her. She said okay, so I took my wife home and gave her the shots, then I went back to the hospital to be with my son.

One night, I came home about three or four in the morning and fell asleep on the couch in front of the fireplace. My wife asked me if I was coming to bed. I said, "Yeah, I'll be there." Then I rolled over and went back to sleep. In the meantime, Susan, my wife's nine-year-old daughter, came over and she asked me if I wanted another rum and coke. She made it and brought it to me, and it happened right there and then. I told Susan that it wasn't right for daddies to do this, but she said, "It's okay, I do this with my Daddy." And she wanted me to go further. She gave me a blow job that night, and she wanted me to go further with her. I came that close to doing it, but then my mind just snapped and I said, "No, I can't." She told me that this is what she does with her daddy, that this is how she shows love for him, and I felt queer at the time and relaxed. But then my mind snapped, and I told my wife what Susan just did and what Susan wanted me to do. I don't really know if my wife believed me or not since she was drowsy because of the medication that I was giving her. So she could have thought I was saying something else.

The next day, we went to see Susan's doctor, and her doctor tells us to don't talk about it, just leave her alone and she will forget it. See, Susan was raped when she was younger, before I came into the picture. It was by a friend of her father's brother. Charges were dropped because he was living with a Child Protective Services worker, and she took care of the case and got everything off. The thing they used to get the guy off was that Susan was handicapped and they couldn't believe her. They told my wife she was lying. Susan is slow in reading, but that's about it. So when the doctor told us to just leave it alone, I let it fly. I should have talked more to my wife, but I didn't.

Susan came to me four other times. I would be sitting in a chair or laying on the couch, and she would come over to me and kiss me and say I'm her boyfriend. Then she'd start playing around and one thing led to another, and she started giving me blow jobs again. I didn't stop it. I hadn't had sex with my wife for so long. I thought about what I was doing, afterwards. I tried to block it out. What got me most scared was once when I was sitting in the chair and she was doing that with me, I had a flashback of when I was a boy. I went back to when I was twelve and the guy first molested me. After that time, that's when I pushed her away. I'd be sitting in that chair, and she'd come over to me, and I'd start getting sick to my stomach. I never thought about Susan being in the same position as I was as a kid, because in my situation it was forced. But I connected the two, because when the police came to the house and took me to the police station, as I was telling them what took place and where it took place, I was telling what had happened to me at the same time.

My wife was the one who called the police. Susan's father was living in his truck on our property, and she asked him if he had ever slept with his daughter. He says yes, and that's when she called the hotline. She didn't know about me, then. Like I said, she was on medication. She didn't expect that Susan would say I did it, too. It wasn't the first time her father was arrested. I really didn't know anything about him. All I knew was that he had been living someplace and got kicked out. I felt sorry for him since he didn't have nowhere to go and the kids didn't want to have nothing to do with him, so I thought I was helping him out by letting him live on our property. When the police arrested me, I was hurting inside and I knew how Susan felt, because I had flashed back to my own experience, but again I couldn't say anything. When I was in the county jail, I broke down and talked to a lady counselor. Since a young age, I always had a problem when I went to hospitals to see doctors. I would not strip in front of a male doctor or even talk to them unless my father was in the room. My father couldn't understand why, and I never said anything, but I would talk to a lady doctor or a nurse, sometimes.

My wife was pregnant before I was taken away to prison and then four months later had another miscarriage. I was talking to her on the phone and broke down and told her about what that guy did to me. It wasn't the best time. I couldn't sleep at night, so I went to the shrink for something to relax. It made me feel really weird. One night at about 11 p.m., that's when I decided to tell my wife about it. She asked why had I waited so long. She knew that there was something wrong, but she couldn't put her finger on it. She said I would wake up in the night crying. She just wished I would have told her. So while I was in jail, she called a person in the phone book who was a rape counselor. The lady explained to her why some men keep it to themselves, because they were embarrassed, so she was able to understand what I was going through.

Now she's divorcing me so the kids can come home. The kids have been in foster care all the time I've been in prison, and they won't give them back to their mom as long as she is married to me. My wife never seen me doing anything with Susan, so she can't say something happened for sure. I copped a plea so Susan wouldn't have to testify. To this day, Susan has forgiven me. My wife still has strong feelings, but she appreciates that instead of seeing Susan go through a lot of hassles and everything, I took the blame. I am responsible—I shouldn't have let it go on. It felt good at the time, but afterwards I was so sick inside—hurt and angry that I let it go on. I can't really blame my wife because she didn't give me blow jobs at the time, because she was sick. So I couldn't force it on her, and with Susan, I didn't have to force; she was always ready to do it. Other than not having oral sex, my relationship with my wife was real good. We have two beautiful sons. I've been a father to them, and a father to my wife's other kids. I was there when Susan wasn't feeling good and had a high fever. I had just come from the hospital from having surgery and I had seven staples in me. I wasn't supposed to carry anything, but Susan wanted me to take her to the hospital. She didn't want Grammy, she didn't want Mommy, she didn't want anybody—she wanted Daddy. I rushed to the doctor's and the doctor said, "What do you want to do to yourself, do you want to pull out your staples? You'll hemorrhage." And so I explained why I did it. And he said, "I guess any father would have done the same thing."

I was in the prison system for two years before they started a group for sex offenders. I got into the group on the first day. I had been there for two years already, and everybody in the dorm already knew what I was there for. Well, somehow it got back to my counselor that I was talking in the dorm, and so they put in that I broke confidentiality. I tried to tell my counselor what happened, but he didn't or wouldn't listen to what I had to say. I tried to explain to him, "How are you going to keep this a secret, especially in a jail?" You can't. So I got transferred for breaking confidentiality. I went to another prison, and there I went to the parole board and I got hit with another two years. I went to see a counselor, and she told me that they did have a treatment program there, but it was too late for me to get into it. One night, they stole my tapes, my tape player, broke into my locker, and did all that. The next night, they set my bed on fire just before the count. I had to get packed up and moved to another dorm. One of the guys that I worked with said, "I like you—I have nothing against you—whatever you did is your business— but I wouldn't want to see you in one of those hospital beds." He says to see the CO and maybe he'll put me in protective custody or get me a transfer. So I ended up here in this prison.

It ain't easy to be a sex offender in prison. I got too relaxed—that's what happened. I let my guard down. Here, I know half the population is sex offenders the same as me. I do feel better, since most of all the fights and stabbings that go on here isn't with us. When I first started out in groups, it was hard because I don't want to trust too many people, so they have to gain my trust. And then when they gain my trust, I had to learn to trust them. I have to trust letting go and opening up—that's what I have to trust. I go to the parole board again next year, and being a sex offender, I know that I won't be getting out. The next year, I will get out for sure, because it will be my third time at the board. So to me, I will have paid for my crime. I spent a lot of time for somebody who had never been in any trouble. Yet I know the other guy, Susan's father, he only got five years probation. And he had been arrested before. This was my first time.

Probation would have helped me more than prison. If I had been out there getting in trouble, then prison would have been good. For someone who hasn't been in trouble in his life, it's not good. When I went to the first court, they asked, "How come you don't got no tickets and everything?" I said, "I live by the rules." But they didn't listen. So here I am. While I been in prison, I have taken advantage of the programs here. Then they took a lot of the programs out of the prison, which hurt a lot of us. They want us to better ourselves so when we get out of prison we can get a job and not come back. Now they took everything away—colleges and all the programs and classes, all gone. Now what do we do, just sit around and do nothing till we get out? Then what will we do?

I don't know what I'll do when I get out. I have to take one day at a time. I think I will still get therapy when I'm out. I'm learning how to open up. Sometimes I do clam up, and when the group leader says something to me, I will get defensive and start yelling at him. My voice goes up because I have to defend myself. I try to just let it go, but it's hard. I'm told I got problems with authority, if it's from a male. It's from me being molested. But it's hard in here, because all the guys in group are men and the counselors in charge are men, too. So I have to get over it.

I'm nervous about this Megan's Law. That can endanger a person who is coming out for that crime, especially if they have worked on themselves and now the community knows what they were in for. They already paid the price. Let them get on with their life. But for guys who do this a lot, who been in prison more than once—I think those three-strikes laws will help. Those people don't care who they hurt. Those notification laws—they can make that worse. If people know they don't have no freedom on the streets, they might do a worse crime just to get sent back to prison 'cause they got no life, anyway.

As for parents, they need to keep a good eye on their kids and find out who their friends are. Once you get involved with your kids, you know the kids by heart. I should have went for counseling and had counseling for the whole family. That's what I should have done. But I didn't. I learned from that. Now I'm focusing on me and taking responsibility for my life. I know that I am strong enough that I can go out there and whatever they say, whatever they do, it's not going to stop me. I know what I have to do, because I'm still a family man. I want to get on with my life and not have to deal with any more of my problems. I won't bother no one. I never bothered no one before, so I won't do it now. I got my family to think of, and that's all that counts to me.

Summary

Greg maintains that he has always "lived by the rules," yet the image that emerges from his story is that of a man who has always been victimized—or at least, considers himself to have been victimized—despite his efforts to create a stable environment for himself and his family. The memories of his childhood rape haunt him. His sexual victimization as a boy turned him into a victim for life.

Ultimately, the major theme that runs throughout Greg's self-narrative is the price of keeping secrets. When Greg was viciously attacked at age twelve, he became the reluctant recipient of a shameful secret. When Greg was seventeen, another event occurred that left him feeling shame and guilt. His father had a heart attack at work, and Greg blamed himself.

Greg tried to exert control over the secrets in his life by living by the rules. He spent two years in the military and pursued a career in security. Along the way, he built a family. Then a string of bad luck added stress to Greg's life that undermined his carefully guarded control. First, his wife miscarried one of their twins. Greg had an accident on his way to work, he lost his job, and the family lost their house. Soon after, Greg's wife went into labor and after a long battle prematurely delivered their tiny son. A few weeks later, his wife developed a blood clot that required round-the-clock vigilance and medication.

Greg blames these misfortunes and stressors as leading to his "sin." One night, exhausted, he got home late and collapsed on the couch. Then Greg claims that Susan, his wife's nine-year-old daughter, approached him sexually. So poor Greg was victimized once again—yet this time, it was by a nine-year-old child, his stepdaughter, a little girl who had been raped previously by a friend of her father's brother and molested by her father as well. It does seem odd that Greg would immediately tell his wife and Susan's doctor about the event when he kept his own childhood molestation a secret. Since Greg's wife didn't seem to grasp the significance and the doctor apparently told Greg "to just leave it alone and it will pass," Greg was not protected from Susan's next four sexual advances.

Greg obviously feels sorry for his actions—or sorry that this happened to him—but still seems to believe that he was just in the wrong place at the wrong time. Greg had tried to play the role of husband, father, and provider for his family, but his festering childhood secret undermined his efforts.

Even though Greg finally shared his secret and has tried to take responsibility for his actions, he is still a victim while in prison. Early on in his sentence, other inmates stole from him and set his bed on fire. So Greg continues to be plagued by misfortune, despite his best efforts. As in the rest of his life, in prison he has been vulnerable to attack. Although Greg considers himself to be a "family man" and a good citizen, he continues to be taken advantage of by other people—people he would like to trust.

~

CHAPTER NINE

Ben—The Defeated Soldier

Ben was a small man, habitually hunched over as though he wanted to close himself off from the world outside his own skin. Missing teeth and painfully thin, he admitted that he didn't eat much, in a passive-aggressive approach to committing suicide. Four years into a six- to twelve-year sentence, Ben's depression was obvious and understandable. Ben's style of communicating was primarily halting and tentative, yet oddly enough, he maintained strong eye contact, which provided a glimpse into past leadership positions he held while serving in the military. Although Ben claimed that he wanted to understand himself and what motivated him to commit his crimes, he still seemed desperate to believe that somehow, some way, the little girls he molested weren't harmed by his abuse. My initial reaction was that Ben's inability to comprehend the enormity of his betrayal probably stemmed from the legacy of sexual abuse he inherited from his own family. As our interview progressed, however, it dawned on me that perhaps an even more potent factor contributed to Ben's difficulty in empathizing with his victims. This was his experiences in the military, specifically in combat situations in the Vietnam War. When Ben joined the army, he had already been emotionally wounded by his uncle's abuse. The military trained Ben to suppress his kinder impulses and instead bring to the surface the half-buried anger he felt as a result of his own victimization. The result was the creation of an efficient soldier, a man who observed that, eventually, killing people got easy.

Ben's Story

I grew up mostly a loner. Mostly, I stayed with my uncle because my mother and father pretty much abandoned me. I come from a big family. My folks had what would have been thirteen kids, but three of them died. I was fourth from the top. Every time my parents got kicked out of their place and had to move, I was one of the first ones to go to a home for kids until my mother and father could get a bigger place or afford to keep me. So my uncle would pick me up and keep me with him most of the time. Sometimes, he'd pick up a few of the other kids, too. He was a wino. So was my mom and dad—they were both alcoholics.

I was put into the home for kids three different times before I was ten years old. My parents just didn't have room and oftentimes didn't have food for all of us. Lots of times, we had a bowl of cereal in the morning and that was it until we came home at night and had a bowl of rice or something like that. My dad worked for the railroad. He'd mark the trains coming through. As I got older, I felt real close to him. When I was with my uncle, he kept me on the farm he worked at. He taught me how to drive the truck and tractors. He also introduced to me drinking. Every time he went down to the bar, he'd take me with him. The only times I was really out of his sight was when I was in bed, but even then I wasn't alone. There were always three or four of us at the same time in the same bed. There just wasn't room for any of us to have our own space. Until my sisters got older and left home and got married or whatever, sometimes one of them would be in the bed with us. So there were no barriers, no boundaries of any kind.

I was probably about eight or nine years old when I got interested in sex. One day when my father was working, I saw my mother having sex with another guy in the living room on the couch. I was home sick from school that day, and when I saw them rolling around, I wondered what the heck they were up to. It made me curious. A little while later, I was walking down the street and ran into a handicapped girl. She couldn't speak or hear. So I got hold of her shorts and pulled them down with her panties. I got a glance at her before her mother came running out and chased me down the street. She never caught me.

This started my obsession with looking at girls. When I was nine, I had a cousin who was about seven years old and asked me if I wanted to have sex with her. I never finished anything with her at that time, but later on, when we were older, I had sex with her for real. I also started messing around with four of my own younger sisters—just practicing with them, not actually penetrating them. I didn't penetrate two of my sisters until I was about seventeen or eighteen years old and they were twelve or thirteen at the time. That was the first time I ever had a virgin—that is, until later on, when I had sex with my nieces. One of them—she was my brother's daughter—stripped right down one time when I was baby-sitting, and it seemed she offered it to me then and there. She was about eleven or twelve, I guess. When I was a kid, I also had sexual intercourse with some of my other cousins. It was a real family affair.

I was in special education classes at school. Once, I wrote a girl and told her that I wanted to have sex with her. I was about thirteen or fourteen at the time. I thought she was probably a virgin, and the only virgins I had had to that point were my sisters. She showed the teacher the note. The teacher figured out it was me. So they called my parents, and I got whipped with the razor strap.

You see, I was just crazy about sex. I didn't know if it was right or wrong—I just knew it was something I wanted to do. My uncle molested me when I was a boy. I was about seven or eight years old at the time. He asked me if I wanted to have sex with him. He said, "Well, let me put it up your rectum and then when I'm done you can put yours up mine." And I said okay. Of course, he had given me a little bit of his wine that day. Just as he got ready to do his thing, his boss pulled up. I had to hurry and get my pants up so he wouldn't catch us. My uncle was constantly fondling me. He was always trying to stick it into me. He didn't get into trouble or anything, so I figured it was an okay thing. But it isn't, is it? I never told anybody about what he was doing. He told me not to tell. I was afraid if I did tell anybody he would probably beat the living daylights out of me. But he was always real gentle when he touched me. He didn't force himself on me; he never penetrated me or squeezed my genitals. But I didn't know what might happen if I said anything about it.

I didn't tell anybody because I didn't know what to say. One day, I picked up one of the kittens we had in the barn and threw it against a wall. I picked it up and looked at it in my hand, then drew my hand back and threw it into the wall. I figured that since cats climbed trees and everything, maybe they'd catch their nails on the board to pull themselves up. But the kitten I threw didn't do that. All it did was shake. I knelt down and cried like a baby. I was thinking about what my uncle was doing to me and I was getting madder, and that's when I picked up the kitten and threw it.

Finally, my uncle left. He joined up with a carnival and started traveling around to different towns and villages. I kept that secret inside of me. A lot of things—most of my feelings—I bottled them all up. Like now, I keep my feelings inside me instead of letting them out. When I'm in group therapy here in the prison, there are a lot of things that I would like to say, but I'm afraid if I put them out there, they are going to come back to me. I'm afraid to tell anybody what I feel because I don't know what might happen.

I was in and out of trouble a lot when I was a kid. I stole things. I even stole from the collection box in our town's church. I also stole from a lot of stores in town. I was so bold, once I even stole some money that a guy had in his wallet. He was working in a gas station, and I just lifted it out of his pants. I was walking across the park, then he realized what had happened and turned around to yell at me. He and another guy ran after me. I just threw the money in the air and kept running, but they caught up with me. They called the cops. My father punished me with a razor strap for that one. I mean, we were brought up real strict, but we just did what we wanted to do anyway, regardless of what our parents said.

When I got into my teens, I started drinking heavily then. I quit school at the age of fifteen and went to work on a farm. It was steady work, and I'd give most of the money that I was making to my mother. The money I kept for myself, I'd use to buy beer. I'd go down to the store, and the guys who worked there knew me because they had seen me with my uncle. So they'd sell me the booze because I'd say it was for him.

A few years later, I went to work for a company in town and still helped out with my mother and father. I continued to live with my parents. At that time, the majority of my brothers and sisters still lived at home. The youngest was roughly about seven years old and the oldest was about twenty-three or twenty-four years old. There were three brothers older than me, then lots of boys and girls younger than me. You just kept on going down the line. I know my mother had sex with other guys, but I don't know if she had any of the kids with them. I do know that my parents liked to argue all the time, especially when my father came home from work and then just sat around drinking his beer. Lots of times, my father had me buy him the beer since I looked older than my brothers did and he and I always got along well together. This was even though I normally used to get blamed most of the time for something somebody else did. I don't know why—maybe because I was the fourth one on the list of the boys, and the older boys would say that I did it. And my father would punish me for it. Lots of times, I just hated being around my older brothers. I was a loner, never played games with them, and maybe that was a reason why they felt that I could get blamed for the things they did.

I was drafted in 1964, just a little bit after the Fourth of July. I spent two years in the army on my draft, and then I reenlisted for six years. At the end of those six years, I turned around and put in for a quick discharge so I could reenlist again. All told, I spent nine years in the regular army, four years of which was over in Vietnam, and then three years in the National Guard. Four years in Vietnam was a long time, let me tell you. I didn't get hurt the first year over there, but I did have friends that I seen get killed, and I still think about it every now and then. If anybody asked me why I kept going back to Vietnam, I'd say that all that training helped me be the best grunt I could be. The honest truth was because I wanted to get myself blown away. I just didn't give a darn.

You see, when I got drafted, my life wasn't going so well. I got married when I was twenty-one and she was eighteen, so we were both too young. My brother had married her sister. We were together about seven or eight months before we got married. Actually, she got pregnant, and then we got married. Then I went down to my permanent unit, which was in Texas. I was down there maybe half a year, and then the whole unit packed up and shipped out to Vietnam. My wife wrote me a letter saying she was going to divorce me because I abandoned her and her child. It wasn't even my baby, but one she had with another guy before she married me. Anyhow, I didn't abandon her—I went over on orders. When I got back home, I showed her the orders and she believed me then, so we got remarried.

When we went over on the boat, I had three other brothers with me on the same ship. One of my brothers was in the navy and then my two other brothers and me were in the army. The commanding officer in charge of the whole group said that three of us had to go back to the States. None of us volunteered to go back, so all four of us went over. I got placed way out in the boonies. One night, my CO asked for a volunteer to do a night maneuver. So I volunteered for it. I went out roughly about half a mile away from the unit and set up an ambush position in case anybody came down the road, so we could stop them from coming in. I didn't mind doing that. In fact, I enjoyed being out there because it was more of a challenge. You didn't have no barbed wire or nothing around you to keep the enemy from getting to you.

During my third year, I had a tragedy. We hit a landmine, but the driver hit on the right-hand side instead of the driver's side, so nobody got hurt too bad. We got bruised up and I hurt my back and leg and the back of my head. The M16 ammo box hit me right in the mouth. That's what knocked my teeth loose; they were just hanging by the roots. I got out and walked around to check on my own men. I didn't even know I was hurt. I got one of my Purple Hearts for that. Then, during the last year I was over in Vietnam, I was out with the military police and we were getting hit right and left. Come to find out the CO who was in charge didn't plot his coordinates right, so we came real close to the enemy, closer than we should have been. But we only had maybe three guys out of that whole platoon get hurt. We were darn lucky. I was darn lucky. But I really didn't want to be so lucky. If the war was still going on after my fourth year, I probably would have kept going over into combat situations. I wanted to get blown away because I didn't care about anything.

It wasn't hard for me to kill other people. There was no problem there. The youngest one I killed was a four-year-old kid. He had a grenade in both his hands, the pins were pulled, and he started drawing back in my direction. I either had to take him out or he was going to take me out. So I killed him with a machine gun. I was shaking. I had to leave the perimeter area and go back into the tent. I had a couple of beers to calm myself and a couple of cigarettes. Then I went back out into the field. Every one after that got easier and easier.

It's kind of funny. All the time I was in the military, I wanted to get myself killed, but at the same time I seemed to really take care of myself. Guys were dying right and left, but I kept on going. I got injured more than once, but never enough to get me shipped home for long. I wanted to die because I kept thinking back to my past, about my family putting me in a home and all that stuff. I was always the first one to go into the home and the first one to get punished by my parents, mainly by my father with the razor strap. But I knew that if I got myself blown away, I'd be hurting a lot of people back in the States.

My youngest brother passed away when he was just turned eighteen. He went out drinking to a bar and had to be taken home. My father gave him a back rub and then found him the next morning in the same place, face down. He had started turning black. According to the death certificate, what killed him was an overdose of Darvon. His death hurt me, too, because he was the youngest of the family and I always felt real close to him. When I came home on furloughs, every time he needed cigarettes, I'd give them to him. He used to go drinking a lot with his friends, and once I got so mad when he came home drunk, I wanted to punch him. But I couldn't bring myself to hit him. Instead, I told him to go up to the bedroom and go to sleep, and then I took his cigarettes away from him so he wouldn't burn the house down. You see, the uncle who molested me as a kid had died in a parking lot. He and his buddy were drinking in an abandoned truck. Evidently, they were smoking and the seat caught on fire when they passed out. The other guy got out, but my uncle was too drunk to wake up. I didn't want my brother to die that way, but he ended up dying, anyway. When my brother died, I was in the National Guard at the time, and I wore my uniform to the funeral home. I walked to the coffin, touched the coffin, and came close to pulling it off the stand it was on. They had to pry my fingers off the coffin. I didn't want to leave my brother that way. He was just a kid.

You know, when my uncle died—the one who molested me—I still loved him. His death didn't hurt me as much as my brother's did, but I still had feelings for my uncle. I still loved him in spite of what he did to me, just like I loved my mother, even though she'd smack me alongside the head or yell at me. Every time I came home on furlough, I always stayed with my mother and father. I'd ask if they needed anything, and then I'd send it to them. My other brothers and sisters never did that. I don't know why they never helped my parents.

So now we are at the point of the story where I talk about my crimes. I have said that before I went into the army, I messed around with my sisters and cousins and pretty much anyone I could get my hands on. When I got out of the military, I just got any job. I worked at a hotel and I worked at a casting company. Other than that, I mostly worked as much as I could just to stay away from people. Anyhow, here it is the middle 1970s, and I started molesting my nieces. I started with my niece Becky. She came over to my parents' house a lot, and sometimes I'd pull Becky onto my lap and touch her breasts or vagina or whatever. I had thought about it a lot before I did anything. Finally, I figured that maybe she wouldn't say anything, so I gradually worked my way up to where she allowed me to put my hands inside her pants. Come to find out that she already had somebody else penetrate her with their fingers. I tried to get her to tell me who did it, but she would never open up about it.

Becky was about five or six years old when it started, and it went on for about five years. She never told anybody about what I was doing to her. I told her that if she told anybody, she would be put into a home and that I'd go to prison. I mean, it never felt like what I was doing to her was wrong, but I knew from what I saw on TV that guys went to jail for molesting and rape and stuff like that. I really didn't care too much or think I'd get caught. I always drank a lot before I did anything to her. I don't know why I drank so much, although I can't blame the booze for what I did. Drinking gave me the courage to go ahead and act out what I wanted to do anyhow. So this went on for a long time. I wasn't involved with any adults at the time. I used to baby-sit for Becky and her younger sister—Katie was about two years younger than Becky—and Becky would talk her sister into performing the act of sodomy with me. She also let me fondle her and perform acts of sodomy on her. From the way Katie was acting, she didn't really want to do it. I asked her if she wanted to do it or not, but she would never answer me. So I can't actually say that she wanted to do it or she didn't, but Katie is the one who eventually turned me in. Her mom, my sister Joy—who was one of the sisters I had sex with when we were younger—also made a statement against me, so

I went to prison for one-and-a-half to three years. My family couldn't believe it. I never admitted to them that I did it, so they didn't believe that my own sister and nieces would say something so bad about me.

After I got out of the state prison, I moved into my other sister's house. This was my sister Dorothy, who was the other one I messed around with when we were kids. Dorothy had gotten real mad with Joy when Joy made a statement against me. She sort of disowned Joy for a while. I was on welfare for the first months after I got out of prison, so while she was at work, I'd watch her two boys. After six months, I got a steady job. I was getting food stamps, but I never seen them; my sister Dorothy was always using them. She was always complaining that I was eating too much. Dorothy and me got into lots of arguments. Finally, I moved upstairs, which was empty. Since I was up there drinking heavily and my beer was always warm, she gave me a refrigerator, couch, and bed, along with pots and pans she didn't want. I don't know what was running through her mind then, but she didn't want me to watch her boys no more. Even though I was on parole, I had been watching her kids and drinking a lot. But I never molested her boys. It was always girls I was attracted to. I knew what the boys looked like, and there was only one way to penetrate a boy, while there were at least a couple of good ways to penetrate a woman or a girl.

When I moved upstairs, I got a check from welfare but I told my caseworker that I had a steady job. She told me to use it since it was in my name, but I sent it back because I didn't want nothing to do with it. Pretty soon, I could afford to get my own car, and my sister started complaining that I was always parking on the wrong side. It was just one more thing we'd argue over. So she finally took her family and moved out.

I went to a rescue mission church every Sunday, and I let it be known that I was looking for somebody to move into my house. Some people told me that they knew someone who needed a place. Turns out it was for the family of a girl I used to fool around with quite a bit when we were little kids. Her name was Kathy. So she moved in with her husband and daughter, Sally. My sisters told me that I'd have problems with them and warned me not to let them move in. I should have listened to them. Sally was about six or seven years old, and she had her own bedroom. Her father and mother's bedroom was straight across from it. There were two bathrooms, one down the hall and the other off Kathy and her husband's bedroom. If Sally had to go to the bathroom at night, she had to go through her father and mother's bedroom and use that one.

I started messing with her pretty quick. She didn't mind. Every time her mother and father had to go someplace, they would leave Sally with me. If I was just getting back home from a day of work, Kathy would ask me if Sally could come upstairs for a while so Joe and her could go to the store. So I had ready access to her. I asked Sally if it would be okay if I touched her, and she said yes. She was a virgin, but she had real problems sleeping at night. When Sally would stay overnight at anybody else's house, she wouldn't sleep. She had that habit way before I ever knew her. Her parents said that she wet the bed every night. So I figured that maybe her father or somebody else might have touched her before I came along, but I could never prove it. I tried to catch them a few times. I thought maybe Joe, Sally's father, might be sneaking into her room to mess around with her. One morning, I know distinctly that I came out and saw Joe running out of Sally's bedroom. The only thing he had on was his underwear. One day, Kathy asked me if I was in Sally's room last night. I said, "No, why?" "Well, Sally was laying there with her leg hanging over the bed when I went in to get her up," Kathy said to me, "and her panties were down." A lot of times when I got really depressed, I'd close my door and keep my dogs in my room and drink a six or twelve pack of beer until I'd pass out. But I didn't recall leaving my room that night.

Kathy wanted to pick up where we left off as kids. She wanted me to have sexual intercourse with her. Her husband, Joe, gave me permission to have sexual intercourse with her if I wanted to. Sometimes, I'd be fondling Kathy, and Sally would be on the other side of me, and I'd be drinking and fondling Sally, too. Kathy had no problem with me doing that to Sally. No problem at all. To this day, I'm sure that Sally's father was messing with her. And her Uncle Bob, too—he got five years' probation or something like that for fondling her. Sally made a statement about how when she'd stay at his place, she'd get up in the night to go to the bathroom, and he'd follow her in there and start feeling her up.

This thing with Kathy and Sally went on for about a year. To be honest, I don't really know what attracted me to Sally. There was just something about her. I feel like all my victims thought I wasn't too bad, that I was an okay person. A few of my victims in the family, like one of my nieces, still write to me in prison. I wrote back to that niece and explained to her everything, right from the beginning of my life all the way up to when I was molested, and told her about all of my victims. I said to her, "You're one of my victims, too." She wrote back to me and said that she didn't remember nothing ever happening, and that whatever did happen was under the bridge and in the past.

Overall, I had roughly about five victims. I can't recall all of their names, but the way I look at it now is that I don't hold no grudges against none of my victims for turning me in and having me arrested. At first, I hated my niece Katie for turning me in, but then I thought about it and saw her point.

When Sally spoke out against me and her mother, I told the cop in charge that if you see Sally, tell her I said thanks, I hold no grudges against her. I said she did the right thing by doing what she did and that she'd be in a better place than when she was with her mother and father. She reported it in school through her counselor, and they called the cops. Underneath, I was very relieved when Sally turned me in. I was feeling guilty, but I was also thinking about making a statement about Joe to have him investigated, because if they asked Sally if her father or anybody else had been touching her, she would never answer. So Kathy got one year's probation and I was put into prison. I was given a six- to twelve-year sentence.

In a way, I think I deserve my sentence. The reason why I say yes is because it gives me more time to work on myself—find out where I made the mistakes, why I did the things I did—so when I get back out on the street, I ain't going to do it again. I know it is going to be a rough life out there. You see, you got that Megan's Law now where they can call the police department and find out if there's any sex offenders in their neighborhood. After I get out there, I ain't going to guarantee myself anything. Once you pass through that gate, there is no guarantee that you ain't going to screw up again. I know that. What I'm most afraid of is what I might do to myself. I know I ain't going to take the pressure out there, especially with Megan's Law and people calling me sex offender, baby raper, or whatever. Like the names they called us when we got back from Vietnam. I can't take that kind of pressure. And then again, I could take it out on somebody else. There is that possibility because I've done it before. When I'm drinking, I'm capable of a lot of stuff.

I have had blackout spells before. Once, I went after my younger brother. It took two of my brothers, my father, and my uncle to pry my hands off his throat. I didn't realize that my hands were around his neck until he started to turn blue. I didn't realize what I was doing. Another time was when I was down in Fort Dix. This was back in the 1970s, when I was still married to my wife. I had her and the two kids down there. I went to a military funeral. A friend of mine had got blown away in Vietnam just before it ended. I turned around and left. I started drinking beer on the way back to the compound. When I got to my house, I told my wife to fix me a drink, and she gave me some whiskey. I downed it and then said for her to make me another one. I downed that, too. After I drank a third one, that's all I remember. Somebody called the military police. I put seven MPs in the hospital, and I don't even remember touching them. The only thing I remember is getting up out of the corner from behind the recliner chair and having an MP ask me if I would come peacefully. I said yes and I got up, and then that's all I remember. I don't know if I threatened my wife or did anything to my two daughters. I don't believe I did, to the best of my knowledge. They took me to jail or a hospital, one or the other first. They had me strapped down. I remember getting my hands loose and unfastening my legs. I was told I hit doctors. How they managed to subdue me, I don't know.

So I don't know what I might do if the pressure's too much. I know in prison you can get booze and drugs if you really want it bad enough. But I stay away from it. Now and then, I think about taking my own life. I told one of my counselors that I'm not afraid of pain. I showed him the scars I have on my arm from playing chicken with my brother. But I don't think of suicide as much now as when I first came into the system. It's not the physical pain that I can't deal with. It's what's inside of me, knowing the things I've done and what other people might do to me. I actually think Megan's Law is a good law because I think that people should be able to know if there's a sex offender in their neighborhood. But as far as some states go, they reveal the names of the offender and even other information. I don't think that is right. That's getting into the person's privacy. If that happens to me, and somebody else doesn't take my life, then I might end up doing it myself. Once I leave that gate, what do I got?

Sex offenders need to be given a lot of time to think about what they did, who they did it with, and why they did it. Plus, they need to get treatment for it. That is the most important thing. If you don't have therapy in prison, then the guy's probably going to go back out into the world and do his crime all over again. In our groups, we got guys talking about their past, which is good. You can listen to other guys talk, and you can pick out a little part in their stories that might pertain to your own life. The most important thing for me is to know myself, know my own shortcomings. If I know what my triggers are, I can work on staying away from them. It might be like giving a child a bath, for instance. When Sally's parents were working, I had to give her a bath every once in a while. So one of my triggers might be seeing a child nude and touching her while washing her. Another thing might be sex books like *Playboy*. That might trigger my impulses to molest a child. I used to read a lot of pornography. I used to watch tapes. As a matter of fact, one night I was watching one when Sally was there. I turned it off. She said, "No, I want to watch it." I don't know why. But I took it out, anyway, and put in a Ninja Turtles tape for her.

I also need to stay away from alcohol and get into an Alcoholics Anonymous group. When I came out of prison after my first bid, I was in an AA group. At that time, I seen people who were in AA go out after they got done talking and go right up the street to the nearest bar for a drink. So I just dropped AA completely and went back to drinking. I need to keep up my sobriety. Here in prison,

I drink nothing but coffee, mostly. Plus, I take an antidepressant to calm my nerves at night, which helps me sleep. I started out at 100 milligrams, but now I'm up to 200 milligrams. I'll stay on 200 milligrams for a couple of months. Then if it don't work and I start waking up two or three times a night again, I'll have them increase it, because every now and then I'll dream about the things that I did in my past. I'll dream about beating my mother and father. I'll dream about beating my brother and seeing him laid out in his coffin. I asked a psychiatrist what that dream means, but he couldn't give me no answer.

So I don't really know what I'll do when I get out. When other guys ask me what I'll do, I tell them I'll sleep on the darn streets in a box until I find a place and a job. What I want to do is get a job on a farm out in the country. If I can get out in the country and away from the city, away from everybody, away from kids and society itself, then I will be happy.

I want everybody to know for a fact that I'm sorry for my crimes. I'm in therapy to help me find out where I made my mistakes and correct them, so that when I get back out there I don't do it again. I need help; I know that. Come hell or high water, I got to find out why I made my mistakes. I have to stay away from my triggers. The way I look at it is that parents should explain to their kids what sex is about. They need to tell their kids to stay away from strangers, don't get too close if a guy asks you a question from a parked car, and if somebody approaches them to tell a teacher or some other grown-up. I'm going to stick to my program and hopefully I can get myself squared away. I don't want to screw up my life all over again.

Summary

Ben presents himself as an ultimately destructive individual, riddled with self-loathing, anger, confusion, and depression. His self-narrative alternately shows him expressing a desire to "do his duty" as a good son and soldier and automatically enacting his warped value system with the most readily available object, preferably a little girl.

From his story, one gets the impression that he has struggled with depression for most of his life. As a child, he lacked privacy and security as he was shuttled back and forth between homes and caregivers. Although his uncle molested Ben as a child and it left him sullen and silent, Ben became obsessed with sex, which seems to have been a fairly common pastime in his family. So Ben grew into a man with conflicting needs. Ben used the military to escape the chaos of his family life and as a source of discipline and a potential way to fulfill his ultimate goal, which was death. Yet although he served tours of duty in the midst of danger, he emerged relatively unscathed, with Purple Hearts to his credit. So while many of his friends and colleagues left Vietnam in body bags, Ben arrived back stateside physically intact but even more emotionally damaged than when he was first drafted.

Aside from military service, Ben exhibits a lack of ambition. Although he took pride in getting off welfare as soon as he could procure a job, he seems to have been content with staying in the same sort of circumstances that characterized his impoverished childhood. Or perhaps he was simply too depressed to have the energy to actively seek out new opportunities. Certainly, he was quick to take advantage of the opportunity to molest a little girl, if she happened to be accessible without much effort on his part. Although his energy may have flagged in other areas of his life, he enthusiastically fulfilled his sexual urges.

These sexual desires seem to have been the major factor controlling Ben's life. As a child, he was surrounded by people with no sexual boundaries. Although he was angry with his parents, his siblings, and the poverty of his environment, he still tried to do the right thing. Then when he was drafted, he did his duty in the service, although "I wanted to get myself blown away." Ben even tried to do his duty by marrying his girlfriend when she was pregnant with another man's child. Ben did not go out of his way, but he was willing to make sacrifices if the opportunity presented itself.

Ben says that he believes he deserved the sentence he received. However, it seems clear that Ben has a long way to go before he will be able to control himself outside of prison. Although Ben seems to wait passively for whatever life throws his way, he admits that he has the tendency to react aggressively to stress. He says that he occasionally thinks about committing suicide, but his self-narrative suggests it would be uncharacteristic for Ben to pursue any action, let alone taking his own life. Whether because he is clinically depressed or due to some personality quirk, Ben doesn't seek out opportunities but accepts them when they become available.

Since Ben has been an opportunistic child molester, he admits that he will have to avoid being alone with children for the rest of his life. However, at this point, Ben doesn't seem strong enough to be able to actively control his impulses, so the outlook is bleak. Unless he can break out of his passive-aggressive approach to life, he seems doomed to be swept along by lethargy and tempted by opportunity.

~

CHAPTER TEN

Matthew—The Lost Boy

Matthew was slight and boyishly good-looking. His prematurely graying hair, worn past his shoulders, served to merely emphasize his youth. He looked like a throwback to the 1980s, with a carefully blow-dried mullet hairstyle that would have seemed incongruous on a college campus, let alone in a prison. His eyes were large and velvety brown; he used them to great effect in a self-conscious effort to be charming. Although Matthew claimed to have had many different jobs since age eighteen, his favorites were disk jockey stints at small-town radio stations, which fed his need for attention and adulation. His radio experience showed in the studiously deep, animated voice that he used when speaking about fairly superficial aspects of his life. When the interview moved to more personal information, the persona seemed to waver, a wary anxiety peering through the apparent confidence. At such times, he looked all of twelve years old, seemingly astounded that he possessed the physical characteristics of an adult. It became obvious to me that Matthew knew how to use his charm to influence and potentially manipulate other people. Lurking beneath the boyish exterior was a man whose motivations were anything but innocent.

Matthew's Story

I probably had my first sexual experience at three years old. I'd play the money-in-the-pocket game with my grandfather. I'd reach into his pocket, and it would be a way of fondling him while trying to reach for a certain coin.

I had no idea it was a sexual thing until I got older. The game basically went on until I was seven or eight years old.

When I was around seven, I went to first grade. I liked to hang around with older kids. I remember when I was seven, there was a kid like a grade higher—maybe he was eight or nine—and I spent the night at his house. I remember him performing anal sex on me more or less, also touching me and having me touch him. It was kind of a weird experience. I didn't really know what to make of it, but I was young and it only happened on one occasion. So life went on.

When I was in high school, at that point, my parents were divorced and my father moved about five minutes down the street. Then my mother couldn't afford the big house we were living in, and we moved about forty minutes away from my dad. They actually got along okay. They still talk today. My father has a girlfriend that he apparently lives with, and my mother is remarried. But at the time it happened, my sister and me—we had no idea that it was going to happen. Me and my sister thought that our parents got along great and that everything was hunky-dory. One day, my mother picked up a dish in the kitchen and threw it at my father and said, "I'm getting a divorce." I think my mom did that because she felt that he spent too much time in front of the TV watching football and going out drinking with his friends. I consider my father an alcoholic. He almost lost one of his jobs through that. He worked pretty high up in government, but then his boss left and he lost his job, too.

During ninth grade, I started hanging out with a new group of friends. I was in a new house by then, and I got to know some of the older crowd as well. I may have been only thirteen, but I was hanging out with fifteen-, six-teen-, seventeen-year-olds because they lived within biking distance from where I lived. One of the kids who was sixteen that I hung out with a lot was Jewish. I was Catholic, so we didn't have much in common, but I would occasionally go to Jewish worship with him to check it out. I would wear one of those hats or whatever they are called on my head. Here was this person who had a father and a mother and an older brother and his grandparents all living together. They were all nice people.

He would sometimes spend the night at my mother's or father's house, and I spent a couple of nights at his house. One night, he was at my father's house with me. When it was time to go to bed—he slept on a cot and I slept on my bed—we got into a conversation about girls. "Do you have a girlfriend?" he asked. I'm like, "Well, no." "Well, have you ever had a blow job?" Oral sex is what he actually said. And I was like, "Ah, no." I didn't even relate back to the other time when I was three with my grandfather. I didn't relate back to that until I was a lot older, like twenty-three or twenty-four. So we continued the conversation about girls and the different things we had done with them, and basically all we had done at that point was give a passionate kiss. I don't know how he jumped into it, but he said, "I could show you how oral sex feels, and if you like it, maybe you could do it to me, too." I was like, "Well, whatever." I didn't find anything wrong with it at the time. I let him perform oral sex on me, and then I eventually tried it on him. There were no orgasms or anything like that. It was just back and forth to each other. I enjoyed it, it felt good, but I didn't know what would come of it. I knew he'd be quiet and ready to throw the covers over me if my father walked out of his room. So I think in the back of my head, I must have thought it was a little bit wrong. After that first incident, it happened on a few more occasions when he'd spend the night. Then his family moved to another state, so he left me.

From that point on, I still wanted it. But I didn't have any girls to go out with, so I started thinking, "Now who can I do this with?" At the time, where I was living, it was all either really young kids, all about three or four or five years old, and one kid I liked who was about ten or eleven. I used to play football with him, and we'd go on rock hunts and stuff in my neighborhood. I recall one day watching TV or something at my house and I said, "I want to show you something." I took him upstairs where I had some dirty magazines, and I let him look through them. I could tell he was being aroused by it. To tell you the truth, I have no idea where I got the magazines. I think someone either gave them to me or maybe I got them from my father's house. I don't think I bought them. They don't sell them to kids that young. Maybe I stole them. I can't really remember.

Wait, let me back up for a second. Before I did anything with this kid, I remember going to a bookstore and buying a book called *Am I Normal?* I still have that book packed away somewhere. It had to do with sexual growing up. I don't know why I bought it; I felt stupid, but I bought it, anyway. So anyhow, I called this kid up to my room and we looked through the magazines. Then I went into the bathroom and stripped down. Usually, I'm not the type to do that—I mean, I never really would plan something like that, but it would just happen. So it's a shock to me today when I realize that I must have planned out that first time. When I walked in, he said, "What are you doing?" "Well," I said, "we're studying the human body in my biology class at school and I want you to take some pictures of me without my clothes on." He just agreed; he wasn't too shocked or anything like that. So he took the pictures and then I said, "Would you let me take some pictures of you?" And he said, "Yeah." So I took a couple of pictures of him, and then he sat down.

He was naked. He started flipping through the magazines, and he had an erection. I went over and touched him. We got into a conversation about whether he had ever had oral sex. I said, "Well, let's make a deal. I'll do it if you do it." I think I went first—yeah, I'm pretty sure I went first. Then he did it to me and we went back and forth. Again, there was no orgasm or ejaculation. To me, it was consensual. I was almost sixteen at the time and he was about eleven, so I mean, I hadn't hit the adulthood point, yet. So we did it off and on for a few months, then he came up and told me that the guidance department at school wanted to talk to him. That was because I got the pictures developed at the drug store. I mean, it's not like I used an instant camera, or then I probably wouldn't be here today. I guess several copies of the prints were sent to the FBI, so I was being watched. Of course, our faces were also in the picture, so they knew who we were.

After he told me that, I took the pictures I had at my house and put them in the fireplace to burn them. I was scared for the next few days. One day, I said to my mother, "I need to tell you something." I knew at this point that something was probably going to happen. I was just one week away from my sixteenth birthday. I was ashamed to bring it to my mother's attention, but I didn't want someone else ringing the doorbell to tell her. She was a little shocked, but I believe she started crying, too. She didn't know how to react at the time. At least she knew, and that made me feel a little bit better. I had no choice at this point to tell her something, because I had the feeling that the knock on the door was coming. I figured I didn't have much time.

So a week went by, and like two days after I turned sixteen, the doorbell rang. This was about 8:30 at night, and it was strange that the doorbell would even be ringing at that time, since it was just me and my mother living in the house, with my sister away at college. So my mother got out of the chair—we were both watching TV—and we're both looking at each other kind of nervously. She headed toward the door. It was a tall figure, so we thought it was our next-door neighbor. Then she opened it up, and three guys came in. They handcuffed me, read my rights, said I was being charged with sexual abuse, and took me to court. This is just as I turned sixteen. My father had no idea. My mother may have talked to him beforehand about it, but I don't think she did. I think she just told him about the whole situation that night. I did not have a very close relationship with him. My mother and father wanted to get me out right away, but since I could not see the judge that night no matter what, I had to spend the night in the county jail.

I got to the county jail about 1 a.m. I was there until 4 p.m. the next day. So it was a long haul—it was about sixteen hours, and it just seemed like the longest night. We went in and out of court for almost a year, and I ended up getting five years' probation. My parents were definitely supportive of me. I was on probation for a good four-and-a-half years with no problem. My father knew some people who kept it out of the newspapers. Then I violated probation. The first violation was a technical violation, and what the hell, I can't recall what the second violation was for. I think it was because I was working out of state and I was in the company of a minor even though the mother was present. I spent thirty-seven days in the county jail. I was older, though, than the first time. Time seemed to go by really slow. I was on a mop gang, so I mopped three times a day. I wasn't in a cell, though. I was put in a dorm, and that again had to do with my father knowing the sheriff who ran the jail. It wasn't too bad. I remember getting punched in the face with somebody's chair. That was probably the worst night I had there. Nobody knew why I was there. I'd just make something up when they asked, something about burglary or drugs.

After I got out of jail that time, my probation became intensive. They needed to know where I was going two or three times a week instead of once a week or every other week. By this time, my mom had gotten remarried and it was me and my sister, two stepbrothers, and two stepsisters. We moved again and got a bigger house. It was really weird at first. We had to deal with all these new personalities, but having two stepbrothers around was kind of good for me. Me and my sister, we got along fairly well. However, I was never able to talk to her about anything. If I had a brother, I probably would have done more talking. And maybe this wouldn't have happened, since I'd have done experimentation with my brother.

We all eventually got adjusted. I continued on probation, so my social life was really terrible. I mean, I worked, and that was about all. I had an 11 p.m. curfew, so it was hard to go out, especially as I got older. It left me with not too many friends. I didn't really get to date much. Back in ninth grade, I had a girlfriend, and we were together for a long time, at least a year. But then again, it wasn't anything big—we just hung out after school. I never went to my junior or senior prom at my own school. I only went to proms at schools where nobody really knew me. I felt awkward with kids at my own school.

I met a lot of girls from other schools at my job, which was down the road from my house. I worked at a skating rink, and attached to it was a nonalcoholic dance club. I started out there as a part-time gate guard on the weekends. Then I took on the part-time/full-time position on the weekends. I was doing Friday nights, all day Saturday, Saturday nights, and all day Sunday as a full-time guard. I did meet a lot of girls there who were my age and a lot younger that looked my age. I worked there for four years, from the time I was seventeen to when I was in my twenties. It was the best job in the world. Being the gate guard, I had total authority. I liked the control aspect of that. I never really had control of things in my life where I was the boss. As the gate guard, I didn't have to answer to anybody. I skated around, and if somebody fell down, I helped them up. I helped some of the younger kids skate around when necessary. I got to blow the whistle at those who were speed skating and screaming. I'd make them sit down, and they would give me a hard time, but it was just little kid stuff. I loved it.

I got violated on probation a second time because there was also some undercover officers that worked security there on their days off. I knew that these guys were police officers, too. Sometimes they brought their kids in with them. One night an officer's kid asked me, "Could you take me next door to get a soda?" We both went to the father and he said, "Yeah, no problem." His father may or may not have known I was on probation—I don't know, probably not. So we went over and got soda and candy. The store was right next door to the rink, but it was winter, so I drove over. We were drinking our soda in the car. Then the kid noticed one of my dirty magazines in the backseat, and so he grabbed it. I had nothing to do with handing it to him or anything like that at this time. I knew I was on probation and was to have no unsupervised contact whatsoever, but I just totally put that in the back of my mind and forgot about it. As long as the cops don't see it, that was justification.

So he saw the magazine and grabbed it, and I kind of grabbed it out of his hands and threw it back into the backseat. He said, "Just let me look at it." So I let him look at it and that was it. That was all that happened. He looked at it and we drove back. A few weeks later, I hopped into my car to go to work. There was an unmarked car waiting for me. They put the flashing light on their car and pulled me over. They wouldn't even let me drive the car back into my driveway; they had it towed and tagged. That pissed me off. I had endangered the welfare of a minor by letting him look at that book. Nothing ever occurred between me and this individual in a sexual manner other than looking at the book. Never had any talks about it or anything. So another three years was added onto my five-year probation.

So I just continued on probation for a while, then I graduated from high school and went to a radio school. I got a job at a radio station, and my probation allowed me to travel back and forth to my job. When I worked there, I got involved with an older woman. I was like nineteen or twenty at the time, and she was like forty-five, and she had what I believe was a nine-year-old son. I believe she became infatuated with me because I worked at the radio station. There wasn't really much appeal for me at first; she was a little bit overweight and I just wasn't really attracted at all. But she asked me to go for a cup of coffee one day, and I said, "okay," you know, as a friend. I got to get known somehow, so she can have coffee with me and then go tell her friends that she had coffee with so-and-so from the radio. So I did that, and then it got to be a dinner thing. Then her son wanted to come over to the station and hang out because it was so cool, you know, to see the equipment or whatever. So he'd see me talk a lot when I was on the air. A couple of times he brought his friends over, and I let them in just to watch. Nothing sexual ever happened with any of them. However, in the back of my mind, I would say now that probably I was thinking down the road that something could happen. But it never came to that point. I never did anything with any of the boys at the roller rink, either. Occasionally, there would be one or two that I might be attracted to, and I tried to get to know them a little more, but that was kind of hard to do.

My relationship with this woman got to be sexual. It did get to the point where I sat down and told her that I was on probation. After that, it turned a little more romantic with her. I tried to have intercourse with her, but it just didn't work out. I couldn't really penetrate her. I couldn't get a full erection. Whether it was because I wasn't really attracted or what the problem was, I'm not sure. She was also sitting there saying, "Go on, I want to have your baby, I want to have your baby." It was freaking me out, you know. She was saying she loved me and all this stuff, and I was just like, "Well, I don't love this woman." I think that I was just trying to do it because I hadn't had intercourse in my life, and I was at the point where I had to try it and get it over with.

Maybe I just wanted to be with her because she had a son. I definitely enjoyed doing things with him. Anyway, it was found out from probation— either through her or the authorities, I don't know—that I was doing things with her and her son, so I was brought down to probation. As soon as I walked into the room, boom, they handcuffed me and brought me up for the violation in front of the judge at town court. I was bailed out right away and back at work later on that day. I guessed that really pissed off my probation officer because he called me at work. He's like, "Hey, how are you doing? There's going to be a court date down the road. Oh, and by the way, there are a couple of things I need to see you about tomorrow." I thought, "Oh no." So I went down the next day, and they handcuffed me again and this time took me to county court. They violated me through town court, and the probation officer didn't like that I got right out, so the next day they violated me through the county court. This guy hated me. Disliked me terribly. He made sure that I ended up going to prison this time.

Thanks to people my father knew, I only had to spend a week at the county jail before I got transferred into the prison. My father made sure I got into a program that was just started there for sex offenders. Up until this point, both of my parents didn't think it was a problem. They just thought it had been a one-time thing. I did not feel safe at all there. You'd be in the general population first, and then they would pack you up and put you in the sex offenders' dorm, so everybody knew. The sex offenders went to chow together and had a table together, so everybody knew what we had done. I never had any problems, but I did know of other people I talked with who did. I did four months there, and then I was able to get transferred to another correctional facility. I spent about eight months there. The chaplain liked me and was very nice to me. I attended services there and was confirmed. My family came up for that. Since I had a good relationship with this chaplain and he knew someone on the board, I guess he put in a good word for me and I made the first parole board. No other sex offender was making the board, but I did. So I did less than a year on my one- to three-year conviction, then got out and violated with this new charge that I'm here for. After getting out on parole, I lived at home for a while and I went to college. While I was on probation, I worked at a campground, I worked at the mall, I worked at a couple of radio stations. I became well known by everybody; all the kids at the major schools in the area knew me. They all caught my radio show. At a career day at one school, I was one of the speakers. Nobody knew I was on probation as a sex offender. Everybody knew me under my radio-personality name, so I was basically safe.

Another thing that made me popular in the area was having newspaper articles printed about my radio career. There was one caller that I talked out of suicide. After the newspaper article appeared about me, I got involved with the family of this lady I went to college with. She was seeing this guy who had a son and a daughter, and they would come over to this lady's house a lot while I was over there hanging out. I became friends with the whole family, and the son would accompany me to the radio station. He'd be there until like one or two in the morning when I worked, and then they would close the station down for the night. Since it was so late, most of the time he would spend the night at my apartment. He slept on the cot, and I slept on the bed. I never was involved with him—no oral sex—but I believe I wanted that. I just never brought up that fact.

I remember once he grabbed himself and made a wise remark to me. It was just kidding around, and I said something like, "Well, take it out and bury it." And he took it out and showed it to me. That was basically the extent that things went with him at the time. However, I said to myself, "Well, this kid showed me his private area. If he did this, how far could he go?" So I was trying to think of ways where I could convince him that it was okay. I had to come up with a new technique other than the girlfriend routine because he had already told me that a girl gave him oral sex when he was real young, like five. I can't remember what I was saying, but he came out with the question, "Well, are you gay?" And I said, "No, no, no." I stopped it right there. This was because I think I was asking him to do some wild stuff, like strip and run down the back staircase in my apartment building. It was really weird. I was trying to think of ways that could lead into something happening, but I just didn't feel comfortable for some reason. I couldn't do it. When I was up on this new charge, this kid stated to the authorities that once when he fell asleep I pulled down the covers and had my hand on his leg. Then I went up under the underwear and touched one of his testicles. To be totally honest, I do not remember doing this. He also stated that I went by his stomach and touched his penis. Now, I don't call it denial, but I don't remember anything. I know that I am capable of doing it, and probably I did do it. I don't know if I am blocking it out or where it is in my memory, but I don't recall doing that at all. However, I went along with it and admitted that I had done it.

I've never really done anything like go to a schoolyard, park, or drive by anywhere to see any kid that might be attractive. I've had driving restrictions on me, but I'm not like that at all. In all of my incidences, it had to do with kids I've known. Basically, the relationships are based on our common personalities. Like this one kid in my apartment building—that didn't happen until his father clearly knew me well enough and was reassured by his girlfriend that I was okay. All my relationships I've known people at least a year before anything ever took place. I had to get to know them first. Let them show me that they really cared or loved me or were just really happy when I was around and listening to them and doing stuff with them. That was the main thing that I wanted. It wasn't that I just wanted the sexual encounter. I wanted someone to look up to me. I wanted the kid to look up to me and give me the attention that I wasn't getting elsewhere from my mother or father or peers or whatever. Or even a girlfriend. I wasn't getting any attention there, so I would seek it elsewhere, around boys that were ten or eleven years old. Like this kid. He looked up to me and thought I was great—I was on the radio and a popular guy, a celebrity, you know. I felt really good about that.

This time, my parole was worse because they put me on a strict curfew. I couldn't do anything with friends. I couldn't leave the state to do anything. I even had to call if I wanted to go twenty minutes to my father's house, which was across the county line. I had driving restrictions as well. When these charges came out, I don't know what my friend's reaction was, since it was with her boyfriend's son. I never knew. When I went to the county jail on the parole violation, I wrote a twelve-page letter—my whole life history and how I felt bad about what I did, and if there was any way I could help, let me know. I never got a response.

One weekend, I went to an AA [Alcoholics Anonymous] dance with another friend. We weren't having alcohol problems, but my friend was the deejay there. I met this girl. She didn't have an alcohol problem, either; she was with a friend. She was like sixteen or seventeen at the time when I met her and we danced. Later, I met everybody in her family. And they are still supportive of me today. Her mother still writes to me occasionally. We were together for about a year. I found her attractive. There was oral sex between us. It was a good relationship. Her basic reason for breaking up with me was that they ended up knowing my whole story. Her nephews were questioned by local authorities to see if I did anything to them. One of them said no and one of them said yes. They were eight and eleven, I believe. The one that said yes was the eleven-year-old. I did touch him on one occasion when he was kind of halfway asleep. I just let it happen. So that threw a big hate between my girlfriend's sister, who is this boy's mother, and me. She just couldn't stand me; she said she wanted to kill me.

Today, again we have a good relationship. When I was out of prison last time, all of us went out to eat: my girlfriend's mother, sister, and grandmother. We'd all go to bingo together or go on a hike or whatever. Sometimes the kids would be there, and sometimes they wouldn't. One time, I had to sleep on their couch because I was there kind of late. They even let me sleep on the couch when everybody was there. So her sister doesn't have any more hard feelings toward me. When the authorities asked her last time if she wanted to press charges, she said, "Well, it looks like he will have to do time for the other kid who is my son's friend, so no, I don't want to." I think I am more of a love addict than a sex addict. I don't necessarily need that sexual gratification right away. I need love and the emotional, caring kind of support. I wasn't doing it as hatred or malice or to be in control. I was doing it as a way to show that I care for them and I wanted them to do the same to show how much they cared for me. I didn't think of it as a game or anything; it had to be something we both agreed on. I'm not the type of person that forces a person. I didn't get enough of that kind of love from my girlfriend. She was very moody. She was also kind of going back and forth to her first love—I'll call him Brandon. She would say, "Well, I'm just going out with you as friends," and she would play games with me and stuff like that. It got to the point where last year when we weren't going out, I was still doing things with her mother and sister, and her and Brandon would be there, too. She would make out with Brandon in front of me, so it was a real awkward situation. I felt really stupid.

I've always felt kind of stupid around girls. I remember when I was around twelve years old and I was in a room with this girl. She tried to give me this big long tongue kiss. I don't know if I choked then or what I was doing, but I pulled away. She was older, like sixteen or seventeen, and she kind of laughed. She decided to make fun of me and tell everybody about it. That was really painful, and it hurt my self-esteem. It came to the point where I was kissing my hand trying to do it right. I even asked my sister once, "Well, how do you make out?" I remember my sister going up to this tree and trying to show me how to make out.

I liked girls, though. But I had a relationship with a guy once. We worked at the same radio station together. He talked with a real high voice, the kind of voice that you would never think would be on the radio. But it was a small radio station, and they hired him for part time. We got to talk since he was there during my shift. There were times I worked so much I'd take a blanket and crash in the conference room overnight because I wasn't going to drive back and forth. He'd work the overnight a lot, too, so we got to know each other pretty well. He spent a couple of nights at my parents' house, and I spent some time at his house. Now, I didn't think of him as gay at this point, because he had a girlfriend for like two years he recently broke up with. I just talked to him the other day.

It did get to the point with him where there was touching and oral sex. I mooned him one day when we were down in my basement, and he kind of ran up and pulled out his dick and slapped my butt or something like that. That led to touching and oral sex, and I think I had anal sex with him once. That happened on a few occasions, and then we stopped. It would happen after we went to bed. He would lay down and pretend he was asleep, and I would do it. But then it got to the point where I didn't want to do it anymore. I wasn't getting anything out of it, really. It wasn't feeding my craving or whatever. And then it stopped after that.

I don't masturbate to guy stuff. My counselor told me I must be fantasizing about kids when I masturbate, but I don't really do that. Even in prison, I'm not really fantasizing about kids. There will be times when I'm sleeping and I'll get to the point where I think I'll have a wet dream and yeah, in the dream I might think about a male child having oral sex. It will get to the point where I'm about to ejaculate without even touching myself. I've been masturbating a couple of times a week so I won't have that kind of wet dream. Masturbation is nothing. It's just a release for me. It's just something I've got to do or I'll have wet dreams about kids. But that's not fantasizing. I mean, I don't sit down and deliberately get turned on by thinking about boys.

I don't know why I am the way I am. I believe it has something to do with not getting enough attention from my father growing up. I got quite a bit of attention from my mother. I remember that my father wasn't there even when he was home. Like, my mother would say, "He's in front of the TV." And he'd say, "Oh, hi, how are you?" and then go back to watching his show. That was it—there wasn't any emotional tie. Even today, there isn't. His way of showing us that he loves us is that he'll take my sister and me out to dinner once a month.

I have accomplished a lot this time I've been in prison. I feel a big accomplishment is that we've gotten out of the stage of a "one-time thing" to "this is a problem." Even though I know it is wrong, somewhere along the line I gave myself justification to do it. In the future, I have to pursue a living arrangement with another friend or something like that. When I was alone, I got kind of lonely. I'd go home to an empty apartment—just me and my cat. I would want to have people over. If kids wanted to come and use my microphones and speakers, they could come over and do it. I think it's because I didn't have the affection that I needed when I was growing up. I was always looking for that. Now that I know that I have the problem, I have to look at ways of keeping myself safe. Now that I know what the problem is, I can work on it. I'm aware of it. So I have to get the kind of support and love I look for in a relationship with a female. I'll have to be more aggressive in that way. I need to leave time open for a social life. In all my jobs, I always worked the night shifts so I wouldn't get out in time to go anywhere or do anything.

I wish I had left more time to go out with people, like this girl Melissa I went to high school with. I really liked her. I should have pursued something with her, but I didn't have the feeling she felt the same way. After she got involved with this other guy, she told me, "All during high school, I had a crush on you." I said, "Well, it's too late now, but you should have told me. I mean, I have a problem with my attention span—I don't pick up things very easily. You should have said, look, I have a crush on you. I'd take it from there." So I could have had a more meaningful relationship with her. She knows everything about me, everything I have been through. To this day, my mother will say, "Well, you must be gay." I told Melissa this, and she called my mother and said, "He's not gay. We've done a few things." I don't consider myself bisexual, either. I'm not really attracted to men my age or older. I don't even fantasize about it. I mean, it happened on occasion, but that was it, and I think maybe it happened because I felt it was a safer way than finding a minor to do it with.

Until the last program I had, none of the other programs I went into worked. I had therapists tell my parents, "He doesn't have a problem." I convinced them that I didn't have a problem. But the last program was where I hit bottom. I know I don't want to go back to prison. I go to SAL [Sex and Love Addicts] and SAA [Sex Addicts Anonymous] groups and those are more effective than any individual counseling I have been in. You're in a group setting—you don't have some therapist telling you what to do. You have other people that have been in the same situation, and you can all talk about your stories. Prison was not what I needed. I think I needed a long-term residential-type program. I needed to have some sort of living arrangement where I would have an apartment but go on a daily basis to a program after being an in-patient for a couple of weeks. That would keep me in line so I wouldn't think about going out and getting in trouble. Now what I need is to find a woman or something like that, and if she has kids, tell her straight up what the deal is. Tell her I shouldn't be around them. Well, maybe I shouldn't find a woman with kids.

Prison has not done a lot to help me. Absolutely not. I can talk fairly honestly in my sex offender group, but that is only to a point. Sex offenders face a lot of problems when they are in prison. I can't be open and talk to anybody else. You are not going to trust another inmate—you can only say so much. I can't be open because it gets out there and, boom, you're a victim yourself due to harassment. People come to you and tell you they want your stuff, that they want you to do sexual things.

As for when I'm out, I think that Megan's Law is good because if I put myself in a situation—say, I go to a town park and I go over to the swings and try to get close to someone I've seen at a distance—it's good that someone knows. I disagree with other parts of it, though, like where some states can make you put up a sign on your front lawn or something. I read about a guy who had to put up a sign, like a for-sale sign, on his lawn saying he was a child molester, and they burned his house down. So there are problems.

I just don't agree with passing out stuff with your picture on it. It's fine if the police department knows—that doesn't bother me. The school district can know, too, that's fine, but I don't feel that the school district should give my name or picture out to the parents in the neighborhood I'm living in. They might say that you have someone living in your neighborhood who has past crimes dealing with minors, but we can't tell you his name. I read an article last night that prison is not helping us. I mean, sex offenders have to come out of prison. I feel if I had the right treatment the first time around, I wouldn't be here. Now that I know I have this problem, I can deal with it. I'm not hiding from anything. My mother knows, and my father and sister, and some of my relatives. They know I won't be sneaking around doing these things. I feel safer knowing that I have to have an alibi wherever I go.

One thing I want to say is that we're not all bad monsters like people think we are. I didn't grow up and plan on going out and abusing children. It was a long thing where I was abused as a child, and that affected me. If you don't have a great childhood or traumatic things happen to you, like sexual abuse or divorce or other things, that can have a big impact on how you are going to act in life. Your parents are the ones that have to teach you how to be an adult and how to succeed in society. Seeing that I didn't have all the things that I needed while I was growing up—that I was used as a toy and abused by my grandfather—that screwed up my head. Also, a lot of sex offenders have different disorders, like I had with my speech and my attention span. I've had tests that show my brain waves are a little bit abnormal in certain situations. Maybe that's where I blocked everything out and said, "Okay, let's do this." Now that I'm aware of it, I can change. I do believe that sex offenders can change if they really want to. People say that alcoholics can never be cured, that they're always alcoholics, but they can stay sober for quite a long time. Forever, if they want. I've never been violent with anybody. And I'm a very caring person, according to my family and friends. I'm one of the most caring persons in the world, very generous and nice. I don't think people think of me as a monster.

Summary

Matthew presents himself as a sort of Peter Pan who halfheartedly recognizes the value of growing up but clings to youth. Three major themes emerge from his self-narrative. First, Matthew claims that he has always sought out affection, since he didn't get what he needed during his childhood. However, although Matthew claims that his grandfather sexually molested him from age three to seven or eight, it does not seem as though his parents abused or neglected him. In fact, his parents appear to have actively supported Matthew, perhaps even enabled him, since his father helped from behind the scenes to influence how Matthew was treated when he was arrested.

Second, Matthew believes that he might have physical and emotional problems that contributed to the poor judgment he has shown in the past. "A lot of sex offenders have different disorders, like I had with my speech and my attention span. . . . Maybe that's where I blocked everything out and said, 'Okay, let's do this.'"

The third theme that underscores Matthew's story is his craving for attention. He believes that he is a "love addict" rather than a "sex addict." He wanted the boys he molested to show how much they adored him through oral sex. This desire for attention is certainly expressed in the career path he chose. As a radio deejay, he was able to get the affection and attention he craved as well as ready access to young boys who were impressed by his career.

After Matthew's first arrest, even while on probation, he was able to spend time around boys, since he had various jobs where youngsters congregated, such as a skating rink and a mall. When he was nineteen or twenty, he became romantically involved with a forty-five-year-old woman with whom he had oral sex, but chances are he was more interested in her nine-year-old son. Later, after spending more time in prison, he became involved with another female, this time a teenage girl whom Matthew actually found physically appealing. Matthew took advantage of the access he had to her young nephews and their friends.

Overall, this seems to have been Matthew's pattern—to seek out situations where opportunities might occur. Matthew never trolled for victims in parks and on playgrounds, but he put himself into positions where he had access to potential victims. Once he became involved with families that had young boys, he was able to take advantage of the chance to spend time with the boys and hopefully arrange an opportunity to sexually molest them.

At this point in Matthew's life, it seems clear that he is destined to molest more boys, given the opportunity. Although he believes that having a sexual relationship with a woman will keep him from reoffending, he already tried that, and it didn't work. The other aspect to Matthew's pattern of molestation that makes it likely he will reoffend is that he doesn't seem to need a victim's willing participation. He admits to having fondled victims in their sleep. Even in the relationship he had with an adult male, Matthew performed fellatio on the man while he pretended to sleep.

So what might the future hold for Matthew? He claims that he has much more insight about his motivation during this last stint in prison. But as long as he manages to squeak by on charm and his father's influence, then it doesn't seem likely he will grow up and come to consider himself truly an adult. At this point, his relative youth and boyish charm are attractive qualities. Yet as his youth fades and he can no longer rely on this appeal to attract people to him, he may find it increasingly difficult to fulfill his need for affection and attention, and he may more actively seek out potential victims.

~

CHAPTER ELEVEN

Rick—The User

Tall and rangy, with thinning fair hair and a haunted expression, Rick exuded a quiet, desperate dignity. By the time I spoke with him, he had served eight long years in prison, and it showed in the droop of his shoulders and his dazed expression. His past addictions to drugs and alcohol seemed to have prematurely aged him; he was in his late forties, but looked at least ten years older. Rick was one of the last men I interviewed in prison. He wasn't willing to speak to me until he felt he could trust me, so I had seen him interact in a group setting for quite some time before I had the chance to talk with him one-on-one. More than anything, Rick seemed sad. His sadness didn't seem to spring from self-pity, but from a weary recognition that he had dictated the events of his life that led him to prison. He claimed responsibility for his actions, but at times it was a struggle, perhaps because it would be easier to sleep nights if he could believe someone else was at fault. He didn't look like he slept much. Although he could have taken something to help him relax—if there is one thing a prison has in abundance, it's a wide variety of pharmaceuticals—he didn't want to slip back into the cycle of addiction. So Rick was well and truly sober, at a time when he would have welcomed drug-induced oblivion.

Rick's Story

I never knew my dad. He left when I was a year old. I had a stepfather from the time I was two years old, right up until a few years ago, when he died. He was an alcoholic, and he was very abusive. I never got disciplinary action in the family—I was never spanked or beat—but he verbally abused me all the time. When he got drunk, he would pick on me. I would laugh at him as I got older, which would make him even madder. I got two stepsisters; they weren't treated the same. My one sister is probably about five years younger than me, and there's seventeen years' difference between [me and] the next one. When I was fifteen or sixteen, that's when I'd say most of the verbal abuse took place. My youngest sister wasn't born yet.

My stepfather would come home drunk a lot. He worked hard—never missed a day of work. It bothered me at first when he'd tease me, but I got used to it. He would get me anything I wanted, though. He had to quit school when he was eight or nine years old and help fix cellars with his dad. He never had no childhood and I'm sure he never even tossed a baseball, so he never even thought of doing it with me.

As I got older, the relationship changed. He became like a good friend. Maybe he teased me like that when I was younger because I was the stepson, and I guess he wanted a real son. Those are the things I never got a chance to ask him. When I got older and when I married my first wife—I've been married three times—he cried at the reception. I told my sister, "I wish he was like that when I was younger." Other than that, I got everything that I wanted; I was spoiled. My parents went without so me and my sister could have Christmas presents, school clothes, and new bicycles.

I think my mom knew what was going on with him. He would verbally abuse her, and I would intervene and call him names when they would get in arguments. Even though my sister got all my stepdad's attention, my relationship with her was real good. I'd always take her with me. She was like one of the guys. We're close. She looks out for me and gets me anything I want. She comes to visit me every two or three weeks. When I got arrested for this, it was the last thing she thought I would be arrested for. I've been dealing drugs for twenty-five years, large quantities. And that was what I think they expected me to get arrested for, but this statutory rape and sodomy was the last thing that they would expect. My sister still stood by me. She knows that the victim was my wife's niece. My family knows who to blame, although at first there was a little blame on my niece because she was sexually active. I told my sister I was at fault—"the girl don't know any better"— you know what I mean. She was abused by her stepfather and experimented with sex when she was nine or ten with her godfather's son, who must have been around the same age. I knew these things, and I should have known better than to use her. But I did. I guess my sister respects me for bringing out a lot of this embarrassing stuff to the family and owning up to it.

Anyway, back to my childhood. I'm not sure when I had my first sexual experience. I was abused by a baby-sitter, an older girl about fifteen or sixteen, best as I can remember. I would be in bed sleeping early in the morning, and she would come over right after my mother went to work, around 7 a.m. And this girl was laying in bed with me and fondling me and having me fondle her. I don't see what damage it did. That went on probably for two or three months. Not that I was ejaculating or anything, but it felt good to me, and it felt good touching her. It ended when we moved out of that neighborhood to the west side of town. Then after that, my next sexual experience was probably when I was fourteen or fifteen and going steady.

My first girlfriend was a year younger than me. It was six to eight months of courting before I even touched the back of her bra. We ended up going together for four years, and then we got married. We were married for thirteen years, but in the meantime I was very cold to her. Yeah, I was cheating, even when we were in high school. The girls that I was going out with, they knew that Jennifer was my steady. They must have known I was just using them for sex on a Saturday or Tuesday night. There were three girls at the same time that I was having sexual intercourse with and one more I was trying to get into the sack. I don't know why I did it. I had a girlfriend, so it didn't make sense. They were nice girls, too. Just one couldn't satisfy me.

Maybe it was a challenge to me. I'd go all out to get them. I wasn't forcing anyone, but I guess it is still using force when you're manipulating people to meet your needs. And they knew it. Looking back, I don't understand why they would want somebody to use them. Back in the sixties, when I was in school, to have sex, you had to go steady with the girl. You would kiss them and start rubbing their back and put your hand down, and that was it for the night. Then the next time, you'd say, "If you love me, you'll let me do it." Then after a while you'd feel their breasts, and then after a while you're down in their pants, and then. . . . But it wasn't just like that. It took months. I would have been satisfied just French kissing and maybe rubbing their backs.

The year Jennifer and I graduated, we eloped. Since she's Italian and I'm Irish–Polish, she heard a lot of "Why don't you marry someone Italian?" My grandmother was always saying, "What do you want a Dago for? Your stepfather is Italian, and he's no good." So we ran away and got married. We got a house. I was working good jobs, and she was working as a secretary. We experimented with drugs together. The first time we smoked marijuana was at a party a year or two after we got married. We started buying ounces for our own use. Then, instead of buying one ounce, I said, "Let's buy two ounces and then I'll sell one ounce—that way we can smoke for nothing." Eventually, it

got to the point where we were making a little money, and finally I went partners with guys buying forty to sixty pounds at a time. We were making big
money then. In the meantime, I bought a pound of acid from the local college. And then a couple of years later, we got into cocaine.

We weren't just selling all these drugs, either. We were using them. I
would try not to trip more than once a week, because I knew we could burn
our brains out, and I didn't want to end up a vegetable. I tried to take care of
myself. When I would start to come down from the peak end on the edge, I
would take two cocktails to counteract the strychnine. Then I would take
barbiturates to go to sleep, although that wasn't such a good thing to do. All
the time I was doing the drugs, I was drinking. I'd have terrible hangovers,
and then I couldn't drink for a couple of days; but then two days later I'd get
drunk all over again.

All the while, I was maintaining my job. I'd carry a little pill bottle—you
know, one of those flat little pill bottles like the ones ladies carry makeup
in—and I'd have Valiums in them or whatever I thought I'd need to get me
through the day. In the morning, I'd leave before my wife would, so most of
the time I'd leave a couple lines of cocaine for her to help wake her up. So
the drug dealing gave me the money to do the drugs myself. It got to the
point where I wouldn't even sell ounces. I'd sell pounds of the stuff. I was in
the upper class of drug users or whatever you call them. I was very promiscuous, too. I'd go to the people I had contacts with; a lot of girls would buy
drugs then. There would be some nice girls, and I would take advantage of
them. Jennifer knew. She wasn't stupid.

Jennifer may have known that I was messing around, but she stuck by me
until she finally just had enough. I was getting worse with the drug use; I was
shooting barbiturates by then. I was verbally abusing her. I slapped her a couple of times, but mostly I abused her with my words. I'm sure her mother and
girlfriends were telling her that I was messing around on her. When she finally left me, our son was about three or four years old. I had a nervous breakdown when she left. I was so depressed that I don't even think I was getting
high off the drugs I was taking. I kept begging her to come back. I was so hurt
and lost with her gone. But I wasn't thinking about what I did to drive her
away. That didn't come for years. At the time, I'm thinking, "Who the hell
are you to leave me?" My sister and my friends could see that I was getting
suicidal, so they admitted me to the hospital. For the four weeks I was in the
hospital, I kept thinking I was okay. I signed out without the doctor's permission. He told me I wasn't ready to go, and I really wasn't—I was still depressed and on all kinds of legal drugs by then for the depression. So I added
in my marijuana and drinking and was really goofed up for a couple of years,

feeling sorry for myself. I lost my job—I didn't care. I supported myself on welfare and unemployment for as long as that lasted. I even quit dealing drugs. I put a lot of weight on, not going anywhere.

Finally, one of my uncles confronted me. We were real close. He took all my medicine and threw it in the river. The next day, when I went to look for it, it was gone. I got all mad at him, but that was the one way that I finally got off of it. My uncle made me stay with him for like a week. He just let me wallow in self-pity and do the drugs. After a while, I started to see myself the way he must've seen me, so I started coming off all that junk that I was taking. That was when I could see the light.

About a year later, I married my second wife. This was about two years after I got divorced from Jennifer and a year after I stopped doing all that garbage. I still wasn't really over Jennifer, so that marriage didn't work out. Again, I picked a nice, pretty girl, and she'd do anything for me. But then my big mouth got in the way. I was expecting Anita to be like Jennifer—you know, cook like Jennifer, dress like Jennifer. She ended up leaving. We broke up once when she was pregnant—she had a boy—then I got her back. I thought we'd try it again. Soon she couldn't take no more of it. She left again, then I got her back again, and about a year later we thought we'd try to have another kid. She got pregnant again; we had Heather. Then she left me again. It was my big mouth.

There was about a seven-year absence when Anita and I didn't have no regular contact. I wasn't the ex-husband or father I should have been, but we still wrote and talked once in a while on the phone. Even after I was married to my third wife and I was in prison, Anita would write. Anita would encourage the kids to write to me, and I would write to them. And then my son found her dead three years ago. I think she committed suicide. They say it was a heart attack, but I think she just gave up. She remarried, and her marriage didn't work out. Anita was a good girl—she really was. She married another guy who she got a bum deal from. He ended up leaving her for a younger girl, even after they had twins together. Anita and I were writing right up to that point, and she wasn't mentioning being sick or anything. I know she was a little depressed. She didn't do drugs; she wouldn't even do drugs when we were married and I was getting high a lot. She didn't like it when I was doing the drugs. I would just say, "It's my life and my business. You got to put up with it, and you got to live with it or leave." She finally left me, but more because of my verbal abuse. I wonder what made me so verbally abusive. Maybe it was because my stepfather always treated my mother, my grandmother, and my aunts really ugly. I would want a woman that treated her men good—that's who I would want for a partner. But I just couldn't understand why I could treat strangers so good and want to have a relationship with a nice lady, and then be so damn mouthy.

After my second wife left, I was trying to change certain behavior. With Anita, I wasn't nowhere as promiscuous, running around. I had one affair in three years, which was good for me. I finally recognized that what I did behind Jennifer's back was what caused her to leave me—having sex with her stepsister and her girlfriend, one-night stands, whatever. I didn't want the same thing happening to Anita and me. So when I met Dana, this was probably three years after Anita and I split up for good. Dana and me had my son Jimmy, but we didn't get married for about two years after we had Jim. I was trying to control my verbal abuse and stuff. It was still there, but not as bad. I had a chance to cheat on Dana, but I didn't. I was working as a foreman in a warehouse, and there were a lot of women. Dana was very jealous. I would try to reassure her, tell her that my cheating was with my first wife Jennifer and I'm not into that no more. We had what I would say was a good relationship for five or six years. We got along good even though there was a big age difference. I was fourteen years older than she was.

We bought an old farmhouse, and I worked on fixing it up. That's when Dana's niece comes into the picture. Dana's got a niece who was abused by her stepfather up in Maine. Her stepfather was in the navy. Katie's mother left her stepfather because of this, but they got back together, and they were going to make another try at the marriage. Katie couldn't come onto the naval base where he got transferred, so somebody in the family had to take Katie in. Katie was twelve or just turned thirteen at the time. Dana thought she could sort of straighten Katie out and be a disciplinary figure for her. So we went down to pick her up and bring her back with us. We stayed a couple of days. I had no sexual thoughts about her. She needed a place to live, and I was going to try to be a disciplinary figure for her, you know, get her away from the crowd she was with.

Everybody knew Katie had been molested before. I think there were even charges filed, but they were dropped because Katie recanted the story or something. Maybe the government took care of it because the stepfather was in the navy. I just knew that as long as he lived on a navy base, he wouldn't be able to have Katie there. I didn't get into details about it. I didn't care. When Katie moved in, I tried to treat her just like she was my son or daughter; my son was six at the time, and my daughter was four. I tried to make Katie feel welcome. I didn't start thinking about sex with her until probably the sixth or seventh month she was living with us. Not that it hadn't been mentioned, you know. I'm not trying to minimize and put the blame on her. My eyes were looking. She was pretty well developed and she was menstruating and everything, and she would brag about having sex and not being a virgin. I would tell her, "Please, when company comes over, don't bring it up in front of them. I don't want people thinking that you are a little tramp." Swear to God on my kids. I didn't want people thinking bad of her, you know.

Katie never talked about her stepfather; mostly she talked about the first time with her godfather's son. And then I guess there were other boys in school, maybe older. All I said is, "I don't want to hear it. I don't want you doing these things." She'd come downstairs, like on a weekend or during the night after she got home from school, in one of those long T-shirts that teenagers wore, with no bra on, and I would see her nipples sticking out. Dana would tell her not to walk around the house like that, in case somebody came over, I guess, but probably for me, too, because I was watching, and I'm sure my wife could see that. I mean, you don't want somebody like that, even your own daughter, walking around like that in front of anybody, even Dad. Those are things that you should be covering up. When Dana was working, Katie would always come down without the bra on or in shorter nighties. After a while I just said, "If you like it, why shouldn't you look?" I guess I was justifying. It started progressing, my sexual desire for her. There was another room off the bathroom, and I kept some tools and stuff in there. I would walk in there and try to take a peek in the shower. I know now at this point I shouldn't have been thinking of going in there, regardless of what I needed. But I was trying to look.

One time, I come home, and I don't know if I was drinking or high—I think I was—but I was going to see if she was just bragging or how far she would go. She was sitting on the floor with me. I think I was rolling a joint—I did let her get high a couple of times. I said something like, "You're pulling crap or you're just bragging, and you never did have sex." And she said something on the line of, "Oh, yes, I did. Go ahead." I turned around and she was sitting on the couch with her legs apart. She had a nightie on, and I could see her underpants. I started going up her leg, and I expected her to stop me at any second. If she had stopped me, that might have been it right then, for a time. But when she didn't stop me, I got all the way up to her crotch, and that was it—I was off. We had sex. Intercourse, yeah. With all her boasting, it was probably just typical teenage stuff, you know—the French kisses and all that. But I took it a different way, thinking she was coming on to me or something, and when I tried and she didn't stop me, I just went all the way. She would give me oral sex; I would give her oral sex. She would climax. She didn't have pubic hairs, and I got addicted to that. This went on until my wife caught us. I would say it happened at least two or three times a week, probably sometimes more than that. When I went to court, they said fifty-one counts over seventeen months. But it was way more than that.

My wife had to suspect. I wasn't performing my, you know, my duties with her as much as I should have. I think I was still trying to be slick, covering up everything, by still trying to do the disciplinary action. I wasn't showing Katie no favoritism, but I wouldn't encourage her to put the bras on, anymore; in fact, I would encourage her to take them off, even when my wife was there. I would make excuses to go places and take Katie with me. Since my wife is a nurse, she would work split shifts, so that would give me all the opportunity to, you know, use Katie. I always made sure the other kids were in bed before we did anything.

The night my wife caught me, she came home early. I think that she suspected something was going on, and she looked in the living room window. We were on the couch, and she seen us. She called me a piece of shit. "How can I compete with a teenager?" she said, with tears running down her eyes. And I said, "You didn't see nothing, Dana; we weren't doing nothing." I felt scared and embarrassed and ashamed that I got caught. Dana got me up for work the next morning, and it seemed like she wasn't even mad, although I know now that she cried all night long. I was at work about two hours when the state police came and arrested me. Two days later, Dana and my sister bailed me out. I had to tell them everything that happened. It hurt telling Dana, not so much because I did it, but because I know I hurt her so bad. I figured I could get out of it somehow. So when they set the bail at first at $25,000, I thought, "Oooooh, I'm in a lot of trouble." I had been arrested two or three times before for assault. They suspected that I had been dealing drugs for years, but they couldn't catch me, because I only dealt with a certain few dealers who dealt to other people. There was still that code among drug dealers where you didn't give up somebody else if you got busted for a deal. So the guys who were getting drugs from me, if they ever did get arrested, never gave me up. The police knew I was dealing drugs; they just didn't have any sales to prove it.

So here it was, two days after my arrest, and I was in jail. I was really embarrassed. The only other time I ever spent in jail was in the city lockup for a fight. I wasn't scared; it was just missing the things that you are used to. And here I had to tell my wife and my sister the truth. How long it's been going on and what I did and everything. Otherwise, they were going to leave me there in jail. When I got caught, though, I felt a big relief. I didn't want to be in jail—I'm not going to lie about that—but it was just a relief not to sneak around anymore. After I would do stuff with my niece, I would feel guilty. Sometimes I would try to make believe I was sleeping, but then the need overpowered me and I just continued. Naturally, after I climaxed, I'd really feel guilty, because now I was satisfied. It hadn't gotten into my head 100 percent yet that I was guilty because she was so young. It was more because I was cheating on my wife. I know that it was against the law, what I was doing, and I naturally wouldn't want anybody doing the same thing to my daughter and my nieces or anybody else. But I crossed the line with her because I knew she was sexually active.

I'm not saying that I didn't look at television and say "That's a pretty girl or teenager." No, a lot of my friends had teenage girls, I got teenage cousins and nieces, and I never thought of them in a sexual way. I did with Katie, I know now, because she was—to use my counselor's words—damaged goods. She had already been abused, she already had sex, so that helped me justify doing it.

When Dana told me why she called the police, she said it was because she knew that Katie wouldn't admit that we had been having sex. When I was at work that morning, Dana had to slap and choke her to get it out of her. So in the meantime, Dana is already making plans to send Katie back to her mother. Dana's got power of attorney or whatever you call it, so she's got to tell her sister that Rick and Katie have been having sex together for the last year and a half or however long it's been. Dana was feeling jealous of Katie, and angry, too. She blamed both of us. Dana was hurt because here's her husband—we've been together for six years—and then I do something like that. At times when Katie and me were having sex—or I was having sex with Katie—I would tell her that we shouldn't be doing this. Now I don't know if at the time I was doing it to justify it to myself or warning her not to say nothing to nobody. What I said is that it is against the law, and I could spend a lot of time in jail; then she would tell me that the laws are stupid and things like that. I didn't love Katie, but I did tell her a few times that I loved her, out of compassion. I grew attached to her through sex. I think that Katie thought she loved me. I was treating her like a woman my age, and I'm sure that she loved it. I was forty-one when it started, and she was thirteen.

Dana sent Katie away. Katie went down to Texas and stayed with her grandmother. They subpoenaed Katie; the DA threatened her with conspiracy and contempt of court, perjury, and jail if she didn't come back to testify, so she did. Even on the stand during testimony, Katie said she learned about how to do blow jobs in school. The only thing the prosecution could bring up was that, since she had been molested by her stepfather but later said it wasn't true, she was lying about me, too. That hurt. All I wished was that I could do this trip all over again, go back to when I was fourteen and all my crap started. You know, when you're a teenager, you think you know everything. When you're in your forties, you realize that you don't. There's a lot of things I learned in programs here in prison about how the body responds to pleasures and stuff. She wasn't saying, "Hey, I want to go to bed with you." She was saying she was sexually active, but it was me doing everything else. She was being a typical abused teenage kid, okay? And I didn't know what an abused teenage kid was.

I think about that baby-sitter who abused me—to the best of my knowledge she was about fourteen or fifteen. What I realize now is that Katie was about the same age. Hearing that Katie was sexually active is what set me off. Set the alarms, my libido, or whatever. It could have been some girl who was thirty, and it would have been the same thing: me wanting satisfaction for myself. But there is a big difference between thirteen and thirty. I don't know why I crossed the line. Maybe it could be the age difference like the baby-sitter; maybe the fact that I was very promiscuous and sexually active in my teens when I was just a few years older than Katie was. Maybe it was due to some hidden stress at that time going on, like bills and selling the house and stuff. I don't know—maybe my wife put on a few pounds, maybe I was drinking a little more. It's a combination of a lot of stuff. I don't believe that it was just one, because I didn't try to coach or groom any of my friend's kids. It wasn't even in my thoughts. The minute there was a sexually active teenager in my house, that was it.

So they sentenced me, and they gave me the max on everything. Now I've been working on what triggers me, on thought switching, thought stopping, and not putting myself around teenage girls. I don't think I would ever do that again, but I wouldn't want to put myself in that position. I don't want to do the drugs anymore. I don't want to drink. I got diabetes, I got high blood pressure; I don't want any more of that. I had a pretty good run with them for twenty-some years, but I don't want to say it was a good run. If I could go back and change that, I would. I'd have a lot more money, and my relationships would have been better.

My wife Dana stayed with me for six-and-a-half years, but she left me last October for another man. She met somebody else. I've been gone a long time. She's sorry. She just came up to visit last week with the kids. My relationship with my kids is good, real good. I don't know where Jennifer is. My sister now and then sees her. My son is twenty-three or twenty-four now. When my sister saw Jennifer, she asked my sister how I was doing, which to me is a step. I mean, I got to eventually see her and tell her that I'm sorry. I've never owned up to her on that. I never come to terms with that until I started taking programs in prison.

You got lots of time to think in here. Twelve-step programs, relapses, triggers—I never faced them until I came here. But I don't think I got a fair

sentence for what I did. It was my first time, and I got the max. It was pay-
back for everything illegal that I did. I hold no animosity toward the DA or
anything, but why would he have to threaten your witness with contempt of
court, perjury, and jail if she don't come back and testify? I mean, here you
are, you are thirteen, you been abused twice or more, and now you're hearing somebody who is supposed to help you threaten you if you don't help put
this terrible person in jail. The DA didn't even ask for fourteen years; he
asked for two-and-a-third to seven. The judge figured he's going to teach me
a lesson. Yeah, I should have come to jail. But I don't believe I should have
gotten fourteen years. I'm not coming out of here bitter, but I'm coming out
of here still embarrassed, still ashamed, still carrying all this in me. It's never
going to go away. I'm never going to forget what I did.

If I had only gotten a year or two, I wouldn't have had all the programs
that I've had. And being honest with you, I don't think I would have gotten
to this point. I appreciate people who come in with concerns with the victims, but also for the offenders. Naturally, you don't want any more victims,
so you have to find something out there that can stop offenders without having to come to this. A lot of offenders I've talked to, if there was some kind
of help without them having to turn themselves in and [getting] sent to
prison, they would have taken it. If there was a point before prison when
somebody says, "Yeah, you know, I'm a sex offender, can you help me? I really want to stop." Sure, there are groups like that springing up, but after guys
have been to jail. From what I understand—say if I had been offending for a
year, and all of a sudden I want to stop—if I went and joined a group and
came out and said, "Yeah, I've been doing this for a year," they could arrest
me and put me in prison. Why is somebody going to want to go there? You've
seen the size of the sex offender groups here—there's five or six guys. And
there's hundreds of offenders in here. I'm not saying to give us a medal because we've come to a program, but gee, give us something. You know, put us
in a probationary halfway house, like the ones for drug offenders. They would
get a lot more offenders in prison to look at themselves and what they have
done if there was some kind of merit for coming to these programs. We're not
talking about someone dealing dope; we're talking about damaging some little kid's life.

As for giving us harsher sentences—I don't think that is going to stop the
problem. If that would be a cure to the crime, sure. But I don't think that it
is going to work. I think that what is going to happen is that you are going
to have more Sara Woods[1] or Polly Klaases,[2] because people are going to say,
"The hell with it, I'm taking a chance, so if you're going to tell on me, I might
as well kill you." That's a shame. I mean, I'd kill those guys myself for doing

something like that. And about community notification—now I'm going to have to go to the police station, and I've got to tell them, "Here's Rick the sex offender." Yeah, that's going to hurt, but put a sign on me across my forehead—I don't care. I'm not going to do it again—I'm going to try not to do it again. But if somebody comes and messes with me? Say, if somebody throws a stone at me, I'm going to try not to throw a stone back at him. But there's no guarantees. I mean, I don't want it to happen. I can see the point, but I don't want a drug dealer living next to me, either.

I don't try to make any excuses with anybody. I'm not proud of what I did, but in turn, I don't want you to worry that I'm going to try to grab your ass if you're not looking or something. Yeah, you're going to be a little nervous, but you should be. Be relieved that I'm working on myself so I don't step over that line again.

A lot of people out there think of sex offenders as being guys in raincoats hanging out at parks or wherever, waiting to jump out and grab kids. They are, and some do. Like I said, I wouldn't ever want my kids, at whatever age, molested. So me being a parent, I'd go to any extremes to try and prevent it. Yeah, I can see where statistics show some people are doing it no matter how many times they are locked up. So there's proof right there that if they did it once, they might do it again. I did it once, so there is always a chance that I'd do it again. It's like an ex-alcoholic, you know: once you pick up another beer, there is the possibility that you are off and running. For the record, I just want to say that I'm sorry I did what I did, and I'm not the same person I was before. I'm sorry for Katie, sorry for my family, and naturally, I'm sorry for myself. That's it.

Summary

Rick's self-narrative focuses on the power of addiction and the ways in which his own addictions controlled his life. These addictions to sex, drugs, and alcohol left him incapable of resisting temptation for long, especially when the source of temptation was readily accessible. So although, in broad terms, Rick did not fantasize about having sex with teenage girls, when an apparently sexually active girl ended up living under his roof, Rick took advantage of her availability. Before long, he became obsessed with having sex with his young niece and added her to his already lengthy list of addictions.

A recurring theme in Rick's story is how he "used" drugs and people. When he was dating his first wife, he used other girls at school for sex. He used his drug addiction to make money by dealing drugs to other people. He used his power as a drug dealer to force women who wanted to buy drugs to have sex with him. He used his wives as vessels for all the verbal abuse he suffered as a child from his stepfather. Rick used drugs and his power as an adult caregiver to sexually take advantage of his wife's niece. He used the excuse that Katie was "damaged goods" to molest her. To gain her acquiescence, or perhaps just to make himself feel less guilty for having sex with her, Rick told Katie that he loved her.

Rick admits that if he had not spent so much time in prison, he would not have taken advantage of the programs offered to help him change his ways. The events of his life, and the way in which he manipulated people and events for his own gain, have caught up with him, and now he is in a position to make amends to the people he used. Rick believes that if he can avoid drugs and alcohol, along with teenage girls, then he ought to be able to avoid reoffending when he is finally released from prison. "But I'm coming out of here still embarrassed, still ashamed, still carrying all this in me. . . . I'm never going to forget what I did. . . . Be relieved that I'm working on myself so I don't step over that line again."

Notes

1. Sara Wood, age twelve, disappeared in August 1993 near Utica, New York. Lewis Lent Jr. was convicted of her kidnapping and murder, although her body was never found. Lent was sentenced to twenty-five years to life, but was returned to Massachusetts to serve a previous life sentence for the murder of a twelve-year-old boy, Jimmy Bernardo. Interestingly, while Lent was in Concord Prison in Massachusetts, he wrote a letter on behalf of himself and John Geoghan, the former Catholic priest, sixteen months before Geoghan was murdered by an inmate in a different facility. The *Boston Herald* reported that, in the letter, which was sent to U.S. Senator Edward M. Kennedy and U.S. Representative Edward Markey, Lent complained that the "illegal behavior" of a particular guard could lead to an attack on himself or the ex-priest. Geoghan, who in 2002 was sentenced to nine-to-ten years in state prison for groping a ten-year-old boy in a swimming pool (although his attacks on children spanned thirty years), was later transferred to Souza-Baranowski Correctional Center, a maximum-security facility, where he was killed by Joseph L. Druce on August 23, 2003.

2. In October 1993, twelve-year-old Polly Klaas was abducted at knifepoint from her home in Petaluma, California. After a massive hunt, her body was discovered in December 1993. In 1996, Richard Allen Davis was convicted and sentenced to death for her murder.

CHAPTER TWELVE

~

Making Sense of the Senseless

If you've now read all of these offender self-narratives, you are to be congratulated. It is no easy feat to peer into the mind of a child molester, when most of us would rather believe such individuals did not even exist. Yet it should have become clear from their stories that these men are not monsters. The crimes they committed were monstrous, but there were very real, powerful, and perhaps understandable aspects of their personalities and environments that led to their deviant behaviors. You might have even felt some affinity with a few of these men; I know I did. Considering my own childhood victimization, I ought to be one of the last people to feel empathy for a child molester. But however painful and confusing my sexual abuse might have been, I am able to look back with an adult's perspective and try to see the situation through my abuser's eyes. I may not understand exactly what motivated The Man Who Molested Me, but I know he had reasons for doing what he did. These reasons may have been embedded in his childhood or acquired as an adult; I will never know the truth, because he has been dead for twenty years. Yet I can glimpse his motivations through the actions of these other men. Being willing to *hear* their voices and really try to *listen* is a significant step toward combating the crime.

So now that we have delved into the self-narratives of these convicted child molesters, how are we supposed to make sense of their stories? How do their perceptions reflect the social constructions of sexual practices and power in our culture? Sexual offenses against children are horrifying to contemplate. Yet the most current statistics regarding child molesters hint that they might be able to be rehabilitated or, at the very least, taught how to control their impulses. According to the U.S. Department of Justice, Bureau of Justice Statistics, on any given day in 1994 there were approximately 234,000 offenders convicted of rape or sexual assault who were under the care, custody, or control of corrections agencies; nearly 60 percent of these were under conditional supervision in the community. Approximately 4,300 child molesters were released from prison in fifteen states in 1994. Among these offenders, 60 percent had been in prison for molesting children thirteen years old or younger. An estimated 3.3 percent of these 4,300 were rearrested for another sex crime against a child within three years of release from prison. Although even 3 percent is too much, consider how the recidivism rate of sex offenders measures up against that of other criminals. Of the 272,111 persons released from prisons in fifteen states in 1994, 67.5 percent were rearrested within three years. Sex offenders were less likely than non–sex offenders to be rearrested for any offense (43 percent of sex offenders versus 69 percent of non–sex offenders), although sex offenders were four times more likely than non–sex offenders to be arrested for another sex crime.[1] Yet the myth remains that child molesters have a vastly higher recidivism rate than any other type of offender.

Perhaps this myth persists because we simply don't have proof regarding what sort of punishment or rehabilitation works for a child molester. Until very recently, we haven't been able to complete any long-term studies of formerly incarcerated sex offenders who had some sort of substantial therapy while in prison, primarily because the treatment programs that do exist in some prisons are so new. In March 2004, a Canadian study was released that tracked a group of 724 sex offenders serving federal prison terms in British Columbia beginning in the early 1980s. Of these, 403 inmates received treatment while 321 did not. After twelve years, the offenders who underwent a treatment program had slightly lower recidivism rates, but the differences were so negligible that researchers said they were not significant. Approximately 21.1 percent of sex offenders who received treatment went on to commit another sex crime, compared to 21.8 percent of those who were not treated. "It is reasonable to conclude that the overall [treatment] program did not have any meaningful effect on recidivism rates," said the researchers in an article published in the *Canadian Journal of Behavioural Sciences*. However, "we still have . . . much to learn about how best to intervene with sexual offenders."[2]

The main difficulty behind the dearth of long-term studies has been finding random subjects to study. Sex offenders make up a small portion of convicted criminals. In addition, in-prison treatment programs have only sprung up in the past decade or so, and they have not been available to a majority of convicted sex offenders. The concept of rehabilitating convicted child molesters through pharmacological and/or cognitive therapies is not widely accepted. Even within prisons that offer treatment programs, attending them has often been optional due to a lack of available funding and counseling staff, and many offenders who don't receive treatment have refused it. So if a child molester reoffends when he is released from prison, it is difficult to say whether it was because he didn't receive treatment or because he wasn't motivated to change in the first place.

Thus, to assuage our fears that child molesters exist in huge numbers and obsessively repeat their crimes, we rely upon notification policies and Megan's Law to keep us safe. Yet the logistical demands of making Megan's Law work has been a nightmare in some states. In New York, for example, a 1998 federal court ruling required the state to provide court hearings when determining what risk level should be assigned to sex offenders, with Level 3 offenders at the greatest risk of committing a new crime and Level 1 at the lowest risk. Yet between 1998 and 2004, thousands of offenders who needed hearings created an unwieldy backlog, and in the meantime, their risk levels were all reduced to Level 1, regardless of their crimes.[3] In an attempt to cut through this complicated procedure, in March 2004, New York governor George E. Pataki proposed legislation that would put the names of all sex offenders on the Internet, regardless of their risk level, and make it a crime for sex offenders not to annually register their addresses with the police. Although proponents of Governor Pataki's plan claimed that this bill would strengthen Megan's Law by giving parents, communities, and law enforcement the tools they needed to keep children safe, opponents argued that the bill would subject all sex offenders to an additional penalty.

This additional penalty would certainly add to the problems that convicted child molesters face when they are released from prison. Just finding a place to live can be a dilemma for both sex offenders and corrections officials when the offenders are released. Many convicted offenders have been driven out of communities when residents protested the offenders' presence. For example, one repeat sex offender in California did his time in jail, then in a mental health facility; finally, to win his release, he agreed to chemical castration and electronic monitoring. Nevertheless, he was pushed out of one California town after another as the state tried to find him a place to live. The problem began when California officials did not forewarn local residents or local police of the man's pending arrival in the four communities where they tried to place him. Once the residents discovered him, they protested his residency until officials had to relocate him. This was the second time the state of California had problems with releasing an individual who went through its sex offender commitment program. Eventually, the first man ended up living in a trailer on state prison property.[4]

Admittedly, communities have a vested interest in keeping violent sex offenders from moving into their neighborhoods. However, it is important to note that, as of 2004, many states' versions of Megan's Law did not distinguish between the types of offenders. There was no distinction between the repeat pedophile and a nineteen-year-old who had sex with his high school sweetheart who was under fifteen. Oftentimes, these notification policies lump all convicted sex offenders together in an indistinguishable mass, and all offenders—no matter the severity of their crimes—reap the consequences, which can range from difficulties finding employment to vigilantism by irate neighbors. This does not provide much incentive for convicted sex offenders to work on rehabilitating themselves while in prison. Although they might have served their prison time, convicted sex offenders still face rejection by a society that refuses to accept the possibility of their redemption. No matter how long a sentence they served or how dearly they paid for their crimes, they are punished for life. This lifetime punishment may occur even when they were fortunate enough to be incarcerated in a facility that offered some form of treatment. Even when they might have been subjected to some form of chemical castration or were civilly committed to a mental health facility after they served their prison terms, the widely accepted assumption is that they are eager to repeat their offenses. So what is the point? Why bother?

Hopefully, the narratives presented in this book help illuminate why we should care and give credence to the idea that some child molesters can be rehabilitated. If all child molesters fit into that safely alien category of "Other," then we can continue to reject them out of hand. However, the vast majority of child molesters are more like "Us" than "Them." They may lead fairly ordinary lives—they may even be respected members of the community—aside from their crimes. Simply from a practical standpoint, it makes sense to focus on determining potentially effective forms of treatment. It is expensive and impractical to incarcerate child molesters for life, and since child molestation does not constitute a capital crime, we can't just kill them (it sounds flippant to even mention the possibility, but enough people seem to believe that murdering child molesters is morally justifiable). These facts, when viewed in light of the realities of the offenses and offenders, should make evident the value of understanding what motivates a person to molest children. If we want to keep our communities safe, then we need to be certain we've done all we can to help offenders control their deviant impulses.

Interpreting Offender Self-Narratives

As expressed in chapter 2, one means of exploring the social construction of these offenders' self-narratives is through viewing the personal, situational, organizational, and cultural/historical aspects expressed by the stories. Even though each man's narrative possesses unique elements, there are also similarities among their justifications and observations. Pinpointing these similarities and where they diverge from each other can contribute to formulating a broad perspective of offender motivations.

Personal Level

On the personal level, each man's self-narrative represents an attempt to fashion his own comprehensible identity, given his experiences and understanding of how the events in his life fit into the social milieu. Since being convicted and entered into the prison system, each offender has been exhorted to tell his story, over and over again, in a recognizable structure with the express purpose of identifying who he is and how he ended up committing his crimes. When the offender was arrested and his story was entered into the corrections system, this became his identity for law enforcement officials, counselors, peers, and the community. Yet the offender has not possessed the ultimate control over this narrative, since only the elements in his story that seem to fit into an acceptable, expected, socially constructed framework are given any credence. So these men have struggled to develop an understanding of their personal identities aside from the account dictated by their scripts as convicted child molesters. This is no easy task when these offenders are constrained by their environment and the society beyond, which has already assumed who they are from the basis of the crimes they committed.

The fundamental question always asked of a criminal is why he or she committed the offense. Since many offenders act out of impulse, this is a thorny issue. The logical assumption is that if they knew why they did it, then most of them wouldn't have done it in the first place—or would they? Did these child molesters possess the ability to control their actions? Or were their actions the inevitable result of the cognitive capacities and situational stresses that controlled them? In an effort to offer an acceptable motive for their crimes, most of these offenders have tried to find the answer in their childhoods. Yet attempting to pinpoint a cause in their youth does not fit comfortably into the social assumption that child molesters are somehow not quite human. To perceive a child molester as a child himself goes contrary to the expectation that he is a monster, since when we see him as someone who was once vulnerable and perhaps even innocent, suddenly it becomes more difficult to hold on to the image of him as irrevocably evil. If we recognize that the impulses of some of these men were shaped by their experiences as children—in circumstances they had no control over—then we have to take responsibility for creating, or at the very least perpetuating, the environments that spawn such behavior. And what society wants to do that?

Although not all of these men were physically or sexually abused as children, some of them were, and they have tried to determine if this abuse helped create their impulses to molest children. Red and Billy describe horrific physical abuse by their fathers and passive mothers who did not protect their children from their fathers' rage. Certainly in these instances, if the children in these families were terrified of their fathers, then it is reasonable to assume that their mothers were frightened as well. So Red and Billy grew up angry, although Red buried his anger in a veneer of self-righteousness and self-loathing, while Billy became an "animal" who functioned on instinct. Ben does not directly state that he was physically abused, but he was shuffled back and forth between caregivers and spent the majority of his childhood living with an uncle who sexually molested him. Ben, too, carried a lot of anger out of his childhood as a result. He told no one about his uncle's actions, because he didn't think it would matter anyhow, but the anger translated into depression that shadowed him for most of his adult life. Abe claims that he cannot remember "a time of innocence" in his life, since he was physically, emotionally, and verbally abused from the time he was a child. Abe's father had heart problems, which made it easier for his mother, and later his stepmother, to torment Abe. Although once Abe entered school there were clear signs that he was disturbed, his father held back from getting Abe professional help, since "he had a fear that there was something wrong in our family and didn't want to know about it." Yet Abe claims the abuse that occurred in his family was not unusual, since corporal punishment and sexual molestation were rampant in the town he was raised in.

Although we would like to believe that abused children don't become abusers as adults, it is reasonable to assume that some abused kids can grow up to repeat the cycle, abusing other people in turn. Yet other men interviewed in these pages say that their childhoods were overall fairly unremarkable. Tony complains that his father verbally abused him, and Rick, too, claims that his stepfather was verbally abusive, but they were not physically beaten or molested. Although he notes that his grandfather played sexual games with him, Matthew's casual description of the event leaves the impression that it did not particularly traumatize him. Matthew also complains that his parents' divorce was a shock, but the pain he felt doesn't seem to be especially intense or even unusual. Undoubtedly, divorce is a traumatic experience for children, but Matthew admits that his parents stayed connected and were supportive of him, even when he was in prison. So although Matthew hints that his parents were abusive, possibly because his own crimes might make more sense that way, it doesn't seem convincing.

Greg and Darrell also describe their families as being fairly ordinary. Darrell's father abandoned him when he was very young, so Darrell took over as the man of the family, which put a lot of pressure on him but doesn't seem unusually abusive. The event that shaped his later actions was his sexual molestation by a priest who was also a close family friend. Since Darrell says he viewed the priest as a father figure—both literally and metaphorically—the priest's betrayal of that relationship was devastating, and the experience deeply wounded Darrell. Greg insists that he had a perfectly ordinary childhood in a large middle-class family with parents who loved him. When a neighbor viciously raped Greg, he didn't tell his parents because, ultimately, he believed he was protecting them. The man threatened his family with violence if Greg revealed the rape, and so Greg harbored this dreadful secret. Even though his behavior at school changed after that experience, and he must have shown some signs of distress, he kept silent about the abuse and told no one for years, until his own arrest for molesting his stepdaughter.

So at the personal level, the ways in which these offenders describe their lives reflect their desires to find explanations for their crimes—crimes that they are well aware society views as particularly heinous. Their self-narratives reflect this struggle between their personal sense of self and the identity that society attributes to men labeled as child molesters. Ultimately, as they relate their stories over and over, generally in the corrections system as a means of defining their "triggers" and motivation for molesting children, they increasingly attempt to fit their own experiences into the socially constructed assumptions about child sexual abuse. They try to relate the events of their lives into a sequential pattern that lends the veneer of rationality to their motivations and gives the impression that they were able to make significant choices about their behavior. Yet, for some of these men, it seems evident that the circumstances of their childhood and the influence of certain people in their lives limited their capacity as adults to choose what actions they enacted—or repeated. They were caught up in a cycle, without the cognitive and emotional tools to escape, trapped by their own limitations and situational factors that conspired to dictate their destinies.

Situational Level

At the situational level, narrators explore the processes through which they transform themselves into social objects. This is the point at which the offenders attempt to show how the events of their lives and their understanding of the social world help them create a mythic persona, an identity they adapt that communicates the roles they perceive for themselves. These roles, and the scripts they enact as a result of environmental pressures, form the basis for determining sources of attribution, motivation, and accountability for their crimes.

It is possible to extrapolate the roles these men perceive themselves as playing from the themes that emerge from their narratives. Tony, Greg, and Ben present similar themes of attempting to "do their duty" as men. Tony considers himself to have been a good citizen, a man who claimed all the elements of respectability, such as a good job, a nice wife, children, and a home in the suburbs. He completed his education, served his country in the military, and settled down to reap the benefits of earnest efforts to pursue what he perceived was the American dream. Yet there was another side to Tony's personality, one that was insecure and lascivious. By exposing himself to young girls, he sought reinforcement for his sagging self-esteem; yet he was also titillated by the drama of sneaking around to fulfill his fantasies. Tony was able to put his acting skills to good use in disguising his dark side. For a while, he was able to immerse himself in the role of good family man and provider, and he might even have been able to convince himself that this wasn't an act. But then the insecurities would magnify, and his need for attention (and perhaps a measure of self-destructiveness as well) overcame his ability to sustain the role. So in a large sense, Tony's behaviors were controlled by situational stresses. As long as he felt secure in his role as husband and provider, he wasn't motivated to expose himself.

Greg also considers himself to have been a good husband and father. Greg tried to keep his family together, taking on myriad roles of caregiver, provider, and model citizen. Before his arrest for molesting his stepdaughter, Greg had not received so much as a speeding ticket. All his life until he ended up in prison, Greg tried to personify the traditionally masculine male whose major duty is to serve and protect. Perhaps he would have been able to accomplish this task as an adult had not his neighbor raped him when he was a child. The rape became a gnawing secret for Greg, and a source of insecurity, since he was determined to protect his parents from the neighbor's wrath. As time went on, it became increasingly difficult to even contemplate expressing his secret to anyone, including his wife, although he exhibited a variety of clues. The secret remained buried beneath his efforts to play the role of protector and provider. His secret burden made him vulnerable to his stepdaughter's advances (or so he believes). Greg thinks that, had he not been the strong silent type and told about the rape earlier on, he probably would not have ended up in prison. Protecting other people by keeping his secret was a burden he had to bear, but the weight of it eventually overwhelmed him.

The circumstances of Ben's life seem to have made it difficult, if not impossible, for him to emerge unscathed. He was raised in an environment that appears to have been devoid of boundaries—moral, physical, sexual, or otherwise. The values he learned from his youth stemmed from his experiences with adults who were sexually promiscuous, alcoholic, and slovenly, and naturally their children adopted those behaviors as well. Ben, who developed an avid interest in sex early on, had any number of opportunities to indulge his appetites, especially with members of his own family. But this morally bankrupt childhood did not totally squelch Ben's desire to do his duty. He tried to be a good son and took care of his parents to the best of his ability. Ben tried to do his duty by serving his country, although he admits that when he was drafted he also viewed it as a chance to leave his dysfunctional family behind. Yet Vietnam and the military were hardly means of healing Ben of his warped childhood. If anything, his military experience intensified Ben's depression, since the values Ben needed to survive combat were the very same values he was trying to outrun.

Some of the other men also describe their lives in terms of doing their duty, yet out of perhaps more egotistical motives. Red views himself to be a long-suffering savior, a well-meaning man whose impoverished environment and poor choice of friends undermined his efforts to do good. Although he was limited by circumstances such as abuse and poverty, he considered himself to be somehow above his family members and peers. Red did not molest children out of some base, animal instinct. The children made themselves available to him when he was vulnerable, weary with the struggle of trying to bring the people in his life up to his level of moral development. Because Red wanted to make other people happy, he went along with their desires. Now that he is in prison, he has magnanimously forgiven the children who spoke out against him. He seems to view suffering as a significant aspect of his self-image.

Abe, too, describes himself and the events of his life in an oddly religious tone. I wouldn't go so far as to say that Abe also views himself as a savior, but perhaps he saw himself as a pilgrim seeking salvation. Abe claims to have worshipped the children he molested, or at the very least, their genitals. As he observes, "One of the things I used to like to do was to lay on my side and just look at their genitals. It was almost like a prayer to me. Looking at it from the standpoint of worship saved me from killing people. It saved me from doing other more horrendous things. I didn't see molesting as pleasure. It was

God to me." For Abe, children represented "something pure, something perfect and safe." Therefore, he was drawn to children who had been molested, tainted by some sort of abuse. These children were "extraordinarily attractive" to Abe. To extend this metaphor a bit further, it does seem evident that suffering is an inherent part of many religions. Catholicism, for one, venerates saints who, like Jesus Christ, were persecuted and tortured for their faith. Abe saw a source of salvation for himself in these abused children, perhaps because on some level they represented the abused, tormented child he once was.

Darrell is another offender who views his motivations through the guise of religion and sacrifice. On a literal level, a priest molested Darrell when he was young and then continued to prey on Darrell when he was an adult. So for Darrell, the church was, paradoxically, a source of sanctuary and succor and of betrayal and hypocrisy. After Darrell's arrest, the church factored in as an even larger part of his life, since the very priest who molested him gained control of Darrell's freedom by taking charge of both his counseling and his probation. Just as the church harbored this priest and his secret crimes, Darrell had his own secret to bear: his homosexuality. Knowing that his mother disapproved and that his faith preached against homosexuality, Darrell hid his identity as a homosexual. Darrell claims that finally being able to embrace his homosexuality while in prison has saved him, although he is still fated to suffer with his deep-seated desires to molest boys. As he notes, "I'm a homosexual, but I'm also a child molester. If I just accept that I'm a homosexual but not that I'm a pedophile, then I'm in danger. I can't keep secrets anymore."

Although, superficially, Billy and Rick might seem to have very different motives for committing their crimes, at a deeper level there are potent similarities in the image they paint of themselves. Both men seem to have spent the greater part of their lives reacting on instinct, without much introspection or self-evaluation. Billy describes himself as a "great big animal" and an "ape." During the first incident with his niece, Cindy, Billy did have moments where he felt guilty about molesting her, but his desire for sexual satisfaction was more pressing. Like Abe, Billy observes that molesting a child was a substitute for more heinous crimes, such as murder. As he says, "I was so angry at everything at that time. I think if I had had a gun, I'd have shot everybody in sight. . . . So I don't know, I guess I was just pretty crazy."

Rick, too, seemed to do what he felt at the time he felt it, not bothering to explore the ethical or moral implications of his actions. He dealt drugs to give himself more money to do drugs. He slept with other women during his marriages because he had the opportunity to do so. He became sexually interested in his third wife's niece because she was right there in front of him.

Instead of curbing Rick's impulse to have sex with Katie, the knowledge that she had been molested before actually made her seem more available to him. Even during the first time, when he discovered she probably was less sexually precocious than he thought, it didn't stop him from using her. So, as with Billy, Rick's motives were dictated by the situation rather than his own sense of right and wrong. Rick also claims to have felt some guilt during the time he molested Katie, but the guilt occurred only when he wasn't in the act of sex. When Billy and Rick's victims were easily accessible, they automatically took advantage of the opportunity.

Which leaves us with Matthew—immature, self-absorbed, bringing to adult pursuits the moral understanding of a child. Like Tony, Matthew is adept at playing roles. He has the confused boy role down pat, as he hypothesizes that his mental and emotional problems might have removed his inhibitions. Throughout his life, Matthew has used this persona of childishness to good effect. His innate sense of drama parlayed itself into radio jobs, where he was able to gain the adulation of fans and ready access to potential victims. Being able to invite boys into the studio to show off the technical marvels of a radio station was certainly handy. His public acclaim combined with his boyish good looks made it easy to attract attention. Like Billy, Matthew expresses the emotional capacity of a child. Like Billy and Rick, Matthew seems to function on instinct, whether he lacks the cognitive ability to attach moral value to his actions or simply does not care to think that deeply. Unlike Billy and Rick, however, Matthew does not seem concerned about truly understanding his crimes and taking steps to avoid committing more in the future. Even Billy, who probably has a lower overall I.Q. than Matthew, says that he is trying to grow up and make changes in his life so that he doesn't hurt anyone else. Matthew, though, doesn't seem to want to grow up. Using his boyish charm to attract people (and potential victims) and then having his parents take care of him, even when he is in prison, works for him, since he can use it to his advantage.

Identifying the themes and commonalities expressed in the offender self-narratives can give insight into how each man views himself as a social object. The identities these men fashioned were in large part constructed by their environment. The circumstances of their childhoods dictated their identities, later expressed in adulthood through their attitudes and actions. Perhaps it is true that some sex offenders lack the cognitive capacity to control their behavior. Then again, perhaps the choices that some offenders make are dependent on the circumstances in which they find themselves at any point in time. Certainly, the ways in which these men committed their crimes reflect both their thought processes and reactions to situational stresses.

Organizational Level

To gain insight on how the offenders' cognitive capacities and situational stresses contributed to their crimes, it is helpful look at the ways in which they structure their self-narratives. The organizational level focuses on how the plots and patterns in offenders' self-narratives reflect the ways in which they were able to commit their crimes, as well as the potential reasons for doing so. Identifying potential similarities between stories can help highlight how social expectations and constraints influenced the narrators' cognitive and emotional development and how these elements contributed to their actions.

Although it is important not to perceive these offenders as symbolic representatives of some concrete typology, applying A. Nicholas Groth's categories[5] to the self-narratives can illuminate the psychological implications of the crime. We can then highlight the legal assumptions that contribute to a social understanding of sexual abuse by showing where these men fit into the FBI's categories of sex offenders.[6]

Groth distinguishes between *fixated* and *regressed* sex offenders. Fixated child molesters, who have been attracted to children throughout their lives, have been unable to attain any degree of psychosexual maturity. Abe and Ben express characteristics of the fixated child molester. Each man claims that he was sexually molested as a child, and this experience might have influenced his later obsession with children. Tony, Red, Billy, Greg, and Rick all show evidence of being regressed child molesters. Although each had relationships with adult women, they turned their sexual interests to children during times of stress or when potential victims were readily accessible.

Tony admits that his obsession with exhibitionism began as an expression of his own insecurities and then intensified as time went on. Red became sexually interested in his stepchildren because his relationship with his wife, sexual and otherwise, was unfulfilling. Billy was an opportunistic regressed offender who took advantage of accessibility more than anything else. He doesn't seem to have been exclusively attracted to young girls, but had sex with them anyway if they were in his field of vision. Greg says that he never had any desire to have sex with a child until he was in the midst of a family crisis, in which his roles as caregiver to his wife and children were exhausting him. Greg seems to believe that, had his stepdaughter not offered herself to him, he would not have availed himself of the opportunity, but he was under a lot of stress, and she took advantage of his vulnerability. Rick was an equal opportunity user when it came to sex. At many times in his life, he was unremittingly promiscuous, and Katie just happened to be ripe for conquest since she was living in his house.

Darrell and Matthew appear to be hybrids of the fixated and regressed of-fender. Although Darrell had intense sexual encounters with young boys and even claims to have been in love with one of them, Darrell considers his at-traction to boys to have been merely a more acceptable form of sexual ex-pression than homosexuality. Matthew also fits into both categories because, although he appears to have been sexually fixated enough on young boys to have spent considerable time grooming them, he thinks that his fixation might be due to his lack of sexual experience with adult women.

Groth next makes distinctions between the types of force used to commit the offenses. In a *sex-pressure offense*, the offender uses enticement or entrap-ment to ensnare a potential victim. Although some of the men may have used verbal threats to encourage their victims to keep silent about the abuse, the majority of offenders in this study engaged in sex-pressure offenses. Tony, Red, Darrell, Matthew, Abe, Ben, Greg, and Rick all actively pursued their victims and used sex-pressure approaches to commit their crimes.

Tony began his exhibitionism tentatively, ready to withdraw if he saw any potential resistance in the girls he exposed himself to. Although he actively sought out victims, and in greater numbers over the years, Tony would not pursue the girls unless he perceived some interest on their part. Red used a sex-pressure approach as well. The girls and boys he sexually abused were readily available to him, and he even convinced himself that they wanted him to molest them. Red told his victims that they would face severe conse-quences if they told anyone, but he did not physically threaten them, al-though as he was an adult caregiver, the threat was certainly implied. Darrell and Matthew groomed their victims. They carefully concocted scenarios in which they could be alone with the boys who sexually intrigued them. Al-though Darrell and Matthew worked to create opportunities to molest their victims, they would not force a seduction if they sensed reluctance or un-willingness.

Abe and Ben engaged in sex-pressure offenses as well. Although they were both sexually oriented toward children and even fairly indiscriminate in choosing their potential victims, they did not physically threaten the chil-dren. They might have hinted to the victims that they would be in serious trouble if anyone found out about the abuse, but they did not use physical force. Nor did Greg or Rick, who actually seemed indifferent to sex with chil-dren before their particular offenses. Both opportunistically took advantage of their victims since the girls seemed to be sexually available. Greg says that he actually did not expend much energy on convincing his victim to keep quiet. In fact, Greg claims that he even attempted to tell his wife and his stepdaughter's doctor what had occurred—that his stepdaughter, who had been molested before and was sexually aggressive as a result, was attempting to seduce him—but they did not take his confession seriously. Rick, in contrast, seized the opportunity to have sex with his wife's niece, since she had been molested before and was "damaged goods." Rick encouraged Katie not to tell anyone because he didn't want to hurt his wife. He also admits that, out of "compassion," he told Katie he loved her, although this was more likely a strategic ploy to encourage her cooperation.

A *sex-force offense* is more openly violent, as the offender employs intimidation, direct threats, and/or physical aggression to molest a victim. Of the nine men profiled in this book, only Billy committed a sex-force offense per Groth's definition. Billy says that he was just like an animal, "a great big ape," when he violently sodomized his stepdaughter. He admits that he was angry with her because she was openly resistant to his sexual advances, especially since he perceived that his niece, whom he had previously molested, had been compliant. Billy's graphic description of the time in which he sodomized Annie is chilling. When asked how he got Annie to go along with his sexual demands, Billy readily confesses, "I told her to do it or I'd beat the shit out of her."

To further flesh out the similarities and divergent elements within the offenders' self-narratives, we can expand Groth's categories with the FBI's typology of offender characteristics. The *situational* child molester does not exhibit a defined sexual preference for children and includes:

- *regressed* offenders, who are immature, socially inept individuals who turn to children in times of stress;
- *morally indiscriminate* offenders, who choose their victims for their vulnerability and out of opportunity;
- *sexually indiscriminate* offenders, who will experiment with almost any type of sexual behavior; and
- *inadequate* offenders, who are social misfits and use children to satisfy their sexual curiosity.

Tony, Red, Greg, Billy, Matthew, and Rick are clearly situational child molesters. Tony, Red, and Greg are regressed situational offenders. Although these men might have seemed to be socially adept, even respectable members of the community, they all turned their sexual desires to children during times of stress. Billy is an inadequate situational offender who wanted to satisfy his sexual curiosity and was willing to engage in physical force to do so. Matthew appears to be a combination of regressed and inadequate. Because Matthew was immature and unable to relate to peers, he took advantage of available victims when the opportunity presented itself, although he did spend some time planning the "opportunity." Rick fits into the morally indiscriminate category of situational offenders since he chose his victim on the basis of availability and vulnerability.

Ben could fit the definition of a situational child molester, since he was opportunistic and morally indiscriminate in his pursuits, but he also admits that he finds young girls sexually appealing, so he shows evidence of being a preferential offender as well. *Preferential* child molesters are similar to the fixated category in Groth's typology and show marked sexual preference for children through their lives. Preferential child molesters include the following types:

- *seduction*, referring to those who court and groom children they know;
- *introverted*, or those who are not socially adept enough to be seductive with potential victims and thus prey on very young children or strangers; and
- *sadistic*, or those who need to inflict pain in order to achieve sexual satisfaction.

Aside from Ben, who seems to straddle both categories, Darrell and Abe fit the definition of preferential child molesters. Both engaged in seduction to accomplish their molestations, as they would carefully groom potential victims in order to convince themselves that the victims cared about them. Darrell even believed he had a love affair with his first victim and years later reminisces about the experience with nostalgia. Abe fits the definition of both seduction and introverted, since he would carefully groom potential victims but also become romantically involved with women in order to have access to their children.

Matthew also exhibits characteristics of the preferential child molester. Although Matthew claims that he has always been attracted to adult women, this seems doubtful given his apparent immaturity and admitted psychological limitations. He managed to engage in seductive behavior in order to molest his victims, but this was dependent upon whether he already had access to them, which fits the definition of an introverted preferential offender. It is evident from Matthew's narrative that he became romantically involved with one woman in order to gain access to her son and later took advantage of a girlfriend's family by sexually molesting her nephew and the boy's friend.

Obviously, if the men whose self-narratives are presented in these pages are any indication of the common sort of child molester that exists in our society, then most cases of molestation do not involve severe levels of physical force. By physical force, I mean the type of force that would fit the stereotype of a child molester as being willing to kidnap, injure, and even kill a victim. Billy is the only offender in this group who admits to having physically attacked his victim. In fact, Billy is the only offender who admits to having sexually molested his victim out of anger. Billy observes that, at the time he sodomized Annie, he was capable of any sort of violence since, "I didn't care if I was hurting her or not. . . . It was just like, all right, you got the hole and I'm taking it."

The other men relied upon various levels of verbal coaxing and implied threat to gain their victims' cooperation. This is not to say that their offenses were not as serious as Billy's. In fact, their seductive approaches may have been even more damaging to their victims in the long term, since they lured their victims into potentially believing that the victims actually participated in their own abuse. As studies on adult survivors of childhood sexual abuse attest, many experience lingering feelings of guilt because their offenders left them with the impression that they were at fault for being molested. However, if our punitive approaches to dealing with child molesters spring from the assumption that these criminals are dangerous because they always use physical force, then we don't truly understand the dynamics of this complex crime. The source of these misperceptions can be examined in an analysis of the cultural/historical level surrounding child sexual abuse and sexual abusers.

Cultural/Historical Level

Primarily, the self-narratives presented in this book are offshoots of the movement to break the silence surrounding rape and sexual abuse that began in the 1970s. Indeed, the very core of each man's identity can also be traced back to this time, at least in terms of its social construction. Ultimately, the details of each man's crime are most significant when we fit his self-narrative into the social narrative we have about child sexual abuse. So let's briefly revisit the timeline of public interest in the crime and its victims.

Over the past thirty years, the overarching focus has been on "threatened children"[7] and tormented adults who once were those threatened children, abused and forced into silence for so long. In the 1970s, the early rhetoric of child sexual abuse focused on "breaking the silence." This outcry emerged out of feminists' efforts to raise consciousness about rape and sexual abuse. Feminists claimed that these forms of sexual repression were used by patriarchy to shape women and children into "docile bodies" that reflected the dominant hierarchy of sex and gender. Although the stories of rape and sexual abuse began tentatively, by the end of the decade they became a roar of outrage.

As the 1970s spilled into the 1980s, the rhetorical focus changed slightly but significantly. Rather than individuals and isolated incidents, tales of mass molestation, often as a result of weird or satanic rituals, captured attention. Considering that the Freudians always believed sex was expressed subconsciously through odd symbols and fantastic imagery, the bizarre descriptions given of sexual molestations occurring in child-care centers and other venues seemed somehow appropriate, if difficult to believe. Yet, for quite some time, the public did believe these stories, and the smaller, less dramatic, more poignant tales told by individual sexual abuse survivors threatened to get lost in the shuffle. Sometime in the midst of the hubbub over ritual abuse arose the Recovered Memory movement, which held as its premise that sexual abuse victims might not even recall their experiences, but that they could be retrieved through hypnotism or therapy. As the popular self-help book *The Courage to Heal* stated firmly to readers who might wonder, "If you are unable to remember any specific instances . . . but still have a feeling that something abusive happened to you, it probably did."[8]

Mass media in the 1980s and early 1990s took advantage of these sensational (and dare I say "sexy"?) stories by exploiting them in newspapers, magazines, and television talk shows hosted by the likes of Geraldo Rivera, Sally Jessy Raphael, and Oprah Winfrey. Rivera seemed especially interested in dwelling on salacious and alarming stories of satanic ritual abuse and hosted a number of shows on the subject. Oprah Winfrey even admitted publicly that she, too, was a victim of child sexual abuse and in 1992 hosted a TV special, *Scared Silent: Exposing and Ending Child Sexual Abuse*. Winfrey did not limit herself to just talking about the issue, however. Winfrey became politically active, and in 1993, President Clinton signed the "Oprah Bill," aimed at creating a national database of convicted child abusers.

In the midst of this cacophony of narratives regarding child sexual abuse, a backlash began to occur against the credulity given these fantastic and ultimately discredited tales of mass ritual abuse. The backlash widened to include the Recovered Memory movement as well, since stories emerged of parents, particularly fathers, falsely accused by their grown children of molesting them when they were young. In the mid-1990s, as more light was shed on people falsely accused and sometimes convicted of child sexual abuse, even Geraldo Rivera publicly recanted his belief that ritual abuse was widespread in America. Yet, although the backlash forced some of the more sensational stories of abuse back into silence, there remained public confusion over the prevalence of the crime. The majority of people still seemed convinced that child molesters could be found under every rock and on every street corner, and politically popular means of combating them such as Megan's Law were the result.

As the 1990s faded and the twenty-first century dawned, some confusion arose as to the realistic numbers of sexual abuse victims and perpetrators, not to mention the nature of most of these crimes. Some scholars, such as Peter Jenkins in his 1998 book *Moral Panic: Changing Concepts of the Child Molester in Modern America* and James Kincaid in his 1998 book *Erotic Innocence: The Culture of Child Molesting*, focused on the ways in which the frenzy over sexual abuse and sexual abusers was in large part created and sustained through media. Although Megan's Law had been in effect in most states since the mid-1990s, it was becoming increasingly clear that monitoring convicted sex offenders was rife with pitfalls. Then the pedophile priest crisis in the Catholic Church revived the panic over sexual abuse, and once again the fear that child molesters surrounded us built to a crescendo.

The self-narratives told by the convicted offenders in this book reflect these social and cultural understandings of child sexual abuse. After all, stories can be told only when they can be heard.[9] Perpetrators of child molestation have been constrained on two counts. First, the social construction of child sexual abuse rests on the premise that the crime is unmotivated. Child molesters, in effect, have no history; their existence is spontaneous—it occurs the moment they commit their crimes. As a result, the second aspect of the social construction of sexual abuse is that perpetrators are irredeemable and even subhuman. Common knowledge is that sexual abusers mindlessly repeat their crimes, and therefore, for convicted offenders, there is no hope for treatment and no hope for their reintegration into society once they are released from prison.

Thus, until recently—and perhaps even today—there has been no context for these offender stories. The public (and indeed, even politicians who take action on this issue and sometimes those in the corrections field as well) has constructed a single framework for their narratives, one that allows for no understanding of motivation and accountability. We assume that these perverts molest children because they are depraved. There can be no logical explanation or, God forbid, any reason for a crime so heinous. Therefore, efforts at treatment, particularly therapeutic forms of intervention that focus on expressing and potentially restructuring offender self-narratives, have been sparse and halfhearted. More attention has been given to controlling offender behavior through aversion therapy (using penile transducers to register sexual arousal to stimuli such as slides, videotapes, or audiotapes), drugs (such as Depo-Provera, which is a form of chemical castration), and notification policies such as Megan's Law.

Thankfully, there have been voices in the wilderness from some corrections officials and counselors who try to set up programs that focus on individual and group therapies. These experts recognize that a large portion of offenders can be termed as regressed, since they tend to commit their crimes during times of stress. The emotional reactions to stress have roots in the offenders' self-histories, since oftentimes it is possible to trace offenders' adult motivations to their childhood experiences. Even fixated offenders often developed their desires out of childhood events that radically affected them. Of all the men I met during the course of this study, I can say with surety that only one man was what I would term "pedo-sexual"—that is, an unrepentant pedophile who claimed that from earliest memory his sexual desires focused solely on children. Yet even he was able to learn behavioral modifications to control his impulses—although the desire still remained—through a mixture of pharmacological and therapeutic interventions.

So although child molesters' stories provide a wealth of information regarding the forces that shape sexual abusers, we haven't been willing to listen to the offenders, because we have assumed they have nothing to say (or nothing we want to hear). Yet it is obvious that key aspects of the socially constructed narrative we have of child sexual abuse have been hastily assumed during fits of panic. Although they contradict the socially constructed assumption, a few caveats have emerged from research over the past few years:

1. Widespread ritual abuse is a myth. The panic over day-care centers staffed by satanists perhaps has its roots in a backlash against working mothers and dual-income families.
2. Some "recovered" memories of sexual abuse may be false.
3. The majority of sexual abuse victims are molested by people they know. The perpetrators of child sexual abuse are generally not strangers, but individuals who have access to victims and take advantage of that accessibility.
4. Most child molesters are not murderers, although some murderers molest children.
5. Convicted perpetrators of sexual abuse have lower overall recidivism rates than offenders convicted of other crimes.

Although the self-narratives of convicted offenders have the potential of giving lie to the mythic aspects of our socially constructed images of the "Child Molester," they have been stifled, perhaps as a result of the workings of power in our culture. As Foucault famously asserted, nowadays there is an "incitement" to discourse, since discourse about sex and sexuality has functioned as an apparatus of power:

Western man has been drawn for three centuries to the task of telling everything concerning his sex. . . . Not only were the boundaries of what one could say about sex enlarged, and men compelled to hear it said; but more important, discourse was connected to sex by a complex organization with varying effects, by a deployment that cannot be adequately explained merely by referring to it as a law of prohibition. A censorship of sex? There was rather an apparatus for producing an ever-greater quantity of discourse about sex, capable of functioning and taking effect in its very economy.[10]

But Foucault's argument about the deployment of discursive strategies and their role in the dance of power and knowledge lumps all these sexual stories together and does not address the ways in which there are dominant—that is, the most socially acceptable—stories that are more empowering than others. These dominant stories tend to determine not which narratives about sex can be spoken, but which will be heard. Indeed, I believe that the dominant narratives about sex in our society actually contribute to the existence of abuse by dictating which stories are legitimated.

Once we have exposed the myths, it is possible to recognize how the dominant discourse that has constructed child sexual abuse does not illuminate the most efficacious means of combating the crime. By being willing to truly understand the dynamics of sexual abuse from the offenders' perspective, we can use the self-narratives of offenders to highlight the most useful ways in which to address the crime. The roots of offenders' impulses to molest children are found in their stories—not so much in the objective facts of their lives, but in their perceptions of events and circumstances. We fashion our identities and the subsequent ways in which we interact with and react to stimuli through a two-pronged process. First, we develop our sense of self not only on a cognitive level but from our environment as well. The circumstances of our youth, particularly our relationships with significant others, contribute to the ways in which we construct our self-image. Second, we operationalize that sense of self by gauging it against our perceptions of the social world. This is hardly a novel explanation of how we come to be social beings, but it has particular salience when applied to a convicted child molester, given the one-dimensional view we tend to hold of this type of offender. By approaching the crime on this basis, we can see how externally driven measures that seek to control offenders through behavioral constraints and community-based restrictions such as Megan's Law inevitably have limited success. Unless we address the internal mechanisms that drive offenders to molest children, we cannot hope to truly understand the crime and stop it at its source.

And what is the source of offenders' crimes? It peers out of the stories they relate about their youth. As the self-narratives of the offenders in this book attest, these men did not spontaneously emerge as social beings at the point they molested their first victim. Their impulses to molest children—and willingness to act on those desires—were formed in concert with events from the past. Although not every child molester was molested as a child, many child molesters were abused in some way that profoundly affected their perceptions of the social world and their place in it. So, although we have focused attention on threatened children over the past decades and indeed view child welfare as a significant social issue, somehow we don't extend this interest to what happens to abused children once they are no longer young. Adults who have the time and money to spend on psychoanalysis often end up wrestling with their "inner child." However, as the narratives of the men in this book should attest, some adults who were abused as children do not possess the resources to work out their issues in therapy. When they were young, they didn't receive assistance in working through their abuse, and once they became adults, it was too late.

So am I placing blame for child sexual abuse on a lack of social programs for abused children? Of course not. Although it would be wonderful if we had the ability to spot abused children and whisk them into the appropriate form of treatment to give them the optimum chance for recovery, that is pretty much impossible on a practical level. However, we should recognize the possibility that some child molesters did not arise spontaneously but were created by their childhood experiences as much as by their cognitive capacities and desires. The social construction of child sexual abuse that has prevailed over the past decades has limited our ability to recognize this reality. In fact, the few times an observation has been tentatively offered that many child molesters were abused as children, the comment has been buried in a wave of outrage from sexual abuse survivors who strongly resent the implication that they might end up repeating the cycle. Yet this outrage has limited our ability to potentially combat sexual abuse. We're not defusing the repressive power of child sexual abuse by favoring the social construction of the problem over the more mundane realities. We are merely ignoring its source.

Ultimately, the factor that inflames public understanding of child sexual abuse is the way in which "Truth," or perceptions that construct it as a social problem, is valued over "truth"—the objective facts of its existence. A postmodern perspective maintains that "truth" is always relative, anyhow, since postmodernism focuses on multiple sources of knowledge. So given this focus, it isn't even important that we debunk the myths of child sexual abuse with statistics, facts, and other forms of empirical proof. Assuming that what is most significant about child sexual abuse is the image it takes in society—the way in which its social construction gives legitimacy to its presence and effects—then we concede that perceptions are the source of its power. Consequently, the ways in which we approach the problem on an individual and social basis should stem from this assumption. We can find the means to combat child sexual abuse in the rhetoric that surrounds it. On an individual level, we can view interpreting the self-narratives of victims as well as perpetrators as means of understanding the impact of child sexual abuse on self-image and self-expression. These narratives ought not to exist independently of each other, since they both construct and reflect the realities of the event for the actors involved. Being willing to listen and attend to the narratives of both survivors and perpetrators can then allow us to construct a new cultural understanding of child sexual abuse. These narratives are the source of how child sexual abuse functions in our society, since they communicate one way in which sex, sexuality, and sexual practices are means of power. Recognizing the way in which the system of sexual abuse is self-perpetuating can draw attention from superficial, external means of combating the crime and focus our vision where it belongs: on the victims and on the adults who were once victims themselves and the ways in which they have dumbly repeated the cycle.

The movement toward restorative justice promises to have potentially inestimable value for working with child molesters. In contrast to retributive justice, in which crime is viewed as a violation of the state and justice focuses on punishment, restorative justice considers crime to be a violation of people and relationships. Restorative justice seeks to promote repair and reconciliation between the victim, offender, and community. From this perspective, the blunt accounting of who did what to whom is insufficient to understand the crime's psychological and emotional impact on victims and perpetrators, including what social factors contribute to its existence. Focusing attention on the ways in which victims and offenders relate their self-narratives can illuminate the ways in which child sexual abuse reflects the workings of power and domination in our culture.

From the standpoint of restorative justice, we can use offenders' self-narratives as means of helping them to refashion their stories and, thus, their personal and social identities. As Erving Goffman observed in *Stigma: Notes on the Management of Spoiled Identity* (1963), "The stigmatized individual in our society acquires identity standards which he applies to himself in spite of failing to conform to them."[11] Since narratives are shaped by the interview as well as the symbolic interaction that is storytelling, they allow the narrators to project an ideal moral self; therefore, to understand the identities of offenders, "we must understand how they emplot these accounts."[12] So programs that feature narrative means of therapeutic intervention and rehabilitation may allow offenders to deconstruct their old identities and potentially construct new ones. Viewing offender narratives as being as essential as victim narratives can help us develop an alternative rhetoric that highlights the relational nature of the crime and guides us to more effective means of addressing it.

As this book draws to a close, I probably ought to offer some pithy summary couched in my own experience as a sexual abuse victim. Yet if I have learned anything in the years I've spent living with sexual abuse and studying the stories of sexual offenders, it is this: *being a victim does not gift a person with the only version of the truth that matters.* The crime that was committed against me was part of a cycle—a cycle that was born of social pressures beyond the comprehension of The Man Who Molested Me. If we want to truly combat this crime, then we have to accept the premise that truth is relative and perceptions are paramount in the social constructions of sex and power that dominate our lives. Listening to the stories told by the victims of sexual abuse is only half the battle. Being willing to listen to the stories of offenders can help us win the war.

Notes

1. U.S. Department of Justice, Office of Justice Programs, Bureau of Justice Statistics, www.ojp.usdoj.gov/bjs/crimoff.htm#sex (accessed March 31, 2004).

2. Jane Armstrong, "Sex Offender Treatment Queried," *Toronto Globe and Mail*, March 31, 2004, at www.globeandmail.com (accessed March 31, 2004).

3. Joel Stashenko, "Slaying Victim's Family Faults Pataki Administration for Killing," *Newsday.com*, March 29, 2004, at www.newsday.com (accessed March 31, 2004).

4. Barbara Grady, "U.S. Ponders What to Do with Freed Sex Offenders," Reuters, March 24, 2004, at www.reuters.com/newsArticle.jhtml (accessed March 31, 2004).

5. A. Nicholas Groth, *Men Who Rape: The Psychology of the Offender* (New York: Plenum, 1979), 142–43.

6. Kenneth V. Lanning, *Child Molesters: A Behavioral Analysis for Law Enforcement Officers Investigating Cases of Child Exploitation*, 1992, at www.skeptictank.org/nc70.pdf (accessed February 18, 2004), 6–9.

7. See Joel Best, *Threatened Children: Rhetoric and Concern about Child-Victims* (Chicago: University of Chicago Press, 1990), for a thorough explication of the rise of interest in child maltreatment in the United States.

8. Ellen Bass and Laura Davis, *The Courage to Heal: A Guide for Women Survivors of Child Sexual Abuse* (New York: Harper and Row, 1988), 21.

9. Ken Plummer, *Telling Sexual Stories: Power, Change and Social Worlds* (London: Routledge, 1995), 120.

10. Michel Foucault, *The History of Sexuality, Vol. 1: An Introduction* (New York: Penguin, 1981).

11. Erving Goffman, *Stigma: Notes on the Management of Spoiled Identity* (Englewood Cliffs, NJ: Prentice–Hall, 1963), 106.

12. Lois Presser, "Stories of Violent Men" (Ph.D. diss., University of Cincinnati, 2002), 200.

APPENDIX

~

Offender Interview Questionnaire

I. Background

This line of questions is focused on having the subject elucidate his background, including his relationships with family and peers. The subject's past may offer insight into what led him to sexually molest his victim[s].

- Describe your childhood. What was your relationship with your mother and father? With other family members?
- What was the relationship between your mother and father?
- What types of relationships did you have with friends and peers?
- What was your relationship with members of the opposite sex? With members of the same sex?
- How did you do in school? What kind of grades did you receive? Were you involved in any extracurricular activities?
- Looking back on your childhood, do you have a favorite memory? A least favorite memory?
- Picture yourself as a child. What image do you have of that child today?
- If you could change something about your childhood, what would it be?
- When did you start developing sexual feelings? How would you describe those feelings?

II. Molestation

These questions are aimed at uncovering the subject's pattern of molestations. An important point here will be to compare the subject's interpretation of his activities against the actual description in his record.

- How old were you when you molested your first victim?
- How many victims did you have?
- How old were your victims?
- Were the victims male or female?
- How would you choose your victims?
- What type of relationship did you have with your victims? Did you know them before you molested them, or were they strangers?
- In what way would you molest your victims?
- What were you feeling before, during, and after you molested a victim?
- Did you ever try to control your impulse to molest children? If so, in what way?
- Were you ever violent with your victims? Did you ever tell them not to tell anyone what happened or threaten them with violence if they told?

III. Disclosure, Arrest, Incarceration

These questions focus on the events leading to the subject's arrest and subsequent incarceration.

- How were you finally caught? Did a victim tell on you?
- How did you feel when you were arrested?
- Did you resist arrest? Did you expect it?
- What did you plea to the charge (did you go to trial)?
- If the case went to trial, did any of your victims testify in court? If so, how did you feel about their testimony?
- What was the sentence? How much of the sentence have you served?

IV. Rationale/Understanding of Crime

These questions cover the subject's interpretation of his crime and how he rationalizes his activities, as well as what he is doing to rehabilitate himself (if anything).

- Have you sought out therapy while in prison? If so, how long have you been in treatment, and what does the therapy involve? What have you learned from this treatment? What do you expect to get out of therapy?
- What triggers your "tug" to molest? Why do you think you are sexually attracted to children?
- How do you rationalize your crime?
- Why do you think some adults sexually molest children? What do you think they get out of it? What did you get out of it?

V. Future Plans

These questions are aimed at discerning how the subject plans to avoid re-peating his crimes and what he intends to accomplish with his life.

- What do you intend to do once you are released from prison?
- How do you intend to control your tugs to molest children?
- When you find yourself sexually attracted to a child in the future, what will you do?
- Do you have anyone to help you readjust to life outside of prison?
- Do you intend to pursue more therapy after you are released?

VI. Prevention

These questions ask how the subject believes society can combat the crime of child sexual abuse. After all, who better to recommend prevention strate-gies than the perpetrators?

- How can parents protect their children from being sexually molested?
- What do you think of sex offender notification policies?
- What do you think of the move toward giving child molesters stiffer prison sentences? Would it deter adults from molesting children?

Bibliography

Allen, Craig M. *Women and Men Who Sexually Abuse Children: A Comparative Analysis.* Orwell, VT: Safer Society, 1991.

American Association for the Protection of Children. *Highlights of Child Neglect and Abuse Reporting.* Denver, CO: American Association for the Protection of Children, 1988.

American Psychiatric Association. *Diagnostic and Statistical Manual of Mental Disorders.* 4th ed. Washington, DC: American Psychiatric Association, 1994.

Anderson, Kathryn, Susan Armitage, Dana Jack, and Judith Wittner. "Beginning Where We Are: Feminist Methodology in Oral History." *Oral History Review* 15 (1987): 103–127.

Anderson, Peter B., and Cindy Struckman-Johnson. *Sexually Aggressive Women: Current Perspectives and Controversies.* London: Guilford, 1998.

Armstrong, Jane. "Sex Offender Treatment Queried." *Toronto Globe and Mail,* March 31, 2004, at www.globeandmail.com (accessed March 31, 2004).

Association for the Treatment of Sexual Abusers. *Reducing Sexual Abuse Through Treatment and Intervention with Abusers.* Policy and Position Statement, 1996, at www.atsa.com/pptreatment.htm (accessed January 16, 2004).

Bakhtin, Mikhail M. *Speech Genres and Other Late Essays.* Translated by Vern W. McGee. Edited by Caryl Emerson and Michael Holquist. Austin: University of Texas Press, 1987.

Bass, Ellen, and Laura Davis. *The Courage to Heal.* New York: Harper & Row, 1988.

Beckett, Katherine. "Culture and the Politics of Signification: The Case of Child Sexual Abuse." *Social Problems* 43 (1996): 57–76.

Berger, Peter L., and Thomas Luckmann. *The Social Construction of Reality: A Treatise in the Sociology of Knowledge.* New York: Anchor, 1967.

Best, Joel. *Threatened Children: Rhetoric and Concern about Child-Victims*. Chicago: University of Chicago Press, 1990.

Broussard, Sylvia D., and William G. Wagner. "Child Abuse: Who Is to Blame?" *Child Abuse and Neglect* 12 (1988): 563–69.

Browne, Angela, and David Finkelhor. "Impact of Child Sexual Abuse: A Review of the Research." *Psychological Bulletin* 99 (1986): 66–77.

Brown, Jodi M., Darrell K. Gilliard, Tracy L. Snell, James J. Stephan, and Doris James Wilson. *Correctional Populations in the United States, 1994*. Washington, DC: U.S. Department of Justice, Bureau of Justice Statistics, 1996, at www.ojp.gov/bjs /pub/pdf/cpius94.pdf (accessed March 10, 2004).

Cook, Judith A., and Mary Margaret Fonow. "Knowledge and Women's Interest: Issues of Epistemology and Methodology in Feminist Sociological Research." *Sociological Inquiry* 56 (1986): 2–27.

Crewdson, John. *By Silence Betrayed: Sexual Abuse of Children in America*. Boston: Little, Brown, 1988.

Davin, Patricia, Julia C. R. Hishop, and Teresa Dunbar. *The Female Sexual Abuser: Three Views*. Brandon, VT: Safer Society, 1999.

Davis, Joseph E. "Social Movements and Strategic Narratives: Creating the Sexual Abuse Survivor Account," [n.d.], at www.unc.edu/~aperrin/narratives/papers/ davis_social_movements_strategic_narratives.doc (accessed March 13, 2004).

De Francis, Vincent. *Protecting the Child Victim of Sex Crimes Committed by Adults*. Denver: American Humane Association, Children's Division, 1969.

Denov, Myriam. "To a 'Safer Place': Victims of Sexual Abuse by Females and Their Disclosures to Professionals." *Child Abuse and Neglect* 27 (2003): 47–61.

DeVault, Marjorie L. *Liberating Method: Feminism and Social Research*. Philadelphia: Temple University Press, 1999.

———. "Talking and Listening from Women's Standpoint: Feminist Strategies for Interviewing and Analysis." *Social Problems* 37 (1991): 96–116.

East, W. N. "Sexual Offenders." *Journal of Nervous and Medical Disease* 103 (1946): 626–66.

Edwards, Derek, and Jonathan Potter. *Discursive Psychology*. Newbury Park, CA: Sage, 1992.

English, Kim, Suzanne Pullen, and Linda Jones. "Managing Adult Sex Offenders in the Community: A Containment Approach." *National Institute of Justice Research in Brief*. Washington, DC: U.S. Department of Justice, National Institute of Justice, January 1997.

Epston, David, Michael White, and Kevin Murray. "A Proposal for Re-authoring Therapy: Rose's Revisioning of Her Life and a Commentary." In *Therapy as Social Construction*, ed. Sheila McNamee and Kenneth J. Gergen, 96–115. Newbury Park, CA: Sage, 1992.

"Extent of Sex Abuse by Priests Reported." *Rochester Democrat & Chronicle*, February 28, 2004, 1A, 5A.

Finkelhor, David. *Sexually Victimized Children*. New York: Free Press, 1979.

Finkelhor, David, and Jennifer Dziuba-Leatherman. "Children as Victims of Violence: A National Survey." *Pediatrics* 94 (1994): 413–20.

Finn, Peter. "Sex Offender Community Notification." *National Institute of Justice Research in Action.* Washington, DC: U.S. Department of Justice, Office of Justice Programs, February 1997.

Fisher, Walter R. *Human Communication as Narration: Toward a Philosophy of Reason, Value, and Action.* Columbia: University of South Carolina Press, 1987.

Fitch, J. H. "Men Convicted of Sexual Offenses against Children: A Descriptive Follow-up Study." *British Journal of Criminology* 3 (1962): 18–37.

Foucault, Michel. *Discipline and Punish: The Birth of the Prison.* Translated by Alan Sheridan. New York: Vintage, 1977.

———. *The History of Sexuality, Volume 1: An Introduction.* Translated by Robert Hurley. New York: Penguin, 1981.

Freedman, Alfred M., Harold I. Kaplan, and Benjamin J. Sadock. *Comprehensive Textbook of Psychiatry.* Baltimore: Williams and Wilkins, 1975.

Gebhard, Paul H., John Gagnon, Wardell B. Pomeroy, and Cornelia Christenson. *Sex Offenders: An Analysis of Types.* New York: Harper & Row, 1965.

Gergen, Kenneth. *Realities and Relationships: Soundings in Social Construction.* Cambridge, MA: Harvard University Press, 1997.

———. "Exploring the Postmodern. Perils or Potential?" *American Psychologist* 49 (1994): 412–16.

———. *Toward Transformation in Social Knowledge.* London: Sage, 1994.

Gergen, Kenneth J., and Mary M. Gergen. "Narrative and the Self as Relationship." In *Advances in Experimental Social Psychology, Volume 21,* ed. Leonard Berkowitz, 17–56. San Diego: Academic Press, 1988.

Gergen, Kenneth, and John Kaye. "Beyond Narrative in the Negotiation of Therapeutic Meaning." In *Therapy as Social Construction,* ed. Sheila McNamee and Kenneth J. Gergen, 166–85. Newbury Park, CA: Sage, 1992.

Goffman, Erving. *Stigma: Notes on the Management of Spoiled Identity.* Englewood Cliffs, NJ: Prentice–Hall, 1963.

———. *The Presentation of Self in Everyday Life.* New York: Penguin, 1969.

———. *Forms of Talk.* Oxford: Blackwell, 1981.

Grady, Barbara. "U.S. Ponders What to Do with Freed Sex Offenders." Reuters, March 24, 2004, at www.reuters.com/newsArticle.jhtml (accessed March 31, 2004).

Greenfeld, Lawrence A. *Sex Offenses and Offenders: An Analysis of Data on Rape and Sexual Assault.* Washington, DC: U.S. Department of Justice, Bureau of Justice Statistics, 1997, at www.vaw.umn.edu/documents/sexoff/sexoff.html (accessed December 18, 2003).

Groth, A. Nicholas. "Sexual Trauma in the Life Histories of Rapists and Child Molesters." *Victimology* 4 (1979): 10–16.

———. *Men Who Rape: The Psychology of the Offender.* New York: Plenum, 1979.

Henderson, A. "The Sexual Criminal." *Governing* (August 1995): 35–38.

Herman, Judith L. *Trauma and Recovery.* New York: Basic, 1992.

Hermans, Hubert J. M., and Harry J. G. Kampen. *The Dialogical Self: Meaning as Movement*. San Diego: Academic, 1993.

Holstein, James A., and Jaber F. Gubrium. *The Self We Live By: Narrative Identity in a Postmodern World*. New York: Oxford University Press, 2000.

———. *The Active Interview*. Thousand Oaks, CA: Sage, 1995.

Jenkins, Philip. *Moral Panic: Changing Concepts of the Child Molester in Modern America*. New Haven, CT: Yale University Press, 1998.

Kay, Jack, "Ethical Considerations in Studying Communities of Hate: Using Ethnography to Explore and Critique the White Separatist Movement in the United States." Paper presented at the Fourth National Communication Ethics Conference, Kalamazoo, MI, May 1996.

Kempe, C. Henry, Frederic N. Silverman, Brandt F. Steele, William Droegemueller, and Henry Silver. "The Battered-Child Syndrome." *Journal of the American Medical Association* 181 (1963): 17–24.

Kincaid, James R. *Erotic Innocence: The Culture of Child Molesting*. Durham, NC: Duke University Press, 1998.

Kinsey, Alfred. *Sexual Behavior in the Human Male*. Philadelphia: Saunders, 1948.

Kinsey, Alfred C., Wardell B. Pomeroy, Clyde E. Martin, and Paul H. Gebhard. *Sexual Behavior in the Human Female*. Philadelphia: Saunders, 1953.

Knopp, Fay Honey. *Retraining Adult Sex Offenders: Methods and Models*. Orwell, VT: Safer Society, 1984.

Krafft-Ebing, Richard von. *Psychopathia Sexualis*. New York: Putnam, 1969.

Kvale, Steinar. *InterViews: An Introduction to Qualitative Research Interviewing*. Thousand Oaks, CA: Sage, 1996.

Lanning, Kenneth. V. *Child Molesters: A Behavioral Analysis for Law Enforcement Officers Investigating Cases of Child Sexual Exploitation*. Washington, DC: National Center for Missing and Exploited Children, 1992, at www.skeptictank.org/nc70 .pdf (accessed February 18, 2004).

Laslett, Barbara. "Personal Narratives as Sociology." *Contemporary Sociology* 28 (1999): 391–401.

Lawson, Louanne, and Mark Chaffin. "False Negatives in Sexual Abuse Disclosure Interviews: Incidence and Influence of Caretaker's Belief in Abuse in Cases of Accidental Abuse Discovery by Diagnosis of STD." *Journal of Interpersonal Violence* 7 (1992): 532–42.

Lieb, Roxanne, Vernon Quinsey, and Lucy Berliner. "Sexual Predators and Social Policy." In *Crime and Justice: A Review of Research, Volume 23*, ed. Michael Tonry, 43–114. Chicago, IL: University of Chicago Press, 1998.

"Mad about the Boy." *Time*, February 16, 1998, 103.

Matson, Scott, and Roxanne Lieb. *Sex Offender Registration: A Review of State Laws*. Olympia: Washington State Institute for Public Policy, 1996, at www.sexcriminals .com/library/doc-1029-1.pdf (accessed February 18, 2004).

McCall, C. Sexual Abuse of Children: The Victims, the Offenders, How to Protect Your Family. *Life* (December 1984): 35–62.

Mendel, Matthew Parynik. *The Male Survivor: The Impact of Sexual Abuse*. London: Sage, 1994.

Nelson, Barbara J. *Making an Issue of Child Abuse: Political Agenda Setting for Social Problems*. Chicago: University of Chicago Press, 1984.

Ney, Philip G., Christine Moore, John McPhee, and Penelope Trought. "Child Abuse: A Study of the Child's Perspective." *Child Abuse and Neglect* 10 (1986): 511–18.

Plummer, Ken. *Telling Sexual Stories: Power, Change and Social Worlds*. London: Routledge, 1995.

Presser, Lois. "Stories of Violent Men: Power, Change and Social Worlds." Ph.D. diss., University of Cincinnati, 2002.

Pryor, Douglas W. *Unspeakable Acts: Why Men Sexually Abuse Children*. New York: New York University Press, 1996.

Reinharz, Shulamit. *Feminist Methods in Social Research*. New York: Oxford University Press, 1992.

Riessman, Catherine Kohler. *Narrative Analysis*. Newbury Park, CA: Sage, 1993.

———. "Analysis of Personal Narratives." April 20, 2000, at www.xenia.media.mit.edu/~brooks/storybiz/riessman.pdf (accessed March 6, 2004).

Renzetti, Claire M., and Raymond M. Lee. *Researching Sensitive Topics*. Newbury Park, CA: Sage, 1993.

Revitch, E., and R. Weiss. "The Pedophiliac Offender." *Diseases of the Nervous System* 23 (1962): 73–78.

Rush, Florence. "The Sexual Abuse of Children: A Feminist Point of View." In *Rape: The First Sourcebook for Women*, ed. Noreen Connell and Cassandra Wilson, 64–75. New York: New American Library, 1974.

———. *The Best Kept Secret: Sexual Abuse of Children*. Englewood Cliffs, NJ: Prentice-Hall, 1980.

Russell, Diana. *The Secret Trauma: Incest in the Lives of Girls and Women*. New York: Basic, 1986.

Sarbin, Theodore R. "The Narrative as a Root Metaphor for Psychology." In *Narrative Psychology: The Storied Nature of Human Conduct*, ed. Theodore R. Sarbin, 3–21. New York: Praeger, 1986.

Schlenker, Barry R., Michael F. Weigold, and Kevin Doherty. "Coping with Accountability: Self-Identification and Evaluative Reckonings." In *Handbook of Social and Clinical Psychology: The Health Perspective*, ed. C. R. Snyder and Donelson R. Forsyth, 96–115. New York: Pergamon, 1991.

Scott, Marvin B., and Stanford M. Lyman. "Accounts." *American Sociological Review* 33 (1968): 46–62.

Shotter, John. "The Social Construction of Our Inner Selves." *Journal of Constructivist Psychology* 10 (1997): 7–24.

Snyder, Howard N. *Sexual Assault of Young Children as Reported to Law Enforcement: Victim, Incident and Offender Characteristics*. Washington, DC: U. S. Department of Justice, Bureau of Justice Statistics, 2000, at www.ojp.usdoj.gov/bjs/pub/pdf/saycrle.pdf (accessed January 16, 2004).

Snyder, Mark. "Self-Monitoring of Expressive Behavior." *Journal of Personality and Social Psychology* 30 (1974): 526–37.

Stashenko, Joel. "Slaying Victim's Family Faults Pataki Administration for Killing." *Newsday.com*, March 29, 2004, at newsday.com (accessed March 31, 2004).

Stop It Now! "Child Abuse: A Public Health Epidemic." *About Stop It Now!* at www.stopitnow.com/about.html (accessed April 12, 2004).

U.S. Department of Justice, Office of Justice Programs, Bureau of Justice Statistics. *Criminal Offender Statistics*, at www.ojp.usdoj.gov/bjs/crimoff.htm#sex (accessed March 31, 2004).

Volosinov, V. N. *Marxism and the Philosophy of Language*. Cambridge, MA: Harvard University Press, 1986.

Ward, Tony, Stephen M. Hudson, and Julie McCormack. "Attachment Style, Intimacy Deficits, and Sexual Offending." In *The Sex Offender: New Insights, Treatment Innovations and Legal Developments, Volume II*, ed. Barbara Schwartz and Henry R. Cellini, 2-1–2-14. Kingston, NJ: Civic Research Institute, 1997.

Weinberg, S. Kirson. *Incest Behavior*. New York: Citadel, 1955.

White, Michael, and David Epston. *Narrative Means to Therapeutic Ends*. New York: Norton, 1990.

Wittgenstein, Ludwig. *Philosophical Investigations*. Oxford: Blackwell, 2002.

Index

217

~

About the Author

Pamela D. Schultz is an associate professor in the Communication Studies program at Alfred University. She lives with her family in western New York.